THE SUNDAY GARDENER

THE SUNDAY GARDENER

Edited and with an introduction by

ALAN GEMMELL

ELM TREE BOOKS
HAMISH HAMILTON · LONDON

First published in Great Britain 1973
by Elm Tree Books Limited
90 Great Russell Street London WC1

Copyright © 1973 by Alan Gemmell

SBN *241 02372 6*

Printed in Great Britain by
Ebenezer Baylis and Son Ltd
The Trinity Press, Worcester, and London

CONTENTS

INTRODUCTION

The purpose of this book is to help the gardener who has only a limited time to spend on this hobby either because he is not a gardening enthusiast who wants to be totally submerged in gardening, or because his work, family, or other hobbies also demand some of his time. For this reason I have called the book *The Sunday Gardener*.

This book will explain how it is possible to have an attractive and productive garden even if your free time is limited and will recommend plants and techniques which will ease or reduce work. Mark you, it is important to realize that you cannot produce Kew Gardens on a few hours' work on an odd good week-end and that the return you get from the garden in beauty or in food will depend on the time you spend working at it. Nevertheless, by skilful use of labour and by good planning a worthwhile return can be got from a minimum of effort. And no matter the size of the garden, adequate planning and careful choice of materials will go a long way towards solving the work and time problem.

Gardening, of course, has a long and distinguished history first as an art and latterly as a science. Along the way it has accumulated a vast technical jargon, some of the words being pure science while other are pure 'country'. To help the beginner I have drawn up a kind of dictionary or glossary which appears at the end of the book. In this glossary I have tried to define in simple terms words used by the distinguished authors in their respective chapters, along with a number of other words used in everyday garden talk, in the hope that, by referring to it, you will then be able to make better sense of what is being said.

This brings me to my second point, namely the form of the book. A gardening book is usually the work of a single author who describes his ideas, experience, and prejudices on every aspect of the subject. I decided to do this book differently since only the real experts are able to talk with authority to the absolute beginner. Therefore each chapter had to be written by a different person, each an authority in his own field and well qualified to contribute a special chapter with all the insight of many years' experience.

Each author was given the same brief, namely to write a chapter on a given topic, specifically with the Sunday gardener in mind. The book therefore will not please the specialist grower or the professional for they seek gardening perfection, but Mr. Everyman does not aspire to this and is not willing to devote the necessary time to it. The book does not go into elaborate techniques of, say, pruning, but tells you simply and in straightforward terms what to do, when to do it, and how, to achieve the best results with the least work.

Three of the chapters deserve special comment. There has been an increased awareness of the environment which has moved some people to explore the possibilities of gardening without the use of chemicals, and so Dr. Shewell-Cooper agreed to write an interesting chapter (Chap. 8) on compost or organic gardening. Secondly, I have included a chapter (Chap. 9) on house plants, not because they are a part of gardening, but because they are so very popular and help to light up many a room in our concrete jungles. Many houses too, are having patios, sun-lounges and garden-rooms added to them, all well-lit, airy, and often with central heating. Mr. W. Davidson who is in charge of growing plants commercially for Rochfords has very wide experience of all kinds of house and pot plants and deals in a straightforward and trenchant way with this aspect of growing.

Thirdly, many folk have a small greenhouse or lean-to conservatory, and my colleague, Fred Loads, with his years of practical experience behind him discusses in Chapter 6 the general principles of using a small greenhouse, concentrating on growing tomatoes and chrysanthemums, since other pot plants are considered in Chapter 9.

The other chapters on Lawns, Flowers, Vegetables, Shrubs, etc. are self-explanatory and I hope will give you the necessary information and assistance to get the best from the shortest time in the garden. A chapter on Pests and Diseases (Chap. 7) is included, not so much to help you to identify specific pests and diseases but rather to show you that there are general guidelines along which you can tackle all garden troubles.

GENERAL ADVICE ON WHAT TO GROW

Whether yours is a house with a garden already laid out or a new house with only bare earth and weeds around it, your best plan is to sit down and think. To say this may seem obvious, but it is amazing how many people start off their gardening lives with millstones hanging around their necks because of a lack of thought.

Your thinking should take two lines: (1) what do I want the garden for?, and (2) How much time am I willing to spend in the garden, not just this year but for many years to come? Obviously these two questions are interrelated for if you want to grow flowers for the house, fruit, or vegetables, or have a perfect lawn, shrubbery, etc. then you must be prepared to spend a lot of time. So be very clear what you want before you start, remembering that it is much easier to introduce new aspects to the garden than to get rid of established ones, so don't be too ambitious all at once.

A few generalizations on planning might however be helpful. Most gardens have some kind of lawn. This can be at 'golf-green standard' or 'mown-field standard' depending on you, but once established a lawn is very easily maintained and amply rewarding in appearance. You must be prepared to put some considerable time in for the first year or two, but it will get easier very quickly, and here you have low maintenance *par excellence*. So decide on your lawn area and get it prepared first.

Another very low maintenance area is a shrubbery or shrub-border—even single shrubs dotted in the lawn. If they are chosen and planted with care, little work is necessary after the first year, and, as the Director of the Royal Horticultural Society Gardens points out in Chapter 3, pruning can be simplified down to very basic essentials.

1*

Perennials and flowers form a very pleasing feature since they add colour and sparkle and produce variety in the seasons. They usually require a little more work than lawn and shrubs and so, unless your wife is a keen flower-arranger, they can be reduced to smaller proportions, depending on your available time.

Vegetables are still more demanding of time, since you have digging, planting, thinning, weeding, etc. all to do. But what a treat it is to eat the vegetables you yourself have grown. Be sure however, to ask for the high-quality varieties suggested by Roy Genders in Chapter 2, and don't be fobbed off with the old run-of-the-mill varieties. You see therefore that how you plan your garden is going to affect the time you spend in it.

A further basic tip about planning the garden may not go amiss. Always remember that you will often be inside the house looking out and will want to have some kind of view. Therefore, never plant tall shrubs or trees near the house for not only will they block the view, they will also keep out light and sunshine, and the roots may damage drains. Close to the house have shrubs or flowers and have your taller plants well away.

Many Sunday gardeners are worried about the costs of laying a lawn or buying roses and other shrubs when they have only a little time to look after these valuable assets. It is well, therefore, to realize that, although the initial cost may be high (a good shrub may cost £2), it will be there for many years, if you buy wisely, giving much pleasure for very little further outlay. It is always false economy to buy the cheapest seeds or plants, for in gardening as in everything else you only get what you pay for.

Because the Sunday gardener has little time he does not want to have failures in planting or sowing seed. The moral is, therefore, to be especially careful to get things right in the beginning. If the advice on the packet says 'spread the roots out' or 'sow the seed with 9 inches between the rows' it is good sense to do exactly that in order to obtain good results. And there is an additional bonus, for not only do you have the best immediate results, but you also prepare the soil for future good performance by your plants, and you get a great feeling of satisfaction.

TOOLS AND EQUIPMENT

Here again it is false economy to buy the cheapest. Take that great symbol of gardening, the spade. Spades come in different sizes with varying handles, and may be made of ordinary or stainless steel. The Sunday gardener is certainly not an accomplished digger and hopes he may never become one, so there is a temptation to buy a cheap spade, which will probably be heavy and badly balanced, and have a rough and sticky metal blade, factors all combining to make hard work of any digging operation. It would be far better for him to buy a relatively light spade, certainly of stainless steel, and with a handle which suits his grip. This will make digging much easier, soil will not stick to the blade, and digging will not get progressively heavier. And when that particular piece of digging is over, the stainless steel blade is easy to clean and does not rust or become rough.

Similar points can be made about other tools and the general upshot of the whole argument is that lighter, stainless steel tools are by far the 'best buy'.

In the case of lawn-mowers another principle operates, for you can have a powered machine or a mower you have to push. Obviously a powered machine is by far the best buy if the area of lawn justifies it, since it is much less demanding of energy and can mow a large area in a relatively short time. The chapter on lawns gives excellent advice on this aspect of gardening, and the one thing which cannot be said too often concerns the importance of regular servicing.

I know few things more infuriating than to be all ready to cut the lawn, only to find that the mower won't start. You pull away at the starter or turn the starting-handle until you are exhausted, but the motor will not come to life. By next weekend the grass will be still longer and it may be raining.

The solution to this and similar problems is to get all mechanical tools serviced by someone who knows his business in the autumn or early spring of each year. It is bad policy to leave the servicing until a week before you hope to use the machine, for you may find yourself at the end of a long queue and have to wait some weeks before your machine comes back. It is all so obvious and elementary, but, if you are a Sunday gardener, you don't want to waste hours of your limited time trying to start a machine when you could be cutting the lawn.

Much the same applies to cutting tools such as garden shears, and secateurs; and when you are putting spades and hoes up for the winter give them a rub with an oily rag which will leave a film on the surface to keep the edges keen and bright.

The wooden handles of tools can also do with a rub of linseed oil periodically to keep them springy and in good fettle.

How to Work in the Garden

One of the cardinal errors made by the Sunday gardener is to think that, since he has only a limited number of hours in the garden, he must get on with the job at once and work at top speed. If this is your feeling, then you have planned your garden badly and are giving yourself too much to do in your limited time. All gardening jobs are best done at a leisurely pace. If you watch an experienced gardener working, he never seems to hurry, in fact he seems to spend a longer time leaning on his spade than in digging. This is because he knows that if you rush at it, like a bull at a gate, then you will tire very quickly and in the end you will have accomplished little. If you ask him how he gets so much done while seeming to do so little, the answer will vary but it can be summed up in the word 'rhythm'. Working well within yourself you will find that slowly you will get into the swing of it and you will be astonished how far you can go without too great an effort.

But the Sunday gardener by definition is going to be badly out of condition, with soft hands, weak back, perhaps a slight paunch, and what an old friend of mine used to call 'white legs'. He will therefore find that sustained bouts of digging or hoeing, or any single job at all, can be not only tiring but also boring. In these circumstances it is often useful to have several jobs going at the same time, so that when you get tired of mowing the lawn, you can clip a bit of the hedge or rake a bit of path, or do some other job. This is not the advice I would give to the enthusiast, who should start a job and carry on until he finishes it before starting another; but to the very part-time gardener he might find that variety helps him overcome a back tired from digging.

Another great time-saver is to carry many things with you as you work. The old gardener used to wear an apron with a great pocket in which were a knife, twine, secateurs, maybe a small hammer, trowel, etc. The modern gardener would not dream of wearing an apron, but the idea is sound and a great deal of time and energy can be saved if you load up the wheelbarrow with a variety of gardening tools and equipment and take it out to a convenient position before you start work.

Many of the readers of this book are part-time gardeners because they are reluctant gardeners, and reluctant gardeners are very often only too willing to seize upon any excuse to avoid doing any gardening chores. Thus, if it happens to rain on the day when he has mentally decided to cut the lawn making the grass too wet to put the mower on it, the reluctant man will sit back with a sigh of relief and a clear conscience and do nothing. This is a wonderful way of not gardening, but there are a number of other jobs that can be done in inclement weather. For example, it does no harm to clip a wet hedge, or to prune roses or black-currants, or to tidy up and, if necessary, repot house-plants. If you *think* before you give up the notion of gardening on that day, you will realize that there are many jobs which can be done in any weather, and the Sunday gardener should always try to have one or two jobs in reserve, saved up for a rainy day as it were.

Another tip which works with considerable success is to start off with a simple and, if possible, interesting job. You see, the main hurdle is to get started. Once you are out and working it is easy to carry on. If, therefore, you say to yourself or to your helper (be it wife, child, husband, or friend) that 'You might like to have a go at . . .' (naming a simple task), more than likely when it is finished he or she will come to tell you and ask what they 'can do now', and so you can push them on a bit.

GARDEN SAFETY

Garden safety is beginning to assume an importance that it

did not have some twenty years ago. The dangers which now face gardeners are of three types:

1. To self and family from poisonous chemicals
2. To owner when a mechanical tool is used
3. To the environment in general by pollution.

1. *Poisonous Chemicals:* These may be sprays, fertilizers, or weedkillers which, if poisonous, are clearly marked as such. A number of chemicals such as paraquat are available only to professionals, but sometimes they find their way into the hands of amateurs, and everyone has read of children dying through drinking paraquat or of workers becoming ill after being splashed with the substance.

Poisonous chemicals such as mercury, arsenic, and nicotine have been used for about a hundred years and accidents have always happened, but that does not excuse any of us from taking the maximum care to protect the safety of others, especially children. The first step is to mark all poisonous substances very clearly in two or three places. Such chemicals should ideally be stored in a locked cupboard and should always be out of the reach of a casual passer-by be he child or adult.

It is also very dangerous to transfer liquids from one bottle to another, for the second bottle is rarely designed for storing that particular liquid. Unfortunately, the commonest container is a lemonade bottle and there must be thousands of lemonade bottles in Britain containing a liquid which is *not* lemonade. The owner knows this, but do his children? Dangerous substances, even petrol, should never be stored in lemonade bottles for who can tell what horrible accident may result following unwitting use of the so-called 'lemonade'. Therefore always keep dangerous and especially poisonous chemicals in their own container, clearly marked and labelled, and either locked away or on a high shelf.

Another cause of personal danger is using the substance contrary to instructions. One may feel that a chance may be taken with certain things, but it is always wise to resist such temptations. If it says 'Wash your hands immediately after use' or 'Only dispense wearing rubber gloves', then you should do exactly that, for the makers do not put directions on the label for fun.

Finally, always wash out containers thoroughly before putting them away. If you have been watering a lawn with weedkiller, it would break your heart to water your lettuces using the same can a week or so later, and to find the plants dead the next morning. This does happen, and a good cleaning of the can would have prevented it. The ideal solution to this problem is to have a 'dirty' and a 'clean' watering-can, one to be used for toxic or other chemicals, and the clean can for simple watering with clean water.

2. *Danger from Mechanical Tools:* The danger from mechanical aids is easily seen when you have petrol for a lawn mower in the garage. Petrol should always be stored in a can with a good screw-on cap, in an upright position, in a spot where it cannot easily be knocked over. Such cans should also be out of the reach of children and clearly marked, for people have been seriously burned by using petrol in mistake for paraffin to get a bonfire going.

Another danger from mechanical aids is that the operator may slip and pull the machine on to some part of his body. There is no danger if the machine is used correctly according to the maker's instructions. But it is always wise to take precautions, and a pair of heavy gardening boots may protect toes and give you a firm grip on greasy or slippery surfaces. But follow the maker's advice and you won't go far wrong.

A danger, which could be very serious, lies in using electric tools, such as mowers or hedge-clippers, carelessly. The danger lies in the possibility of cutting the cable and so getting a severe shock. There are various devices to help avoid this danger, but great care should always be taken when dealing with electrical equipment.

This applies also to the handyman who tries to lead electricity to a small greenhouse without employing a properly qualified electrician. Most of the time he may get away with it, but a greenhouse is always wet, and, unless plugs of the correct type

are properly sited and fitted, the greenhouse could become a
death trap. So be careful.

3. *Danger to the Environment:* There is little need to draw
attention to the way in which the environment can be poisoned
or polluted by indiscriminate use of chemicals. The major part of
such pollution can be laid at the door of industry and agriculture,
but the amateur gardener contributes quite a lot as a result of the
indiscriminate use of sprays, weedkillers, etc. The important
word is 'indiscriminate', for the danger to the environment can
be reduced to a minimum by using such preparations only when
necessary and then strictly according to the maker's directions.

It is wise, for example, to use insecticidal sprays only when the
flowers are not open, for then there will be no bees around and
so your spray will not be killing friendly insects. Again, all sprays
should be used at the first sign of trouble, or even before trouble
appears as a kind of insurance. Such an early application will
prevent any infection building up to really harmful proportions
which would then necessitate a much greater use of the chemicals
in question.

I am sure that it would be foolish to live in an age of great
technological advance and not to take advantage of the new
techniques, but at the same time it is always unwise to throw out
tried and trusted techniques before you can use the newer, easier
ones with safety and maximum effect.

Keele
March, 1973   ALAN GEMMELL

1 *The Lawn*

J. R. ESCRITT

The lawn is such an essential part of a garden that I had no hesitation in making it the first chapter. Similarly, I had no hesitation in asking J. R. Escritt to write it.

Mr. Escritt is the Director of the Sports Turf Research Institute, a world-famous organization, with which he has been associated since 1938. This Institute gives advice and conducts fundamental research in all grades of sports turf from golf-course greens to public parks. He is therefore in a unique position to meet all the problems which arise at practically every level of turf-growing.

THE REQUIREMENTS

Most gardeners regard a lawn as an important if not an essential feature of the garden. Interpretations of what lawns should be like, however, are very wide, the only common factor being that they should 'look nice'. Obviously this can mean many things and uniformity is probably the characteristic that is wanted above all else. The lawn should look a good green and be pleasant to walk upon, having a suitable degree of resiliency. Most people like a lawn consisting entirely of grass and we will assume that this is the requirement, although we can sympathize with the minority who don't mind a lawn with a blend of small herbaceous weeds with the grass, or even a nice sprinkling of daisies!

Even when we are talking about a grass lawn people vary in their reactions to different kinds of grasses. Some don't mind what grass it is so long as it is grass, others want fine grass looking like a bowling-green, but the popular requirement is low maintenance and, generally speaking, the fine grasses which make for a fine lawn also grow more slowly and less high than the coarser grasses. On the other hand, the coarser grasses will generally stand a greater degree of neglect and irregular attention.

MAKING A NEW LAWN

When making a new lawn it is important to consider what is really being aimed at and this applies not only to the character of the actual turf but to the shape and levels as well. There is no need for a lawn to be dead flat, nor indeed to be in one plane. It can have a slope and it can have undulations provided these are smooth enough to allow easy mowing. A lot of us like a rectangular lawn because it fits in conveniently with having flower beds around but there are advantages in having an irregular shape instead of the formal rectangle, provided that mowing is kept in mind when doing the shaping.

The remainder of the garden must also be taken into consideration. Try to avoid having a lawn under dense shade from overhanging trees, indeed overhanging shrubs and plants can lead to disease and other troubles.

SITE PREPARATION

In the interests of keeping lawn maintenance to a minimum over future years, it is wise to try one's hardest to make a good lawn in the first place. Thorough preparation is essential if a load of troubles are not to follow. Quick preparation by raking out whatever material is available over a few days and then scattering any old grass seed is a sure way to disaster.

The kind of situation on which the lawn is to be produced obviously varies from site to site and it is impossible to envisage all situations, so perhaps it would help if we describe the conditions we are aiming for. These are a well-cultivated top soil, preferably six inches deep and consisting of a light sandy loam, overlying a local sub-soil that is not so compacted that water penetration is prohibited. In striving towards this, we should work the earth only when it is in a reasonably dry condition.

The general shape and contours required should be decided at an early stage and obviously one works to the existing situation as much as possible. Keeping to the levels which exist saves a lot of work. If, however, a considerable adjustment of levels is required it may be necessary to remove the top soil completely so as to grade in the sub-soil. Only minor adjustments in levels can be obtained by moving top soil around, since this results in uneven depth of soil (perhaps inadequate depth in some places) and lack of uniformity in the resulting lawn. If the levels are reasonable and there is sufficient useful top soil, then the first steps are simple, i.e. digging and cultivation. Quite often, of course, at new houses the site is in the condition left by the builder, and not all builders give attention to garden requirements! The first step then is to burn up any burnable rubbish, and collect and dispose of rubble, concrete, and other materials which are in the way. Any long grass should, of course, be cut down and burnt along with timber, tree roots, etc. and the ashes from such operations spread over the proposed lawn area. A good builder will have left a cover of top soil over the garden area, but if he has not it may be necessary to buy in some sandy loam top soil.

Whereas on existing garden sites straightforward digging to break up the top soil is the first requirement, on new sites double digging to break up the sub-soil as well is almost certainly necessary, or even more positive action such as the use of a sub-soiler hired for the occasion. Ideally, digging is best done in the autumn or early winter, and during the operation any old turf or other vegetable matter should be completed turned in and weed roots and rhizomes of coarse grass species removed as the work proceeds.

Since lawns are seldom used heavily in wet weather, somewhat surprisingly drainage is seldom found necessary but occasionally, especially on heavy land, some simple drainage scheme with land tiles buried to about two feet and covered with ashes may be necessary. Much depends on the circumstances on the site as to how many drains, if any, are required, and some kind of outlet is clearly necessary for drain-pipes. It is best to connect the drains to the sewers or other suitable outfall, if permission can be obtained, since soakaways are not always satisfactory. However, if an outfall cannot be found and drains are considered necessary it may be possible to drain into a soakaway consisting of, say, a hole three feet square and several feet deep (preferably to meet porous material through which the water can percolate), the hole being filled up with stones to within about eight inches of the surface and then blinded with fine gravel or gritty ash before replacing the top soil. On many small lawns a soakaway without any drains may suffice.

By this time (if not before) you should have a good idea of what kind of top soil you are dealing with, and when this has been dug is a good time for making soil improvements. If the soil is very light and sandy then it may be worth while forking in rotted compost or rotted farmyard manure or, more simply, granulated peat, which may be applied at say 4 lb. per sq. yd. On heavy soils peat is also an advantage, but it should be accompanied by other material designed to open up the soil and make it more porous. As little as 10—14 lb. of suitable coarse sand (preferably lime-free) is useful if raked only into the immediate surface, but if six inches of sandy soil is the aim then at least three inches of sand (say 2 cwt. per sq. yd.) needs to be mixed with the top three inches of soil when the original soil is of very heavy texture. Gritty ash if readily available might possibly be used instead of the sand.

Assuming the land was dug in the autumn and the sand and peat are added in dry weather in early spring, cultivation with a Dutch hoe can commence to mix the ameliorants with the top soil and to produce a good tilth through the full six inches or so of top-soil depth. This should be followed by rough raking, paying attention to the smoothness of levels. Grass seed may be sown in the spring but the best time is mid-August to mid-September—'the end of August' is a good expression to keep in mind for sowing. The land which has been brought to a fairly advanced state of preparation in the spring can be fallowed during the summer period with a view to getting rid of broad-leaved weeds and coarse grasses. Fallowing means regular cultivation to promote germination and subsequent destruction of weeds which would otherwise establish themselves in the final seed-bed. This can be done by regular severe raking.

In the final preparation of the seed-bed, alternate raking and light rolling in various directions may be necessary to get the soil into the desired condition, the object of the rolling being not only to firm soft spots and prevent subsequent sinkage, but also to crush soil lumps. If a really good job with a smooth surface at the end is required, the laborious process of 'heeling' the area by tramping over the surface in short (3–4 inches) steps, with the weight thrown on the heels is recommended. This finds out soft spots and air pockets better than the roller. After heeling, the area should again be raked over and if necessary the process repeated. The surface should be checked during this work and any bumps or hollows eliminated, since, once the lawn is seeded or turfed, faults in surface levels will be difficult to correct. A gadget such as the proprietary 'Trulute' can save much work here and is useful for working in later top dressings. Stone-picking should also be done, especially in these later stages; in fact, during the whole of the preparation, stones should be picked and/or raked off as convenient.

TURFING OR SEEDING

A subject which always leads to discussion is the choice between sowing grass-seed or laying turf. Many people are attracted to the idea of turfing because of the 'instant' nature of the result. However, there are definite snags, one of which, of course, is cost. Then, again, good quality turf is not easy to obtain and many people have been disappointed with the turf obtained. Moreover, if one has spent money, time, and labour on preparing a high quality top soil to support a good lawn, then it is rather a pity to spread over it a turf which might have been grown on a very ordinary clay soil. Advantages of turf other than time-saving are, that it does cover a multitude of sins and reduces the necessity for producing a clean seed-bed, since a covering of turf is likely to smother out many weeds.

When buying turf, one has to take the grasses which are present and these are likely to be assorted. When buying grass-seed, one can prescribe what one wants. For a first quality lawn one should use only first quality grasses, and the cost of the seed is a good guide to the quality of proprietary grass-seed mixtures. For a first quality lawn a mixture such as eight parts of a good variety of Chewings fescue with two parts of a good variety of browntop-bent, sown at the rate of 1 oz. per sq. yd. is very suitable, and the best proprietary mixtures are very similar to this. Even if a lawn like a bowling-green is not required, these fine grasses have advantages in requiring relatively little mowing. On the other hand, they do seem to require careful handling and good maintenance, as otherwise they are likely to be replaced by natural invaders including coarse grasses. At the other extreme are the relatively cheap proprietary mixtures containing perennial ryegrass. These are cheap in use not only because of their lower price but also by virtue of the fact that they can be sown at a lower rate, say ½ oz. per sq. yd. They are quick to establish, they will stand rough, careless treatment including irregular mowing and will give a green cover, but they will not provide the first-class lawn that so many would like to see. There are also in-between mixtures which do not contain perennial ryegrass but contain medium/coarse grasses like timothy and smooth-stalked meadow-grass as well as fescue and bent. These are probably suitable for a great many people who don't like the coarseness of ryegrass but have not the time or patience to give a fine grass lawn the attention it needs. Whatever type of mixture is chosen, try and ensure good persistent varieties of the species chosen.

There is a difference in time-scales and degree of preparation as between the two main processes for establishing turf. (There are, of course, other processes, such as the planting of stolons, a sort of intermediate between seeding and turfing, rarely used in this country though much used in other parts of the world.) Sowing grass-seed, as we have said, is best done at the end of August, but it may be done at the end of April. It may be done in the months between April and August with a reasonable chance of success, especially if watering can be carried out. Turfing can be done at any time of the year provided watering facilities are readily available but the best time is usually considered to be the months of October, November, and December.

Whether seeding or turfing, chemical improvement of the land is also required on most occasions. On very acid land a dressing of, say, 4 oz. of ground limestone per sq. yd. may be needed, but this should not be used unless proved necessary by soil tests. A good proprietary fertilizer suitable for the purpose (i.e. pre-seeding or pre-turfing) should be applied at the maker's recommended rate and raked into the seed-bed.

If turf is bought it should be of uniform thickness, say $1\frac{1}{4}$ inches, and in standard pieces, e.g. 1 ft. × 1 ft. or 1 ft. 6 in. × 1 ft. or 2 ft. × 1 ft., by agreement. Turfing should be carried out under reasonably dry conditions and it is usually best to lay at least one run of turves completely round the borders of the lawn and then work from one side so that no walking on the prepared soil is involved, i.e. the new turf is laid from a working position on the already laid turf, using planks to protect the grass. The individual turves should be laid with alternating joints rather like brickwork and pushed closely up to each other but not beaten down. Any unevenness should be rectified in the earth below. After the turf has been laid it should be lightly rolled and then given a dressing of 3 or 4 lb. per sq. yd. of sandy compost material or sandy soil or even sand alone, spread as evenly as possible with a shovel and then worked into the surface by a Trulute or a drag-brush or drag-mat so that it smooths out the surface and gets worked into the joints. Further topdressing to smooth out the surface may be required a few months later.

Sowing grass-seed is undoubtedly the best procedure in the long run as well as the cheapest. Care should be taken in the choice of the grass seed and in getting the right amount of seed having regard to its constitution. The next thing is to get the seed spread evenly, and it is a good plan to divide the seed into portions so that it can be sown in two different directions at right angles. Indeed, for a really good job, it pays to divide the lawn into measured squares and then on each square to sow the weighed amount of seed, again preferably in two directions. Some people go further and mix the seed with sandy soil to provide more bulk. Incidentally, a calm day is a great help to sowing the grass-seed uniformly.

The final operation is to rake lightly in. It is not necessary for every seed to be covered by any means—grass-seed needs only a light cover. If all the seed is left uncovered on the surface, it is likely to shrivel just after germination whilst if the seed is buried too deeply a lot is likely to be too weak to reach the surface. The first two weeks after the grass is sown can be a worrying time because of the birds. Seed can be obtained which has been treated with bird-repellent, but an efficient method is to string out the lawn with black cotton on sticks three or four inches high. The amount of grass-seed the birds eat may not be important in view of the heavy seed rates which are normally used, but the amount of damage they can do in dust-bathing is quite considerable.

EARLY CARE

Assuming that there is a little rain, the new grass should be showing through within about a fortnight. As the days pass by, you will usually find that, despite the fallowing, there is an early crop of weeds, which may cause some unnecessary anxiety since, although they may look bad, they do protect the seedlings from drought and, as most of them are annuals, they quickly disappear once mowing is started. Sometimes, indeed, mowing is a good idea before the grass is really ready just to restrict the weeds, but this must be done very carefully. Some low-growing perennial weeds may persist; they can be tackled with selective weedkiller at a later stage. But tufts of coarse grass should be hand-weeded if you are trying to produce a really fine lawn. The first mowing of the new grass should normally take place when the grass is about two inches high. At this stage pick off any surface stones and give a light rolling, allowing then a day or so for the grass to come back to the vertical. The first mowing should be done with a very sharp mower to prevent tearing out the seedling grass and a mower of the side-wheel type is best. Only about a third of the grass should be cut off at the first cut; as the turf progresses, the cut can be gradually reduced to the height required, but this should take place only slowly over a period of several weeks. In the early weeks it may be found that, as a result of uneven sowing or hand-weeding, some areas are rather short of grass; this position can be rectified by rubbing into the surface a little of the original seed mixed with soil, foresight having been shown in retaining a little for the purpose!

The first full growing season is probably the most important time in a new lawn's existence, whether it has been sown in spring or in late summer. Obviously, the first full growing season for a spring sowing is the year in which it is sown; for a late summer sowing it is the following year. In this first season it is important to give the grass a good deal of attention, particularly in applying fertilizer and regular mowing. The best protection against a great many troubles is a good cover of grass and this is assisted by regular feeding and regular mowing. The principal requirement in this first year is undoubtedly nitrogenous fertilizer and, whilst proprietary fertilizer can be obtained, some people prefer a simple mixture of ½ oz. sulphate of ammonia mixed with 4 oz. sandy soil per sq. yd., applied on two or three times during the season.

During the first growing season year success or otherwise in achieving smooth levels will be observed. For the finest lawns especially occasional top-dressing as described in the maintenance section, using sandy soil or sandy compost and then working it in with a Trulute, a drag-mat or drag-brush, is a good way of producing the smooth surface which looks good and facilitates mowing.

If a lot of perennial weeds appear, treat carefully with selective weedkiller only when the grass is well established.

MAINTENANCE OF THE EXISTING LAWN

There seem to be two main groups of lawn-gardener—those who try too hard and those who don't try at all. The latter presumably won't bother reading this; to the former we would offer caution that overenthusiasm can lead to a *poorer* lawn. Not all the spiking, pricking, raking, feeding, and treatment with conditioners one reads about is necessary by any means. A high quality lawn needs a good deal of care but it does not need to become an obsession.

MOWING

Without any shadow of doubt *regular* mowing is the key operation in getting a good lawn and keeping it 'looking nice'.

The first requirement is a good mower in good condition; it is false economy to buy a cheap mower if you can afford a better one. The better the mower and the better its maintenance, the better the lawn. The best size for your mower obviously depends on the size of the lawn, the storage facilities, and the position of the storage place in relation to the lawn—carrying a heavy mower up steps is no joke. A small hand-mower may well be the most suitable for the average suburban lawn; too large a mower or a heavy power-driven machine may cancel out any advantages through inconvenience. It is true, of course, that most people like a mower wide enough to get through a job quickly.

An important consideration when buying a mower is the type of finish required. For a first-class finish on a first-class lawn a conventional mower with a roller at the front and back is undoubtedly the best. Side-wheel mowers generally do not produce quite as good a finish as the roller mower and are less convenient for working up to lawn edges, but they will tackle the less fine lawn very adequately. Both types of mowers cut the grass by the scissor principle, as the rotating cutter catches the grass against the bottom cutting blade. The so-called rotary machines, however, work on a different principle, for they more or less beat off the grass. In these machines, the cutting cylinder rotates horizontally round a vertical axis. They are all power driven and have the advantage that they will chop off all kinds of grass and all kinds of lengths of grass satisfactorily, and are remarkably tolerant of even rough usage. These mowers are not usually capable of cutting very closely satisfactorily and they bruise individual blades of grass at the tips so that they can mar the appearance of a good quality lawn. Nevertheless, the sale of these 'convenience' mowers is steadily increasing so a lot of people must be finding them satisfactory.

A very important consideration with a conventional cylinder machine is the number of cuts per yard run (the more cuts, the more even the finish), and the really good mower may give as many as 100 cuts per yard while cheaper machines give only fifty or less. The number of cuts depends on the speed of the cutting cylinder relative to the speed of travel and upon the number of blades on the cylinder. For a really smooth finish eight or ten blades are needed.

For most small lawns, however, a hand-mower is quite adequate. Petrol-motor machines are satisfactory and well established, but they may prove difficult to manipulate in awkward situations, and, with irregular use, are sometimes difficult to start. Electric mowers, driven by battery or cable, often give less trouble, once you have learned to operate the cable on the latter.

Any mower must be kept clean, well oiled, and in good sharp condition. Usually, sharpening is necessary at the end of every season. Provided the mower is sharp and correctly adjusted, you should have no trouble in getting a good finish. The main adjustment on any mower is, of course, for the height of cut, and, when choosing your mower, make sure the method provided is simple and efficient. A usual range of heights for a mower is $\frac{1}{4}$–$\frac{3}{4}$ inch—about $\frac{1}{4}$ inch for really fine lawns and fine grasses and $\frac{3}{4}$ inch for mixtures containing ryegrass. Not all machines cut efficiently throughout the full range, a point to bear in mind when buying.

Make sure also that the arrangements for delivering the grass-cuttings into the collector are satisfactory. The container should be light but sufficiently strong to have a useful life and it should be easy to remove and replace. It is wise to arrange for cuttings to be boxed off on all occasions, since allowing them to fly tends to lead to a soft, easily damaged turf, with the spread of weeds and an increased liability to disease and worms. And cuttings make good compost.

Finally, an important factor in buying a machine is to take notice of the safety factor, of most importance perhaps in mowers power operated through an electric cable. On rotary machines there should be an adequate guard against stones being thrown up or the operator's toes being damaged by the rapidly rotating blades.

We would again emphasize the importance of regular mowing.

Obviously most of the mowing is done during the main growing season from the end of April to the beginning of October, and through much of this period really fine lawns should be cut twice a week (even more if there is heavy growth), but lower quality lawns may get by with once-a-week mowing. Even in the period between October and April, if mild weather results in growth, occasional topping with the mower at a slightly higher setting than normal is a good idea to keep things tidy and to minimize disease.

Whenever possible the grass should be mown in dry conditions (brushing off the dew helps on occasion), and worm casts should be dispersed by switching or brushing before the job starts. After mowing, clean the mower; when cuttings are dry a small hand brush will do the job, but when the mower is covered with wet grass a hosepipe is far better.

Whilst on the subject of cutting the grass, it is perhaps worth mentioning the importance of trimming the edges of the lawn. There are various types of equipment for the purpose but many lawn-owners will have to use their ordinary shears. When a lawn edge tends to wander a bit it may have to be trimmed with a straight spade or a half-moon; this can be avoided if an edging material of timber, concrete, or aluminium strip is used. Then all there is to trim is the wispy growth of grass over the top.

FEEDING

It is in this aspect of maintenance that lawn-owners often err. To avoid weeds, worms, and disease it is wise not to use fertilizers which leave an alkaline residue, such as nitrate of soda or nitro-chalk, and to avoid the excessive use of organic fertilizers. A good fertilizer will usually have a suitable blend of organic and inorganic constituents.

Some of the best lawns have had no fertilizer for years, and, of course, more fertilizer usually means more mowing. There is, of course, a considerable variation in the possible needs of the lawn according to the original circumstances and the quality required. A really high-quality lawn receiving maximum attention might need the makers' recommended rate of a fully

balanced fertilizer (i.e. one containing all three main plant foods—
nitrogen, phosphate, and potash) in the spring, followed by two
or three dressings of a summer fertilizer containing nitrogen
only (e.g. sulphate of ammonia at ½ oz. per sq. yd.), but this is
excessive for most people. Many lawns would benefit from an
annual dressing of a complete fertilizer in the spring, but there
are also many lawns that could do without fertilizer for two or
three years at a stretch. If you are one of those who, despite
advice to the contrary, prefer to let your cuttings fly, there will
be less need for fertilizer than if you box off the cuttings. Keeping
up a reasonable degree of fertility by means of fertilizer does
help to keep the grass looking a good colour and it is unfortunate
that this almost automatically means more mowing.

Careful and uniform application of fertilizer is most important.
Uneven application means at best uneven growth and, at worst,
killing off by scorch or disease the patches of grass which get too
much fertilizer. Good results can be obtained by mixing the
fertilizer with 4 oz. sandy soil per sq. yd. and dividing up the
total dressing so that spreading can be carried out in at least
two directions. This bulking is especially important with scorching
materials like sulphate of ammonia. Spreading can be carried
out very satisfactorily by hand, but the purchase of a small
distributor is worth considering, though it must not be assumed
to be foolproof. If no rain falls within forty-eight hours, watering
in of the fertilizer is advisable.

WEEDKILLING

There are no selective grasskillers at the moment so that patches
of coarse grass have to be removed by hand or by patching out
with better turf. Most ordinary weeds can be eliminated by means
of the selective weedkillers which are available in proprietary
form. The best of these are usually those which are applied in
solution, and theoretically the most efficient way of applying
such weedkillers is by means of a suitable sprayer. However, on
small lawns the risk of the weedkiller getting on to the flower-
beds by drift is very large when a sprayer is used. It is, therefore,
recommended that, though the weedkiller thus applied may be a

little less efficient, it is worth while accepting this and applying it diluted to the maker's recommended prescription through a watering-can fitted with a fine rose or with one of the relatively new dribble-bars, so that comparatively large droplets fall on to the turf and do not drift on to roses and other plants. There are many brands of selective weedkiller but it is best to ask for one of the 'broad spectrum' types, which consist of mixtures of chemicals designed to cope with a large variety of weeds. Make sure the watering-can is well washed out after use!

For convenience it is worth considering one of the combined fertilizer/selective weedkiller mixtures which are available. These may not be as good in ensuring the complete elimination of weeds, but they are certainly exceedingly convenient to use.

Of all the weeds which might occur in a lawn, moss is the one which is not susceptible to control by ordinary selective weed-killers. The real answer to moss is to find out why it is there. It can be caused by excess of acidity (shortage of lime), by sheer poverty, or by bad drainage. It can also invade a lawn, which has been severely weakened by drought, once some moisture does come along. If the cause can be discovered, steps can be taken to remedy it. To clear out the moss where no cause can be readily discovered, the proprietary mosskillers, which contain small amounts of mercury compounds, are very satisfactory. Some of them are slow-acting and it may be some time before the moss goes, but these proprietary mosskillers are usually very satisfactory if there is no obvious cause of the moss invasion.

OTHER MATTERS

If a lawn has a weed-free, green appearance, that is all that most people want, but for the perfectionist a few other things are worth mentioning.

Top Dressing. In lawn management, top dressing means the application of bulky material like sand or sandy soil spread at 3–5 lb. per sq. yd., as evenly as possible by means of a shovel or by hand application, followed by working the material into the sole of the turf by a Trulute or drag-brush, so that, instead of trying to get the lawn even by planing off the bumps, one is, in fact, smoothing the surface by filling in the hollows. Obviously one application of top dressing will fill in only minor hollows (smothering must be avoided), but with regular applications, say once or twice a year (spring and autumn), it is amazing what a difference can be made to the smoothness of the lawn, which in turn reflects on the uniformity of the cut. To get a good even cut, a smooth surface is required, and to get a smooth surface, top dressing is the real answer. The top-dressing material need not have very much food value for the turf.

Pests. The principal lawn pest is the earthworm. Earthworms make the surface unsightly and muddy and make mowing difficult. Their casts also act as seed-beds for the seeds of weeds and coarse grasses, inblown or, in fact, brought up in the cast from below by the earthworm. One of the hazards of controlling earthworms is associated with toxicity. The best wormkillers are those which kill underground, like lead arsenate and chlordane, the latter being the most popular these days. Both these toxic materials are persistent and may last for 5–10 years. There are wormkillers which are less toxic, such as those containing the chemical Rotenone (usually described as Derris products) and these are available in proprietary dusts; but even Rotenone is toxic to fish! A new range of proprietary wormkillers of very low toxicity has recently come out and these typically contain the chemical Carbaryl (Sevin). These are quite good but by no means as persistent as, for example, chlordane. There is, however, a certain peace of mind to be obtained by using materials of low toxicity, especially where there are children and pets. There should be no difficulty in obtaining these non-toxic preparations at the local horticultural shop or garden centre.

Diseases. There are several diseases which will attack a lawn and if one is present it is perhaps wise to seek advice. The most common and damaging disease is undoubtedly Fusarium patch, which attacks most lawn grasses but especially annual meadow-grass, which is a common natural invader of almost all lawn turf. It usually appears as yellow circular patches about two inches across, generally showing up first where the grass is longest and most lush. The patches become darker in colour as the grass dies out in the middle, and white mycelial growth may be seen at the edges of the patches. Although it can occur at any time, the disease usually comes in spring and autumn in mild humid conditions, particularly where there has been unwise feeding or where the turf is shaded by trees or overhanging garden plants. Treatment involves the use of one of the proprietary fungicides, some of which are based on mercury which is poisonous, although the treatments are applied in very dilute form, either dry or in solution. Some of the up-to-date fungicides (based on organic chemicals) for Fusarium patch control are much less toxic and are worth enquiring about, even though they may prove more expensive.

Scarification. To produce good playing surfaces on bowling-greens and golf-greens, particularly old established ones, regular surface scarification involving the use of wire rakes or mechanical scarifying equipment is necessary. For most lawns a very limited amount of such raking is needed unless the lawn is very old and has got a great deal of fibrous matted growth at the surface. If this situation occurs vigorous wire-raking to get rid of some of the fibre is a good idea but this should be done at a time when good growth conditions are likely to follow and when demands for a first-class appearance are not too high; thus late summer or early autumn is often a good time. For people with an old-established fine lawn containing a great deal of old matted fibre it is worth considering hiring a suitable scarifying machine to do the job mechanically. Excessive matted fibre at the surface may be caused by excess of acidity (lime deficiency), in which case a dressing of ground limestone (carbonate of lime) at 4 oz. per sq. yd. would be needed.

Even for the ordinary lawn an occasional light raking or brushing helps to keep the grass growing vertically and to bring up the creeping growth of grasses and weeds so that it is cut by the mower. Nevertheless, the importance of this operation can be overemphasized.

Aeration. For heavily-used sports turf areas, regular aeration is almost essential. For the average lawn, aeration is seldom necessary. Only if there is reason to believe the soil has become compacted, so that air and moisture cannot penetrate, is some form of hollow tining or spiking really justified. If the soil has become overcompacted, the most efficient way of relieving the compaction is by hollow tining and on a small lawn this can be done with a special fork manually operated. Some of the spiking and other aerating equipment bought by some lawn-owners does not serve a very useful purpose.

Watering. Most lawns will get by, even in the dry summers which we have had for a year or two, without watering, but, if a green, pleasant appearance is to be maintained, then occasional watering is a good idea. Each watering should be sufficient to penetrate several inches so as to avoid encouraging only shallow-rooted growth and a good watering once a week in dry weather should suffice. Watering helps to maintain a good appearance but it also means more cutting as growth increases! Excessive watering can lower the quality of a lawn and encourage invasion by moss or attack by disease.

Rolling. Superstition has it that all that is necessary for good lawns is regular mowing and regular rolling. This is not far wrong if you forget the regular rolling! Rolling leads to soil compaction which means reduced air and moisture penetration and the need for alleviating these conditions by aeration, and in addition the quality of the lawn can be reduced. Rolling does help to smooth out the surface but obviously this can result only from the compacting of the earth in the bumps. Generally speaking, little or no rolling is needed. Many good lawns have never seen a roller other than the one on the mower, but after a severe winter it is sometimes desirable to take a light roller over the lawn in spring to firm up any upheaval caused by the winter weather.

2   The Vegetable Garden

R. GENDERS

Since many people are now growing their own vegetables, I considered there was no one better than Roy Genders to write this chapter. He has had a very wide and varied experience since he took up commercial fruit-growing in the 1930s, and moved into fruit and vegetable-growing immediately before the war. He is one of the most widely-read gardening authors of today. He has appeared frequently on television and his articles have appeared in the Field, *the* Countryman, *and many gardening magazines. He has written several books on vegetable culture including his latest entitled* The Complete Book of Vegetables and Herbs.

In recent years, vegetable-growing has been changed out of all recognition by the introduction of strains of vegetables possessing hybrid vigour which not only show a marked resistance to disease but bear heavy crops with the minimum of cultivation. Equally important, they will reach maturity days—even weeks, in some cases—before the older varieties. To those growing vegetables in the colder parts of Britain, this may mean all the difference between success and failure especially in a season of adverse weather.

If you plan to make vegetable-growing an important part of your gardening work locate your vegetable plot in an open, sunny situation, as few crops will do well in shade, and mature trees growing near will deprive the soil of moisture and nourishment. For early crops in the open, the soil must be warmed by the spring sunshine before the seed is sown or plants set out. Seed will not germinate in cold, wet soil. If the ground has a gentle slope to the south or west, this will be ideal for the vegetable-garden, for it will ensure good drainage, enabling it to warm up quickly in spring and to be workable as soon as the frost and snow have gone.

Tool Requirements

Those who find digging an irksome task are advised to obtain the Terrex digger. This will eliminate the strain caused by lifting and turning heavy soil; when you realize that a spadeful of soil weighs about 14 lb., it is obvious that the semi-automatic spade can be a great boon.

The digger is merely pushed into the ground until the rear lever is resting on the ground. Then a slight movement of the handle backwards and downwards, it loosens and turns over the soil. There is no laborious lifting, and the tool can be used by a person with one arm.

Those who do not need assistance with their digging should choose a spade with the same care as a cricketer selects his bat, trying several to get the right balance, for all spades differ slightly. And buy one with a stainless steel blade to which the soil will not stick. It will cut through the heaviest soil like a knife through butter, especially if wiped with an oily cloth before (and after) use. The spade is used for trenching and earthing up as well as for digging, and, as a complement, get a fork of stainless steel which you will need for mulching, lifting root crops, and loosening the surface of the soil.

Other tools needed will be an efficient rake for breaking down the surface and making a seed-bed; and a good hoe for breaking up the soil between the rows after rain has caused the surface to consolidate. This is done to enable oxygen and moisture to reach the plant roots. A valuable tool is Wilkinson's swoe, a long-handled tool which is a combination of a scuffler and a hoe, and functions in the same way as both tools. It is useful for thinning turnips and beetroot.

No vegetable-garden is complete without a strong barrow or truck, the all-steel builders' barrow being more durable and lighter to use than a wooden one.

Water is also an important part of successful vegetable culture, and a good water-can, made of galvanized iron or plastic and fitted with a long spout, and having a capacity of 1½–2 gal., is a 'must'. Watering by hand-hose and sprinkler is, of course, easier. An automatic lever-spray nozzle will enable the jet to reach to a considerable distance, and if it is fitted with a metal spike which can be stuck into the ground, part of the garden may be watered while you are working elsewhere.

PLANNING THE GARDEN

Before planting anything, you should make a plan of the vegetable-plot so that the best possible use may be made of it. A four-course rotation of crops should be followed, even if your garden is small, for only then will the crops make the maximum use of the different plant foods stored in the soil in varying amounts. One crop will use up larger amounts of nitrogen, another more potash and phosphates. Again, there are plants that require more lime in the soil than others. You should therefore divide the plot into four sections so that one crop may follow another each year in rotation, and each section should be cropped intensively, every inch being brought into maximum use the whole year round.

Climate will play a part in deciding the cropping programme. Gardeners in the south-west will be able to bring on outdoors crops of lettuce and broccoli in winter to harvest during the spring, followed by French beans and cauliflowers, to be sown or planted early in April when the ground has been cleared. You can follow these with quick-maturing cabbage and broccoli, thus taking three crops from the land.

In less favourable areas, use must be made of cloches to protect early crops, whilst heated frames will contribute to the winter larder. Tomatoes protected by cloches may be planted out fully a month earlier than where there is no protection, whilst plants brought on in frames or under cloches will mature several weeks earlier than normal.

Inter-cropping is also important. Along the earthed-up rows of celery or leeks you may plant lettuce or a small, quick-maturing cabbage. Between rows of potatoes, plant French beans, which will have finished cropping before it is time to earth up the potatoes. Well-cultivated land may be kept continuously productive, and whenever opportunity presents itself, you can take off a quick-maturing 'catch' crop, which may be planted between those vegetables which will be occupying the ground for a longer time.

Always take note of sowing and planting times, when the crops are harvested, and the performance of each variety as this information will prove most valuable for future cropping programmes.

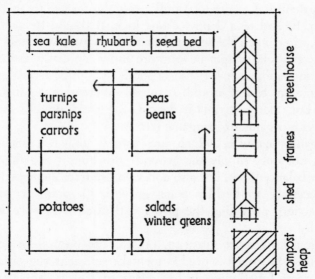

Fig. 1: *Diagram of a vegetable garden showing rotational cropping.*

Preparation of the Soil

Bringing the soil into as friable a condition as possible is the first consideration, for, if the soil is heavy and badly-drained, excess moisture will remain about the plants' roots in winter, causing them to decay, and autumn-sown peas and broad beans will be unable to survive; or, if the soil is dry and sandy, the plants will make little growth during the drier months of summer.

A heavy soil will require the incorporation of ample drainage materials, which may take the form of crushed bricks obtained from a building site or boiler ashes and clinker, whilst the countryman will make use of clearings from ditches. Peat may also be used, for both light and heavy soils require humus, a clay soil so that it will open up and aerate the soil, thus allowing oxygen to reach down to the plant roots, whilst a sandy soil needs humus to bind it and provide a moisture-holding medium.

Humus, such as peat and decayed leaves, may not contain much plant food but it is most useful for the improvement of soil texture. A bale of peat moss (obtainable from garden shops and agricultural merchants) will cover the surface to an area of 200 sq. ft. and to a depth of one inch. It should be applied in early spring when the soil is clear of frost. Peat will hold up to twenty times its weight in moisture and is especially useful for a sandy soil, and, since it is almost sterile, it is to be recommended in preference to leaf mould. A suitable alternative is poplar bark fibre, but, like peat, this is devoid of plant food and must be used with organic or inorganic fertilizers.

Organic manures, which are natural and not chemically made, not only supply the ground with humus and the plants with a balanced diet, but also add valuable trace elements which are necessary to healthy plant growth. Organics are usually slow acting, providing the plants with food over an extended period.

Vegetables require nitrogen, potash, and phosphates as their main diet. Nitrogen is needed to make sufficient vegetation for the correct functioning of the plant so that it will attain its maximum size and will yield abundantly. Phosphates are required not only to bring the plants to maturity but also to stimulate root activity; and potash is required to make a plant grow 'hard', to enable it to withstand adverse weather and disease. It also accentuates the flavour and colour of vegetables.

Farmyard manure, now difficult to obtain, contains each of the important plant foods and is the best of all forms of manure. Now, however, one has to make use of one of several alternatives. For those living near the coast, chopped seaweed, containing **limited** amounts of nitrogen and potash is a valuable source of humus, whilst those gardening in the industrial north will find that wool or cotton shoddy is readily and inexpensively obtainable and clean and easy to use. It has a high nitrogen content. Old mushroom-bed compost is excellent for vegetables, as are used hops, usually obtainable from a brewery for the asking.

If farmyard manure is available, it must be well decayed before use. Well-rotted cow manure is the best of all plant foods, but pig and poultry manure are also valuable with their high potash content. Bone meal, slow acting, has a high phosphatic content and should be used in conjunction with one of the nitrogenous manures.

Another valuable source of humus and plant food is straw, composted with an activator, and material from the garden compost-heap should be constantly in use.

There are various preparations on the market which will help to improve the condition of heavy soils. One is Colimnus which is fortified by plant food; a 28 lb. bag will treat 400 sq. ft. Another is Krillium, whilst Aerosil, a product of British Gypsum Ltd. will help to break up the clay particles of a heavy soil and will bind a sandy soil, besides providing valuable minerals such as calcium and magnesium.

But no amount of fertilizer and soil-conditioner will be of use unless the soil is well worked and has been cleared of all perennial weeds.

When first bringing the soil into condition, a start should be made in autumn when the soil is friable and easily worked. It should be cleared of perennial weeds, the lime content increased if necessary, and the soil drained and aerated. At this stage, double digging will be necessary so that the manures and humus materials may be incorporated to a depth of at least eighteen inches. The soil should also be treated for wireworm and millepedes by dusting with Gamma-BHC powder as the work proceeds, though this preparation must not be used if potatoes are to be planted within twelve months.

To double-dig the ground, first mark out the area into sections each of one square yard, using garden lines (also useful for making trenches and for planting out). Two spits' (or spades') depth of soil is then removed (Fig. 2) from the top (a) of section

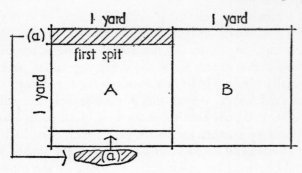

Fig. 2.

(A) and placed at the bottom or side. The next spit is then removed, and put into the trench made available after the first spit has been removed, and so on until the end of the section is reached when the soil removed from (a) is used to fill in the last trench. The digger then moves on to the next section (B) and works across the plot until the operation is complete, all the time shaking out any weeds and incorporating drainage materials and humus-forming manures, thus improving the whole soil structure. If the surface is left rough, winter frosts and winds will break it down to a fine tilth.

The Compost-Heap

To make a compost-heap, erect a strong bin made of wire netting in a corner of the garden. The heap is built up in layers using all the unwanted 'greens' such as pea and bean haulm, the tops of beetroot and carrots, the outer leaves of cabbage and cauliflower, in fact anything except potato and tomato haulm and sprout stems which will be difficult to compost. Potato and tomato haulm and all diseased plants must be burnt and not left lying about.

Build up the heap in six-inch layers, watering with liquid manure or adding a sprinkling of activator. Any poultry or pig manure will increase the richness of the compost. Decayed leaves and lawn-mowings can be added as well as the clearings from ditches and ponds and at the end of six months the heap will have turned a rich greenish-brown and have the consistency of farmyard manure. Vegetables require ample supplies of both humus and plant food, and the ultimate aim with all soils is to bring them to a fine tilth, enriched with moisture-holding humus active in bacteria, which will make it spongy and friable when squeezed in the hand. Such a soil will be well drained in winter and will warm up quickly with the first of the spring sunshine.

Calcareous soils, found in the region of the Chilterns, in the Cotswolds, along the south coast, and in the limestone areas which cover much of north-east England, usually have only a small amount of top soil which dries out rapidly in hot weather with the result that plants make only limited growth. For such a soil, 'green' manuring in August is advisable. After clearing the ground of perennial weeds, thickly sow rape seed on the surface. Rake in and water well. By early October, there will be a thick covering of green top growth and, below ground, a mat of fibrous roots, all which should be dug in as deeply as possible.

Fertilizers for a Balanced Diet

Vegetable plants require a balanced diet to be successful; nitrogen to make sufficient growth and to start a plant growing after a period of inactivity due to cold conditions. Nitrogen is best given in the form of nitrate of soda at the normal rate of 1 oz. per square yard of ground. This will also release the pent-up potash in the soil and, in comparison with sulphate of ammonia, it does not prove so destructive to the lime already present in the soil.

Potash may be given as wood ash, which should have been stored under cover, as the potash content is readily washed away by rain. For this reason, light soils are those mostly lacking in potash and require replenishing more often than heavy soils.

Fish meal, guano, and poultry manure are organics which will provide potash but where the land is in good 'heart', sulphate of potash may be used instead, at planting time, or shortly after, for it is quickly washed down to the plant's roots, Use at a strength of 1 oz. per square yard, preferably during showery weather.

2*

Another valuable fertilizer is liquid manure which is given to growing plants, especially tomatoes, and is readily assimilated by them. It is sold in a concentrated form (Liquinure or Welgo) and diluted as necessary. It is clean to use and free from any unpleasant smell. For best results, after it has been applied to the soil around the plants it should be well watered in, so that there is no loss in evaporation before it reaches the roots.

Lime is all-important as a soil lacking lime will (with the exception of potatoes) never grow good crops. Apart from its ability to correct the acidity of a soil, lime is able to release the various plant foods locked up in the soil. Well-manured land will not confer its full benefits on growing crops unless lime is present to unlock the food content. Again, lime is able to improve the physical condition of a heavy soil by its action on the clay particles.

SUMMARY TABLE OF FERTILIZERS

Fertilizer	Action	Nitrogen Content	Phosphatic Content	Potash Content
Basic Slag	Slow		15%	
Bone Meal	Slow	5%	20%	
Dried Blood	Medium	10%		
Farmyard Manure	Slow	0·5%	0·25%	0·5%
Fish meal	Quick	10%	8%	7%
Guano	Quick	15%	10%	7%
Kainit	Slow			13%
Nitrate of Soda	Quick	16%		
Nitro-Chalk	Quick	16%		
Potassium Nitrate	Quick	14%		40%
Poultry manure	Medium	3%	2%	6%
Rape meal	Slow	5%	2%	1%
Seaweed	Slow	5%		1·5%
Shoddy (Wool)	Slow	12%		
Sulphate of Ammonia	Quick	20%		
Sulphate of Potash	Medium			50%
Superphosphate	Medium		15%	
Used Hops	Slow	4%	2%	

A heavy soil may be more easily worked by giving it an application of unhydrated lime in autumn. This is also known as caustic lime and is obtained from a builders' merchant and *must* be kept *dry* until used. Apply when the soil is reasonably dry, then lightly fork it in. The moisture in the soil will cause a reaction which, combined with winter frosts and wind will put the soil in a friable condition by early spring.

RAISING THE PLANTS

A frame or a small greenhouse will not only enable a greater variety of crops to be grown but tomatoes and cucumbers can be produced earlier than in the open air; and, where some form of heating is available, out-of-season crops may be enjoyed. Tomatoes may be raised early in the year to begin cropping about June 1st; rhubarb may be forced under the greenhouse bench, and, in a frame heated by soil cables, winter lettuce and early beans may be grown.

A sunny position must be selected for the greenhouse so that full advantage may be taken of the early spring sunshine. If artificial heat is available, a greenhouse may be kept in use all the year round.

To calculate the amount of heat required to raise the temperature 25°F above that of the outside temperature, the total area of the glass and base must be ascertained and this is multiplied by ten to give the number of watts required. Where electricity is available, this is the most labour-saving form of heating, and a heater with thermostatic control ensures no wasted heat and low running costs. The heater should be fitted with a fan to circulate air (warm in winter, cool in summer) which is vital for healthy plant growth and will usually prevent an attack of botrytis or mildew which may prove troublesome in a stagnant atmosphere. Where seedlings are being raised, economies may be made by the use of a propagator which will raise the temperature to the 60°–65°F. necessary for rapid germination and with the minimum of expense.

The use of soil-warming wires for use in greenhouse or cold frame is an inexpensive way of raising early salad crops and young plants. A transformer unit which reduces the mains supply to a safe low voltage is used to heat a plastic-covered galvanized wire laid under a bed of soil or sand. When making such an electric hotbed, a minimum of six watts per square foot is allowed and the current switched on at night. When turned off, the soil will remain warm for several hours, there being no rapid fall in temperature as with air heating.

This is a less arduous method of raising seedlings and enjoying early crops than the use of a hotbed made by composting manure or straw with an activator. When the material has generated sufficient heat, the hotbed is made six inches wider than the frame itself. It is well trodden down so that the heat will be retained for as long as possible, and the frame is then placed over it. Sterilized soil (in which the seeds or plants will grow) is then placed in the frame to a depth of 2–3 inches.

It is important when you are raising your own plants in a greenhouse or over a hotbed, that there should be another frame available for the hardening-off of the young plants before planting into the open ground.

SOWING THE SEEDS

Seeds of hardy vegetables, e.g. cabbage, savoy and leeks, may be sown in the open and grown entirely without protection. A prepared seed-bed, brought to a fine tilth, should be made ready for a late summer sowing. The plants may be allowed to spend the winter unprotected in the milder parts or, if the garden is exposed, may be covered with cloches in the rows. The less hardy vegetables, e.g. cauliflower and those which mature late, like celery, should be sown outdoors early in spring, or in a heated greenhouse or frame for planting out when hardened.

For best results, always obtain fresh seed from a seedsman with a reputation to maintain and sow thinly, so that the tiny seedlings will not be overcrowded lest they become 'drawn' and weakly, a condition from which they will not recover. They must have room to develop.

PELLETED SEED

The seed houses now supply the seeds of many vegetable crops treated against a number of the more lethal virus and fungus diseases, whilst the seed of several vegetables, e.g. beetroot and lettuce, is obtainable in pelleted form in which each seed is covered with a coating of plant food. This protects the seed from disease while awaiting germination which may be retarded during a period of cold weather. It also gives the seedlings an additional boost as soon as germination has taken place. The coating is programmed to break down quickly after sowing. Pelleted seed may be sown singly, spacing out at the required distances, thus saving time in thinning and transplanting, and there is also no wasted seed.

Sow outdoors only when the soil is friable and in drills 1 inch deep and in rows 9 inches apart to enable the hoe to be moved between the rows. The drills are best made with the back of a rake, using a garden-line to ensure straightness.

For under-glass sowing, clean boxes or pans should be used, although marrows and cucumbers should be sown in small pots or in half-inch Solo-Gro cubes made of specially prepared plant food and Vermiculite. After germination, the cubes are planted in peat pots containing a suitable compost and grown on without root disturbance.

For indoor sowing, John Innes compost is to be recommended, having been proved reliable over many years. A soil-less compost composed mainly of peat and sand with added nutrients such as Fison's Levington, is easier to handle but needs more care with watering as it dries out rapidly, and experience in its use is needed for best results.

The John Innes sowing compost is made up to this formula:

2 parts	sterilized loam	
1 part	peat (horticultural)	
1 part	sand	per bushel
1½ oz.	superphosphate	
¾ oz.	ground limestone	

Have the compost in the greenhouse (or frame) several days before sowing, to enable it to absorb some warmth and make sure that it is in a moist but friable condition. It should have been made up shortly before use for it deteriorates in quality if stored for any length of time and may become contaminated. Fill the container to just below the edge, make the surface level and after sowing thinly, just cover the seed with compost, and water lightly.

To hasten germination, cover the container with a piece of brown paper or black plastic which you remove for watering and as soon as the seed has germinated.

Transplant the seedlings as soon as they have formed their second pair of leaves and before they have used up the nutrients in the sowing compost. To transplant, have the boxes ready filled with a freshly-prepared compost and, holding the plant with the fingers of one hand, carefully loosen the roots with the other hand with a piece of smooth-ended wood or cane. Then lift with one continuous movement, transferring the plant to the new growing medium and inserting the roots to a depth of about one inch. Plant two inches apart, make comfortably firm, and water in.

The plants should be grown on in a warm but buoyant atmosphere for about four weeks when they should be moved to a frame for gradual hardening. This will take from two–three weeks. From an early February sowing the plants will be ready to set out about mid-April, depending upon situation and weather conditions. Do not plant out if cold winds are troublesome or if the soil is wet and sticky. It is better to wait for more suitable conditions, otherwise the plants will receive a check from which they will take weeks to recover. Planting distances are given under the description of each vegetable. When ready to go out, the plants should be 3–4 inches tall, sturdy, and of a rich green colour. Yellow, sickly-looking plants will never do well.

Early crops of carrots and turnips may be obtained by sowing directly into a seed-bed made in a frame or over a hotbed, and here it is better to sow broadcast, raking in the seeds lightly and keeping the frame closed.

Artichoke, Jerusalem: Introduced into Europe by the French settlers in Canada, its unique flavour should ensure its greater popularity. It prefers a light, sandy soil into which some manure has been incorporated. At the end of March, plant tubers about walnut size in narrow trenches about 6 in. deep, allowing 12 in. between the tubers, with the rows 20 in. apart. Water well if the soil is dry in summer. Earthing up the rows, as for potatoes, will help to increase the yield.

Lift the roots in late October when the foliage has died back and store the tubers in boxes of sand; or lift as required, for freshly dug tubers have the best flavour. The silver-skinned variety is the best and the way to cook is to parboil before removing the skins, and then to bake them.

The tall top growth may need support if the garden is exposed. Before lifting, cut away the stems 6 in. above ground.

Bean, Broad: One of the first of the summer crops, for which reason it is always welcome and makes an appetizing dish, steamed until tender and served with parsley sauce.

Provide a deeply-worked soil and that has been manured for a previous crop. Some decayed manure or old mushroom-bed compost is suitable and the soil must not lack lime.

Two sowings for successional cropping should be made, one in October (and where the garden is exposed, the young plants should be covered with cloches during severe weather); another in March. Sow in a double row 8–9 in. apart so that they may be covered if necessary with a barn-type cloche, and allow the same distance between the beans in the rows. Plant the seeds 2 in. deep, using a trowel.

When the plants begin to grow in spring, earth up at the base and support them when 18 in. high by enclosing with twine fastened to stakes. Early support may be given by inserting twigs about the plants after earthing up.

Black Fly is the most troublesome pest but rarely attacks autumn-sown plants. As the flies congregate at the top of the plant, either pinch out the tops as soon as the plants have set a fair crop or spray fortnightly from the end of April on with derris solution. Slugs may also prove troublesome to young plants, so water the ground with Slugit after sowing.

The Longpod varieties are the hardiest and are sown in autumn, Longfellow being excellent, bearing large crops of

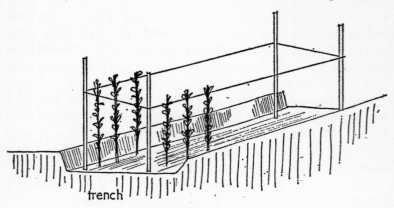

Fig. 3: Staking a double row of broad beans.

straight pods each containing 8–9 beans. The Windsors are the more tender and are sown in spring. Green Windsor has a deliciously mild flavour after cooking.

For a small garden, The Midget, which makes a bush plant 15 in. tall with 3–4 stems covered with beans up to 6 in. long, does well in poor soils.

After cropping, chop off the haulm and move to the compost heap, then dig in the roots which will improve the nitrogenous content of the soil.

Bean, Dwarf: Also known as the French bean and one of the most appreciated of summer vegetables. With their compact habit, freedom of cropping, and quickness to mature, they are ideal to grow between those crops which mature later in the year.

The first sowings should be made under cloches in March; or plants may be raised in gentle heat and set out in April, to be covered by cloches until late May when the risk of frost damage will be gone. Again, plants may be raised in a cold frame and set out at the end of May, for all beans transplant well.

The first unprotected outdoor sowing, should be made towards the end of April and further sowings at monthly intervals until late July. French beans like a light friable soil well enriched with humus-forming manures such as used hops or mushroom-bed compost. For an early sowing, use the quick maturing Earligreen or The Prince, planting the seeds 2 in. deep and 8–9 in. apart in the rows. If sowing a double row, plant 12 in. apart and stagger the planting to allow room for development. The plants will begin to crop within eight weeks of sowing and will continue in bearing for six or seven weeks. It is advisable to pick them each day, whilst young and succulent, to give others the chance to form. So as not to loosen the plants in the soil, remove the beans with scissors. Tread in if the plants have been blown about by strong winds or made loose by careless picking.

For maincrop, Masterpiece does well in all soils, and bears heavy crops of crisp, long, deep green pods, whilst Processor is outstanding for deep freezing, the brittle pods being short and round.

To guard against black fly, dust with derris at fortnightly intervals. If dark brown spots appear on the beans, this may be due to anthracnose which can be troublesome in damp, humid weather; so spray with weak Bordeaux Mixture.

French beans may be forced in a temperature of 65°F, four seeds being planted in a 10 inch pot in a friable compost containing a little decayed manure. Sow early January, syringe the plants regularly; they will begin to crop towards the end of March. For forcing, Canadian Wonder and Earligreen are reliable.

Bean, Runner: This is the prince of vegetables to follow the French beans and is at its best in late summer and autumn. The beans may be grown up laths or canes 6–7 feet tall and set out in rows or arranged in tent fashion—a better method where space is limited (Fig. 4).

Fig. 4: Lathes or canes set out tent-fashion.

The variety, Hammond's Dwarf, may however be grown in rows like the dwarf bean, for it makes a bushy plant 18 in. tall and bears 8–9 pods over a period of 10–12 weeks. It may be grown under barn-cloches.

Runner beans require a rich, well-manured soil. When growing in rows it is usual to take out a trench 10 in. deep and the width of a spade. At the bottom, place material from the compost-heap which is limed and trodden down. Over this, spread a layer of soil and some decayed manure and allow it to settle. The trench should then be filled up with sifted soil to which you have added 1 oz. of superphosphate and ½ oz. of sulphate of potash per yard of trench.

The laths are inserted well into the ground at intervals of 9 in. and are tied in place to a strong wire stretched 4 ft. above soil level and fastened to stout stakes at the ends of the rows. It is usual to have a double row 9 in. apart. Seed is sown 3 in. deep at the base of each lath, mid-May being the time to plant and it is advisable to plant a few extra seeds to fill in where any fail to germinate. Alternatively seeds may be sown in a frame in early May and the plants set out in early June.

The plants must never lack moisture, otherwise the flowers will drop before setting. So water the plants copiously in dry weather and give them an occasional watering with dilute liquid manure to increase the weight of crop and prolong its life. Regular spraying of the foliage will help the flowers to set and keep the plants free from red spider.

A reliable variety is Crusader; the long straight pods grow to 18 in. and are suitable for exhibition; but for table use remove them when 12 in. long when they will be free from any stringiness. Excellent, too, is Dobie's Yardstick, which will grow to 20 in. if required for exhibition.

Heavy pickings may be preserved for winter use by slicing the beans and placing them in an earthenware jar, covering the beans with layers of salt as the jar is filled. When required, wash away the salt and soak for an hour before cooking.

Beetroot: Beetroot is a native of the Mediterranean and slightly tender, so do not sow until May; otherwise the seedlings may be caught by frost. It requires a friable soil which has been manured for a previous crop. Before sowing, dress the ground with 1 oz. of common salt per square yard. Beet seed is now sold in pelleted form which protects it whilst awaiting germination. It also allows the seeds to be sown individually, thus saving time in thinning. Thiram-soaked seed will also guard the seedlings against *Phoma lingam* attack, which makes the seedlings turn brown and decay.

Sow in drills 1 in. deep and 15 in. apart; an ounce of pelleted seed will sow a 30-yard row if the seeds are spaced 2 in. apart.

At all times, keep the soil moist or the beetroot will become coarse and 'woody'; and to suppress annual weeds, place strips of black polythene, held in place by stones, between the rows.

When the plants have reached golf-ball size, remove alternate plants and either pickle or use in salads. This will give those you have left room to develop, and they should be lifted in October before frost and stored in boxes of sand or peat. Lift with care, for the roots will bleed if damaged; to reduce bleeding to a minimum, twist away the leaves rather than cut them off.

Avon Early is one of the best to sow for it does not easily 'bolt' in dry weather. Detroit Globe is also reliable and is free from 'rings' when cooked. Outstanding, too, is the new Burpee's Golden, ready to use within sixty days of sowing, the skin being golden yellow with a mild, sweet flavour, whilst the tops may be cooked like Swiss Chards.

Broccoli, Large Heading: To withstand a hard winter, the plants must be grown well, and, as they usually take twelve months to reach maturity, those wanted for March cutting must be sown the previous March, and so on.

Sow the seed in a frame or in a prepared bed outdoors, either broadcast or in drills 1 in. deep. Thin out if there is overcrowding so that transplanting will not be necessary until the plants are moved to the open ground when about 4 in. tall. If the plants are raised in boxes in gentle heat, they will need transplanting when they have formed their second leaf, being spaced 2 in. apart.

As with sprouts, firm planting out is necessary for the formation of a tight head or 'curd'. Plant 2 ft. apart in well-drained ground into which you have incorporated a slow-acting nitrogenous fertilizer such as wool shoddy or farmyard manure. Additionally, 1 oz. of sulphate of potash per square yard should be given at planting time, for this will help to build up a 'hard' plant.

Keep the hoe moving between the plants and water copiously in dry weather. Should the weather be severe, fold several leaves over the head to give protection.

The first to mature will be Early Penzance, ready to cut at the beginning of winter, and this is followed by Veitch's Self-protecting and Leamington for April and May. To extend the season, Royal Oak makes a dwarf, compact plant, its pure white heads remaining firm in the hottest weather.

The brassicas, and this includes the cabbage and brussels sprout too, suffer from two particularly unpleasant foes, (a) club root disease, also known as 'finger and toe', and (b) the grub of the Cabbage White butterfly which devours the leaves and the 'curds' of cauliflower and broccoli. To control, dust the plants with derris powder once a fortnight from early June, and, as a further precaution, immerse the 'curd' in salt water for an hour before cooking.

Club root is caused by a slime fungus which lives on decayed vegetable matter in the soil. Well-limed land will rarely support the disease but as a precaution, dust the roots of all brassicas with calomel before planting. (See pp. 167–8).

Broccoli, Sprouting: Though growing tall and occupying the ground for several years, there is no more valuable plant, for it gives a continuous supply of white or purple 'sprouts', like tiny cauliflowers, and intense cold will trouble it not.

It requires a deeply worked soil containing plenty of humus-forming manures such as garden compost, farmyard manure, used hops, or shoddy, whilst in their second winter the plants will benefit from a mulch of strawy manure forked in around the plants in spring.

Seed should be sown early in April, the plants being set out 3 ft. apart towards the end of May. Firm planting is essential or they may be blown over by strong winds.

The first shoots will be ready before the year end and should be removed when small and tender. If the plants are regularly picked over and not allowed to run to seed, they will remain productive for several years. Early Purple Sprouting provides a succession of purple shoots which turn green when cooked, whilst Nine Star Perennial bears eight or nine pure white 'curds' like small cauliflowers, each winter.

Brussels Sprouts: This is the most important of winter vegetables for it begins to crop in October and continues until the end of March, giving six months of delicious sprouts during the coldest months of the year. But to have firm 'sprouts', like golf-balls, the plants require a long season to make plenty of growth, a well-manured soil, and firm planting.

Seed may be sown in a frame or in the open in September and the plants set out 2–3 ft. apart early in April. The ground should have been manured as for broccoli and for the formation of tight, crisp sprouts rake in at planting time 1 oz. each of super-phosphate and sulphate of potash per square yard. Plant firmly and as the plants make growth, tread the soil around the base repeatedly. Keep the hoe moving between the rows and, in autumn, remove any decayed leaves from the stems.

Remove the sprouts before they become too large and coarse, by snapping them from the main stem and removing two or three from each plant as they reach the necessary size. At the end of winter, the tops may be used as 'cabbages'.

Avon Cross is a reliable early variety, the sprouts being even in size, and they retain their quality if unpicked; and for later pickings, Peer Gynt is a continuous and heavy bearer.

Cabbage: With its extreme hardiness and ease of cultivation, doing well in all soils, this is an indispensable vegetable for winter and spring, though, by planting for succession, you can have cabbages to cut throughout the year.

With *spring cabbage*, the plants must be advanced sufficiently to withstand a severe winter yet not so advanced that they will 'bolt' in a dry spring. Sow seed in shallow drills in July and move the plants to their permanent quarters in September. The ground should be well manured and given a 2 oz. per square yard dressing of basic slag at planting time. Plant 16 in. apart, keep the hoe moving, and in spring, give a ½ oz. dressing of nitrate of soda per square yard, applying it between the rows, preferably on a rainy day. The plants will be ready to use in late spring or early summer. Unwin's Foremost, Flower of Spring, and Greyhound, with its pointed head, are all reliable.

For autumn, sow seed in September or in a frame in March, moving the plants to the open ground in mid-April. By early autumn, they will have formed heads large enough to cut. Amongst the best are Princess, Golden Acre, and Primo, each being ready within six months of sowing and forming compact heads like small footballs.

For winter cabbage, sow in April and set out 20–24 in. apart in May. These form large heads and require a rich, deeply-worked soil. Give a 4 oz. per square yard dressing of nitro-chalk before planting. Do not sow too early or the plants may run to seed in a cold late spring. Sentinel is one of the best; though the heads may weight 6–7 lb. they are mild of flavour. Winter Keeper is another reliable variety which, when cut, will store throughout winter in an airy shed.

Carrot: For an early crop, sow seed in February in finely-screened soil, over a gentle hotbed in a frame. Sow broadcast and keep the soil moist and the frame closed on all but the mildest days. The young carrots will be ready to pull by early May, the smaller roots being left to mature later. For forcing, use the stump-rooted Sweetheart or Early Gem.

For the maincrop, sow broadcast or in drills 1 in. deep and 9 in. apart, thinning the seedlings to 2 in. apart and later removing alternate plants, which make delicious eating. The soil must be brought to a fine tilth to a depth of 9 in., otherwise the roots may grow forked. Do not use fresh manure but sow in soil that has been manured for a previous crop.

Carrots are not improved by frost, and any still in the ground in November should be lifted, cleaned, and stored in sand.

Carrot fly is the most troublesome of pests, the yellow larvae burrowing into the roots. Before sowing, therefore, dress with Dieldrex-'B' ($\frac{1}{16}$ oz. to an ounce of seed), or dust the soil with Lindex at sowing time.

A reliable variety is Goldinhart which grows 2 in. broad at the top and tapers to a stumpy point. Its orange flesh continues through to the centre.

Cauliflower: For an early summer crop, sow seed in a frame or under cloches in early September, pricking the plants out to another part of the frame when large enough. After sowing, water with Cheshunt Compound to prevent an attack of 'black leg' which causes the seedlings to turn black at the base and die.

After hardening in spring, set out the plants in May, 2 ft. apart, planting firmly to ensure a compact head. The plants require a soil rich in humus and plant food, so dig in material from the compost-heap, or use shoddy or hop manure augmented by 2 oz. of sulphate of potash per square yard at planting time. If the spring is cold and the plants are making slow growth, give a sprinkling of nitrate of soda around each plant on a showery day. In dry weather, water copiously and begin using the 'curds' as soon as they reach a reasonable size, for in warm weather they soon run to seed. For this reason it is better to sow a small amount of seed at monthly intervals rather than all at one time.

For an early crop, Snow King will bear its solid white heads in early July, and to follow there is the compact Dwarf Monarch, followed by Sutton's Superlative, which is ready in November.

Celery: The amateur will find the self-blanching type easier to manage for it needs neither trenching nor much blanching. It is grown on the flat in a well-manured soil containing plenty of humus to retain summer moisture.

Sow in gentle heat in a greenhouse or frame in March, and set the plants out 9 in. apart early in June. Plant firmly and keep them moist during dry weather. The stems are self-folding and no earthing up is necessary, but the sticks will be more tender if pieces of cardboard are fastened round the plants about three weeks before they are required for use. They will then be fully blanched. Celery may be sliced or grated and eaten raw in a salad or stewed and served with meat or game.

Celery fly is the most troublesome pest but may be exterminated by spraying the foliage with quassia solution in June and again three weeks later.

Golden Self-blanching bears rich yellow sticks and hearts well, whilst Greensleeves forms large succulent sticks of lime green which are free from fibre.

Cucumber: If a frame or barn-type cloche is available, 'frame' cucumbers can be grown; where there is no glass, 'ridge' varieties are grown in the milder parts of Britain.

Frame cucumbers may be grown cold in a well-manured bed but will be a month later to fruit than if grown over a hotbed. Fill the frame with manure to a depth of 18 in. and this is topped with 6 in. of soil into which the seed is sown, as the plants resent root disturbance. Two 5 ft. × 4 ft. lights together will accommodate three plants, but sow the seed in pairs 2 in. apart and remove the weakest plants. Sow early in April, keep the frame closed, and maintain a damp atmosphere until the seed has germinated.

As the plants make growth, stop the laterals at the second leaf, training the sub-laterals about the frame. As the sun increases in strength, spray frequently and give plenty of ventilation. When the fruits form, place them on pieces of wood to prevent their coming into contact with the soil.

If growing under cloches, make a trench to the width of the cloches, fill with manure, and top up with soil. Allow 4–5 ft. between the plants.

Topnotch is excellent for frame or cloche culture, the slender dark green fruits having a thin skin and mild flavour. It also does well in a greenhouse.

Ridge cucumbers should be grown over a hotbed in a sunny position, the seed being sown late in April under a cloche, which must be removed in early June. When the plants have formed 2–3 leaves, 'stop' them by pinching out the growing points to encourage the formation of the laterals which will carry the crop. In dry weather, water copiously; an occasional application of dilute manure water will increase the quality and also the crop.

Sutton's Prolific is excellent, being hardy and compact; the medium size fruit has a mild flavour.

Endive: Either cooked or eaten raw, it has a delicate flavour and a crispness, unusual with salad crops. Sow endive where it is to mature for if transplanted, it will run to seed. Sow at fortnightly intervals from early July until early September in a soil well supplied with humus. Make shallow drills 15 in. apart and thin the plants to 9 in. in the rows. If later sowings are covered with cloches, endive may be enjoyed until Christmas.

Blanching is necessary to make a good heart, raffia being tied round the top just before the plants reach maturity; they will be ready to use after three weeks.

Batavian White makes a large heart filled with crisp creamy white leaves.

Leek: Leeks have been grown by people in the north since earliest times, for it withstands intense cold and may be lifted throughout winter.

The best leeks are grown in trenches, in a well-manured soil, and the plants set out in June, having been raised in a frame or in gentle heat in March. Like celery, they require a long season to reach their best.

When planting out, make a hole 6 in. deep and drop the plant in. Do not fill up with soil, but water in. Plant 9 in. apart in a double row and allow the wide part of the leaf, the blade, to fall along the row rather than across it. Leeks are moisture-lovers and need copious amounts of water during dry weather.

By mid-August, the stems will need blanching. Fix corrugated paper, held in place with a rubber band, round the lower part of the stem. Then, as the plants make growth, place soil thrown up from the trench round the stems to complete the blanching. The plants will continue to grow until mid-November when the first liftings are made.

Reliable varieties are Clandon White, early to mature, the 'sticks' having a sweet, mild flavour; and Marble Pillar, pure white when blanched and with a mild delicate flavour.

Lettuce: To grow lettuce one needs a well-limed soil containing plenty of moisture-holding humus. Garden compost or old mushroom-bed manure is suitable, augmented by a liberal dressing of peat if lime is present.

By using a cold frame or cloches for a winter crop, you can have lettuce all the year. For winter, sow Tom Thumb or Trocadero in a seed-bed in early September and plant out in a frame in October 8 in. apart, watering only occasionally and admitting air on all mild days.

For early summer use, sow in a frame in March and plant out 12 in. apart early in April. Constant Heart and Webb's Wonderful, which stands through the hottest weather, may be sown at monthly intervals until July.

For autumn and winter outdoors, sow early in July Arctic King or Winter Marvel, both of which stand the severest weather. These are cabbage lettuce. For a cos lettuce for summer use, grow the self-blanching varieties to reduce garden work to a minimum.

Botrytis, a grey mould and the most troublesome disease, attacks frame-grown plants and those outdoors in a wet summer, causing the leaves to decay. Dusting the young plants with Orthocide Captan will usually prevent an outbreak. For downy mildew, dust with equal parts of hydrated lime and sulphur.

Marrows and Squashes: These require a position of full sun and shelter from cold winds. They resent root disturbance and must be pot grown, the seeds being sown late in March, in small pots over a hotbed or in a warm greenhouse. Use the John Innes compost in which decayed manure is substituted for the peat. Just press the seeds into the compost with the point upwards and keep the compost moist. Early in May, when the plants have formed their second leaves, place in a cold frame and harden gradually, planting out at the month end.

Plant 5–6 ft. apart in a large mound of decayed manure covered with 6 in. of soil and keep well watered. When planting, take care not to break the soil ball. When the plants have made 18 in. of growth, pinch out the leaders to encourage side shoots to form, for these will carry the crop.

Pollination may be by insects, but, for heavier crops, transfer the pollen from the male flowers to the females, using a camel-hair brush, pollinating only when the flowers are dry. (The female has a small swelling beneath the flower which is absent in the males.)

Throughout the summer, spray the foliage often and remove the marrows before they grow too large. At this stage they will be at their best for eating.

Amongst the most reliable are Cocozelle, the Italian marrow, a semi-trailing variety bearing dark green fruits, striped yellow; and Rotherside Orange, of similar habit which bears fruits of the size of a grapefruit. After cooking, place in a refrigerator and serve cold, with ginger.

For a bush marrow, Zucchini bears dark green cylindrical fruits which are at their best when about 8 in. long.

Mustard and Cress: Sow cress four days earlier than mustard; in a temperature of 48°F. both will then be ready to cut together—about three weeks after sowing. Sow in punnets or boxes filled with soil and some decayed manure, cutting when about 3 in. high.

Commercial growers sow rape seed which is quicker to mature and combines the flavour of both. It may be grown all the year, outdoors in summer, in the kitchen window during winter.

Onion: To obtain large bulbous onions which will keep all winter, plant onion sets early in April in a prepared bed. They require a well-worked soil enriched with decayed manure; and a good idea is to rake some bonfire ash into the surface (which should be brought to a fine tilth). Stuttgarter Riesen is the best sort to grow from sets, which should be plump and firm. Press them into the surface 6 in. apart, allowing 12 in. between the rows. As a deterrent to onion fly, dust with calomel after planting.

Keep the hoe moving between the bulbs, and the ground well watered. A weekly application of manure water will help the onions to swell. By mid-August, watering should be with-held to enable them to complete their ripening, which will be helped if the tops are bent over just above the neck.

Towards the end of September, when the soil is dry, lift carefully, shaking off the soil and string up by the tops in an airy shed for use when required.

To have spring onions, sow seed of White Lisbon in October in shallow drills 9 in. apart to pull in May; those from a spring sowing will be ready later in summer. Dust the rows with calomel before sowing.

Parsnip: It requires a long season and a deeply-worked soil. No fresh manure apart from some used hops or old mushroom-compost should be given. Good parsnips may be up to three feet long.

Sow in March, in drills 18 in. apart and thin the seedlings to 6 in. apart in the rows. Use fresh seed and sow thickly. Even if only two years old, the seed will not germinate.

Keep the roots growing by watering in dry weather. They will be ready for lifting in November, but only lift as required, for, like turnips, they are improved by frost.

The only troublesome pest is carrot fly, so dust the rows with Lindex before sowing. In recently-manured land, canker may prove troublesome; where this disease has occurred, sow Avonresister, the roots being small but of good flavour. Hollow Crown also shows resistance to canker and makes a large root with a clear bright skin.

Peas: By planting early, mid-season, and late varieties, you can have peas from early June until well into autumn. Southern gardeners may make a sowing in autumn, covering the plants with cloches in severe weather. The round-seeded varieties, e.g. Histon Mini, should be used for autumn sowing, for they do not hold moisture like the wrinkled or marrowfat varieties which have had some of their starch content converted into sugar.

At the end of March, make the first outdoor sowings, which may be Early Onward or the new Sweetness, to mature in June. Then follow, in April with Onward, and, if Kelvedon Wonder is sown in June, it will crop early in autumn.

Peas enjoy a well-manured soil and one containing plenty of lime, but an excess of nitrogen should be avoided. Take out a shallow trench to the width of a spade and 2 in. deep and, after lining it with peat, sow the seeds 2 in. apart. Sprinkle peat over the peas before covering with soil. Peas are sold by the pint, and half a pint will sow a 10-yard row. Winter-sown seed should be protected from mice by shaking the seed in a tin containing paraffin and red lead. Do not let this mixture come near with children or animals, and wash the hands after using it.

When the plants appear above ground, insert some twiggy

branches near them to allow them to climb up by their tendrils. The varieties mentioned are suitable for a small garden, for they grow less than two feet tall.

The peas are ready to harvest when the pods are filled, and firm when pressed. Remove those low down first, to allow those at the top to mature later.

If Fusarium Wilt has been troublesome, grow resistant varieties such as Recette and Vitalis. Pea moth is eradicated by spraying with Sybol when the plants are coming into bloom and again when the first pods have formed.

Potato: In addition to its food value, the potato is able to crop well in 'dirty' land, provided it is well manured. When the crop is lifted, the ground can be cleaned. Potatoes do not like lime, which causes scab. They require a slightly acid soil and are peat-lovers, whilst decayed farmyard manure suits them well. The land should be limed *after* potatoes in the 4-course rotation.

For an early crop, 'sprout' the potatoes (use Scottish or Irish seed for heaviest crops) in a light, airy room, placing the tubers 'rose', or broad end, downwards, and standing them up in a seed tray. Pack peat around the tubers and, for early April planting, begin the sprouting a month before. The sprouts will then be about an inch long for planting.

To plant, make a V-shaped trench 9 in. deep and place at the bottom some manure and peat. Press the tubers into this, 2 ft. apart, the sprouts or eyes uppermost. Cover with 3–4 in. of soil and, where possible, make the rows run from north to south so that the sun can reach both sides of the plants.

When the haulm is about 6 in. above ground, earth up to a depth of 3–4 in. and again a month later. At the same time spray the foliage with Bordeaux Mixture as a precaution against blight.

Maincrop potatoes should be planted 4–5 weeks later.

Lifting the earlies should begin about July 1st., and the maincrop should be lifted in early autumn when the haulm has died down. When lifting, scrape away the surface soil and lift each root with a fork. Carefully shake away surplus soil before placing the potatoes in a bag or box to exclude light, otherwise the tubers will turn green.

Maincrop varieties must be lifted before the frosts and stored in tea chests in a cellar or shed after exposing to the air to dry off surplus soil. Potatoes lifted when the soil is dry will keep better than when the soil is wet.

Eclipse, Epicure, and Arran Pilot are reliable earlies, bearing white kidney-shaped tubers. Follow with Sutton's Olympic, a heavy cropper of round, pink-skinned tubers; and with Stormont Dawn or Arran Comrade for maincrop. All these varieties possess outstanding flavour and crop well.

Radish: For flavour and appearance, the radish is an important part of every salad but it must be grown quickly, otherwise it will be hard and 'woody'.

The seed-bed must contain plenty of humus to hold moisture, so work in a mixture of peat and decayed manure and bring the surface to a fine tilth. Then sow broadcast or in shallow drills and for succession, making a sowing each month from mid-March until early August.

Pull the radishes when the round types are ½ in. across, when they will be juicy and nutty. Inca forms a cherry-like globe and is crisp and sweet, whilst French Breakfast has long red roots, tipped with white.

Savoy: The largest and hardiest of cabbages, capable of withstanding the severest weather. The crinkled leaves enable the winter rains to drain away so that the hearts never become 'soggy'.

Savoys require a well-manured soil and a long growing season. Sow seed outdoors in drills in early April, setting out the plants in May, 2 ft. apart. They will benefit if the soil receives a 4 oz. per square yard dressing of nitro-chalk before planting.

The best variety for a small garden is Tom Thumb, which makes a compact head and will be ready by Christmas. For later, plant Savoy King and Omega, which will stand until the following spring.

Shallots: For pickling, these small onions make a welcome accompaniment for cold meats. Plant the sets late in March, 10 in. apart, pressing the base into the soil, which should have been enriched with decayed manure and the surface rolled firm before planting. Keep the hoe moving, and in late August, bend over the necks to encourage the clusters of bulbs to ripen. Lift early in October and string up to dry; pickle in vinegar within a month or so.

The best variety is Dutch Yellow; make sure to obtain Dutch-grown bulbs.

Spinach: Sow for succession every three weeks from late March to the end of July. Select a partially-shaded position and provide a soil containing plenty of humus. As soon as the plants make some growth, rake in ½ oz. of nitrate of soda per square yard to encourage them to make leaf.

Sow in shallow drills 12 in. apart and thin the plants to 9 in. in the rows. In dry weather, give frequent waterings and begin to pick the leaves when large enough.

Reliable varieties are Cleanleaf and Victoria Long-Standing; the latter bears thick dark green leaves and does not readily run to seed.

Tomato: One of the most important crops for greenhouse and outdoor culture, the tomato requires a sunny position outdoors and a soil that has been worked 15 in. deep, incorporating garden compost and farmyard manure. Peat and hop manure may be used instead, whilst wood ash (which has been stored dry to preserve its potash content) should be raked into the surface just before planting. Or rake in 1 oz. of sulphate of potash per square yard; this will assist the fruit to ripen. To prevent magnesium deficiency, a sprinkling of Epsom Salts should be scattered around each plant.

Plants are raised by sowing seed in a temperature of 65°F. in January, or by sowing in boxes over a hotbed in March, the plants being set out in early June after hardening.

Space 3 ft. apart, and keep the soil comfortably moist throughout the summer, or bud-drop will result. Plants may also be grown outdoors in large pots, but stand them where they will not be blown over. Plants in pots will require regular watering, at least twice daily in warm weather, whilst all tomatoes will benefit from a weekly application of dilute manure water.

Keep the soil stirred to prevent it 'panning', thus shutting off supplies of oxygen to the roots. A summer mulch will also help to prevent this and those varieties which are being grown as a single cordon (main stem) should have the side shoots removed as they form.

To assist the fruits to set, dust the flowers when dry with a camel-hair brush and spray the foliage on all warm days. When the fruiting trusses form, support them by tying them to the cane which is used to support the main stem. A number of outdoor varieties, however, e.g. Atom and Tiny Tim, will need neither support nor stopping, for they will also bear fruit on the side shoots. As they grow low and bushy, place clean straw round the plants to prevent soil splashing on to the fruit. The later trusses will ripen more quickly if the plant is partially defoliated and not watered.

In a cold, sunless summer, outdoor-grown plants may be troubled with botrytis, but spraying with Shirlan AG at the first signs will give control.

Recommended outdoor varieties include Atom, which may be grown under barn-type cloches and bears heavy crops of golf-ball size fruits; Histon Early, which is tall-growing but short-jointed; and Sleaford Abundance, a F_1 hybrid which bears and ripens large crops with the minimum of sunshine.

For greenhouse culture, Amberley Cross and Eurocross, both highly resistant to 'greenback' and *Cladosporium*, cropped heavily and ripened well in a cold house during the sunless summer of 1972.

Turnip: For an early crop, sow Early White Milan over a hotbed early March, thinning to 6 in. apart. For the main crop, sow in early May to mature in July, the roots being lifted when about tennis-ball size.

Outdoors, turnips require a firm bed and well-manured soil with a high lime content. To guard against turnip fly, dust with derris late in May and again a month later.

For winter use, sow Golden Ball, which has sweet orange flesh and will stand well through winter.

3   Shrubs for Small Gardens

C. D. BRICKELL

C. D. Brickell is at the moment Director of the Royal Horticultural Society's Gardens at Wisley where he has worked since 1958. He has, therefore, been associated with one of the most important botanic gardens in the country, if not the world, and there is no one better qualified than he to write about shrubs for the small garden. Chris Brickell has wide interests in the history of plants and is Vice-Chairman and Secretary of international committees which look after the naming and registration of cultivated plants.

Most of us require from our gardens colour and beauty throughout the year, preferably with the minimum of care and maintenance. One of the most satisfying ways of achieving this aim is by using as the backbone of a garden, whether it be large or small, shrubs which can be relied upon to flower freely or provide foliage colour for long periods. As a result of plant exploration particularly early this century, and often at considerable danger to the plant-hunters concerned, we are now able to obtain through nurseries and garden centres an enormous diversity of shrubs suitable for almost any climate and soil type to be found in the British Isles. Additionally, hybridists have played their part by crossing the natural species after they have been brought into gardens and raising from seed a further host of excellent shrubs. Many shrubs will grow far too large for the average small oblong plot, but there still remains a wide selection of medium and low-growing shrubs from which to choose.

How to choose is a bewildering task which faces the inexperienced gardener and in this chapter my aim is to guide the reader through the maze of catalogue names towards those shrubs which give the best value in the garden throughout the seasons and require only limited attention to thrive for many years.

SOIL PREPARATION

The soil in which the shrubs are to grow is as important as the shrubs themselves and it is essential to know the type of soil in your garden before you consider anything else. Is it a sticky clay, the proverbial medium loam, or a very light sand? If a clay, the drainage may be impeded and so the area might need to be drained; if a sandy soil, it will need a considerable amount of humus added to help retain moisture and nutrients.

Does it contain chalk or lime in any form, or is it an acid soil in which rhododendrons and heathers will thrive? Often one can tell by looking at the plants growing in nearby gardens; if acid-loving plants like rhododendrons are growing next door, it is very likely that your own soil will grow them also. But it is always safer to carry out a simple soil test with one of the relatively inexpensive and easily-used kits on the market.

The acidity or alkalinity of a soil is measured by an apparently mysterious pH scale. These letters are followed by an indicative number and pH 7 represents a neutral soil. Numbers below 7 shows acidity, those above 7 indicate alkalinity.

If you are of a more enquiring mind, a detailed analysis of the soil and its nutrients may be obtained through your County Horticultural Officer. Don't forget also, that even in a small area there may be variations in different parts of the garden and it is best to take samples from several points to obtain an overall picture. The results of the tests will determine to a large extent the type of shrub you can grow most easily.

Adequate preparation of the planting site is very important. It is no use just digging holes, pushing the shrubs in and hastily covering the roots with soil, even if the hole is filled with freshly-prepared or bought-in soil-compost. On a clay soil this merely creates a sump in which the shrub's roots will quickly drown; and on a sandy soil, although initially the shrub may grow well, it will quickly exhaust the food in the prepared soil, and growth may be severely checked when its roots reach the unprepared soil outside the hole. Some plants will thrive in spite of such treatment, but many are likely to fail.

Once it has been decided where the shrubs are to go, the whole area should be dug one or two spits deep depending on one's enthusiasm and energy, and manured, using if possible old, well-rotted cow or horse manure. Failing this, rotted garden compost, leaf-mould, spent hops, or coarse peat which are frequently more easy to obtain may be used. They are equally as useful in providing humus in the soil into which the young roots will grow, but generally speaking contain less nutrients than does cow or horse manure. I prefer to use a coarse grade of peat, particularly for sandy or thin soils, as it takes several years to disintegrate completely in the soil, whereas the finer grades normally last for only a season or so.

If the soil is a sticky clay, it may be necessary to carry out more thorough preparation, incorporating large amounts of humus-forming materials, and perhaps also coarse grit to aid aeration, but most soils do not require the elaborate preparation laid down in many gardening books. A well-dug top spit, a forked over lower spit, and a reasonable quantity of some humus-forming material are the basic requirements.

Even this basic preparation may appear hard work in the beginning, but the shrubs will be in the same position for many years, so the better the preparation the less aftercare they are likely to require.

SELECTION AND PLANTING

Obviously personal choice will play a large part in the selection of the individual shrubs to be grown but there are several points to be borne in mind.

It is very easy to admire a beautiful shrub in a garden open to the public and to rush out and buy a similar specimen from a garden centre. But before doing so, it is always advisable to find out if the plant will grow in your soil, what its ultimate height and spread are likely to be and whether or not it is particular as to its cultural requirements. This may seem ordinary common sense, but it is surprising how often one sees mutilated weeping willows and other plants which have outgrown their positions and been cut hard back in a vain effort to keep them under control. Some vigorous large shrubs, if pruned correctly, can be maintained in a small garden; others are slow-growing and will take many years to overspill their allotted positions. Otherwise, however desirable they may be, they should either be excluded entirely or planted with the definite intention of replacing them after a few years—and few people have the heart to do that!

Usually, too, it is much better to buy a small, but vigorous young plant rather than a tempting larger and older plant of the same species. A few plants, such as rhododendrons, transplant well as old specimens, but many other shrubs treated in the same way may survive but look miserable for years before recovering. And by that time a young plant would have overtaken the older one.

If one is lucky enough to buy properly-grown, large container-ized plants that is a different matter. But beware the large 'container-grown' plant which has been in its container only a few months! The true article may be more expensive but it is far better value than its cheaper rival.

Make sure also that the plants are healthy and vigorous when you pick them out at a nursery or garden centre. If the particular plants you are looking for are 'shop-soiled' and appear tired, wind-damaged, or dry, leave them alone—don't buy just because you feel you must complete the planting that weekend. Apply the housewife's techniques for choosing the weekend vegetables—firm and fresh not flabby and drooping—and you will find that very few replacements are needed. Not all garden centres stock a wide range of varieties but specialist shrub-nurserymen offer excellent plants by post. But be cautious of so-called cheap offers; you will get just what you pay for! Choose bushy, well-furnished specimens with several strong, even, basal shoots. If they are in leaf, make certain the foliage and young shoots are healthy and firm. If they are soft, they are liable to droop and damage easily so that the plants receive a check in growth before they are even in position in the garden.

Depth of planting often worries inexperienced gardeners, and the rule is to plant so that the soil surface is at exactly the same level as the old soil mark on the plant-stem when the plant is received.

In general terms, the needs are a well-worked damp, but not sodden, soil and a planting hole slightly wider and deeper than the maximum root spread of the specimen. The roots should be spread well outwards and downwards avoiding crowding and twisting—stuffing the plant into a small hole is not recommended! A useful tip when planting is to place a rigid bamboo cane across the centre of the planting hole so that it is easy to keep the crown of the plant at the correct level whilst working soil well in and firming it around the spread-out roots. Planting too shallowly will expose the upper roots to frost and drying-out; and deep planting will prevent the surface roots getting air. Finally, firm the soil around the plant by hand or with a gentle foot—but don't use too heavy a boot or you will damage the roots and, on clay, compact the soil badly. Plants need air to live just as we do.

After planting, water in thoroughly for this will help to settle the soil as well as providing moisture to assist establishment. If planting during a dry spell in spring or summer (now possible with containerized shrubs), soak the planting positions some time beforehand and water again after planting. If there is much delay between receiving or purchasing the plants and planting, don't let them dry out but heel them into a spare piece of ground until you can deal with them properly.

PRUNING

Again a worrying problem to many and the best advice is 'when in doubt, don't'. The basic requirements are to dead-head the old flowers, except hydrangeas or shrubs grown for their ornamental fruits, to cut out weak growths, to keep the main branches well spaced to let in air and light, and to remove any dead and diseased wood.

Evergreens, if they require pruning at all, only need to have over-vigorous shoots removed to improve their shape or to prevent their becoming too large for their positions. Such pruning

is best carried out after flowering or, if hard pruning is required
to reshape them completely, this should be dealt with in early
spring.

Deciduous shrubs vary in their flowering habit and one cannot
readily generalize. Where specific pruning is required, this will
be mentioned when the individual shrubs are described later on.
Not many deciduous shrubs really need regular pruning after the
first season or two, when a well-shaped framework should be
built up, but thinning is more important, particularly with
shrubs like forsythias and spiraeas, which quickly make thickets
of growth.

A lazy man's method is to establish a three-year renewal cycle
of pruning, each winter or early spring cutting out or thinning
out one-third of the old shoots so that the plant never contains
wood more than three years old. This means that all the pruning
can be carried out at one time without the bother of remembering
whether the shrub flowers on the current season's growth like
Buddleia davidii, the butterfly bush, which should theoretically be
pruned hard back in early spring, or forms its flowerbuds in late
summer and autumn and blooms in late spring or summer as do
the *Philadelphus*, the mock orange, which should be pruned
immediately after flowering. This method would be frowned
upon by the purist as it does not necessarily give a mass of flower
every season. What it does do is provide the ordinary gardener
bemused by explanations of pruning in books, with a simple
system and a reasonable amount of bloom from a pleasantly-
shaped bush. It falls midway between the tailored look required
by the enthusiast and the unkempt, sparse-flowering shrubs of
the non-gardener.

Some plants will not, of course, respond to this régime but it can
be applied successfully to many commonly-grown shrubs to
good effect. But *please* avoid the 'short back and sides' method,
which may keep the bush neat and tidy but results in sparsely-
produced flowers and plants which have lost all their natural grace.

MULCHING AND FEEDING

Mulching, the provision of a thin blanket of humus-forming

material over the surface of the soil between plants, can be both beneficial to the fertility of the soil and labour saving as a weed-smothering device. Manure, leaf-mould, spent hops, garden compost, peat, chopped bracken, and shredded bark are all excellent materials for mulching provided they are relatively free of weed-seeds. Grass mowings, often used and often used much too thickly, are less beneficial as they tend to heat up rapidly, burning surface roots and are often full of seeds of annual meadow grass and other weeds.

After planting, shrubs can be mulched with a thin two-inch layer of one of the materials listed above and if at all possible the whole area of bare soil between the shrubs should be treated in this way. The treatment should be at least an annual event, preferably carried out in autumn when the soil is moist and warm, so forming a snug layer over the roots during the winter. Spring mulching is often practised but mulches are best not applied when the soil is cold. The mulch acts as an insulator and the cold soil takes longer to warm up so that growth may be retarded. If materials (and funds) allow, a further mulch in late spring to follow the autumn dressing is beneficial, and acts as a weed-smotherer for the remainder of the season. Never mulch if the soil is dry—water the ground first, then apply the mulch.

Apart from peat and bark, the mulching materials previously mentioned supply nutrients to the soil to greater or lesser extents and very little, if any additional feeding is necessary for a number of years after planting provided mulching is carried out regularly. An occasional late spring or summer dressing of 1–2 oz. per sq. yd. of a balanced general fertilizer or a seaweed-based fertilizer will not come amiss but regular application is necessary only on very poor soils, when organic materials are totally lacking, or when a system of rather heavy pruning is used and the plants are called upon to produce a mass of vigorous young growths every season. Shrubs in need of a pick-me-up can be treated individually, and a reasonably economic method is to apply to the leaves one of the several good foliar feeds now available.

Where mulching materials lacking nutrients such as peat and bark are used, regular fertilizer treatment may be necessary to supplement the diet unless the soil is a loam or clay already rich in plant foods.

And now to the plants themselves. Rather than provide an alphabetical catalogue I will deal with the plants season by season.

WINTER

Let us start with winter, a period, for the purposes of this chapter, covering the months November to February or March. Most people do not realize that during the dead of winter there are still many plants which will provide flower or persistent berry.

One of the finest of these is the winter-flowering heather, *Erica carnea* from Southern Europe, which unlike most members of its family will tolerate chalk and grow reasonably well on limy soils. It is also able to put up with atmospheric pollution, a certain degree of sea-spray, and will grow but flower less freely in shade, provided it is given reasonable soil conditions. A most cheering winter sight is to see through snow and ice its deep rose or carmine clusters of flowers a few inches above the ground. The habit of the different garden forms varies, some, like Springwood White, forming vigorous weed-smothering carpets, whilst others, such as the rich purple-red Loughrigg, are more bushy and upright in growth but seldom exceed nine inches or a foot in height. Almost fifty garden varieties have been named and introduced and their flowering periods cover the months November (occasionally October) to April. A selection of reliable varieties which can be grown in almost all gardens includes Springwood White, which flowers from January to March; its pink counterpart, Springwood Pink, with the same flowering season; the deep rose King George, an old favourite, in bloom at Christmas and continuing to March; the cyclamen purple December Red, in bloom from December to March; the dark-foliaged Vivellii, its deep carmine flowers appearing in late January and carrying on into March; with the later-flowering soft purple Loughrigg, of upright growth; and the strong-growing, ground-covering Pink Spangles, a deep rosy-red, completing the season in March and April. Coloured foliage forms of *Erica carnea* are few, and the best so far introduced is the golden Anne Sparkes, with bronze-tinted leaves in winter to complement the carmine flowers in February and March. All these varieties are easily obtained, thrive in any reasonably prepared well-drained soil without difficulty, and are hardy and tolerant.

At the same time of year the hybrid *Erica* × *darleyensis*, which has *E. carnea* as one parent, is in bloom. Again there are many slight variants from white to deep rose-pink and they differ from *E. carnea* in the taller habit, reaching $1\frac{1}{2}$–2 feet eventually. *E.* × *darleyensis* makes an excellent dwarf hedge and, like *E. carnea*, is surprisingly tolerant of a wide range of soils. Two good forms are the white Silberschmelze, in flower from December to April, and Arthur Johnson, a fine deep pink.

The longest flowering of these winter heathers is probably *Erica lusitanica* which deserves much wider cultivation, as it starts flowering in November and continues until April. Coming from Portugal and Spain it is liable to be cut back in severe winters but is undamaged by 10° or 12°F. of frost. In nature it may grow to ten feet in height with erect, feathery branches, but is seldom more than 4–5 feet in this country. The mass of small pink-tinged, buds very gradually open to white, slightly fragrant, narrow bell-shaped flowers and appear quite undamaged by frost. It grows perfectly well in any ordinary garden soil, is lime tolerant, and has produced a slightly hardier but otherwise very similar hybrid *Erica* × *veitchii*.

Heathers generally give excellent value in any garden as, once established, they provide a great deal of beauty and pleasure with relatively little maintenance. Some weeding between the plants at first may be needed but, apart from a mulch and occasional restriction of over-vigorous growth, there is little else to do but sit back and enjoy them.

One of the finest winter-flowering shrubs is *Viburnum fragrans* (now to be called *V. farreri*), a deciduous Chinese species, which if left untended will grow to ten or twelve feet but is quite easily kept to small garden size particularly by the housewife who will constantly be picking its sweetly fragrant, blush-white flower clusters which appear during any mild spell from October to March. In growth it is rather upright, constantly pushing up strong shoots from the base. The pruning out of weak, thin branchlets is generally the only treatment required for a few years, but a system of renewal pruning as suggested earlier can

3*

be established to keep the shoots well-spaced and allow light and air into the plant so that flowerbuds are freely formed. Any reasonable soil will support this lovely plant and its equally good hybrid *V.* × *bodnantense* Dawn, distinguished by its deeper pink flowers. The dwarf form of *V. fragrans*, known as Nanum, is a snare and delusion, a twiggy two-foot bush which is unkempt and flowers only sparsely.

The evergreen Mahonias, once included in *Berberis*, are fine foliage plants with glossy dark green leaves and, with some, the agreeable habit of providing bright yellow, often scented, winter flowers. *M. japonica* has long, spreading, fragrant tassels of bloom from November to March and is a most useful plant, eventually six foot across and high, quite happy in a shaded position on any soil including chalk. By pruning out the top growths for use in home decoration, it is easily kept to reasonable dimensions and apart from mulching requires no other treatment. The similar *M. bealei* with shorter, more upright flower spikes is less valuable, but the recently introduced hybrid Charity is a very fine winter plant. It is more upright in habit and left unchecked can go to twelve or more feet, but like most Mahonias can be pruned quite heavily if required. The large clusters of rich yellow flower sprays are produced in November and more or less continuously until March.

Yellow flowers too from the Witch Hazels or *Hamamelis*, delightful but rather large shrubs with fascinating citron-scented, spidery, frost-resistant flowers in late December and January. Not true small garden plants, as they can reach twenty feet or more across but, provided this is realized and allowed for, probably the best value in winter shrubs. They are not happy on lime-containing soils but otherwise are not difficult, and they will flower freely even as young plants only two or three feet high. The Chinese witch hazel, *H. mollis*, is the best species for general cultivation—but be warned again that eventually they will grow too large for a small garden.

Favourite shrubs with everyone are the Daphnes. *D. mezereum* in rose, purple-red, or white, a small 3-4 foot deciduous bush, the stems of which are sprinkled with scented blooms in February, is a very fine small garden plant. It prefers a cool moist soil but is not too difficult to please and excellent value at this time of year. *Daphne odora* announces its presence when in flower long before you approach it. In cold gardens it is unlikely to thrive but is well worth trying in a warm place in the north of England and is reasonably hardy in the south, forming 2–3 foot mounds of evergreen, glossy leaves, usually margined slightly with yellow. Clusters of white, purple-backed, star-shaped, penetratingly fragrant flowers are produced in February and March.

Several dwarf shrubs retain their brightly coloured berries through the winter in spite of the birds. Chief among these is *Skimmia japonica*, not a happy plant on chalk, but otherwise easily grown, a beautiful small neat shrub with handsome dark evergreen leaves and large clusters of shining red berries. Here is a case where it is essential to obtain a free-berrying form—some are male and will not berry, others female and form no berries without a male! Luckily there are selected hermaphrodite varieties which require only the one plant to produce berries and it is advisable to obtain a specimen from a reliable nurseryman to avoid disappointment. A male plant known as *S. Japonica* Rubella is very ornamental in winter, in this case, for the dense clusters of bronze-red flowerbuds which gradually open as spring advances.

Butcher's Broom, *Ruscus aculeatus*, our British native, tolerant of dense shade and dry soil is also evergreen and capable of producing masses of bright, cherry-like fruits which brighten the winter months. A shrub 2–3 feet high, it suffers like *Skimmia* in having the sexes on different plants but again luckily there is an hermaphrodite form known as Bowles' Hermaphrodite, very free-fruiting and seldom more than 1½ feet tall. An ideal plant for the dry, shaded, spot which occurs in almost everyone's garden.

More exotic is *Pernettya mucronata*, a variable South American shrub for acid soils, intolerant of lime but magnificent in winter with great clusters of soft, glossy, white, pink or rosy-purple berries. A gently suckering habit and some tolerance of shade and a height of only 2–3 feet make this an excellent plant for growing between taller shrubs. To ensure fruits Bell's Seedling, a mahogany red, or the Davis Hybrids, a self-fertile race with berries in a variety of colours, should be obtained.

This by no means exhausts the winter-flowering small shrubs

which can be grown—try the Sweet Box, species of *Sarcococca*
with neat evergreen leaves and small intensely fragrant blooms
in January—but we must pass on to spring to consider shrubs at
their best in March, April, and May.

SPRING

Some of the most beautiful and easy of spring shrubs are the
Japonicas which are botanically grouped under *Chaenomeles* and
often referred to as Cydonias or Japanese Quinces. The colour
range goes from blood-red to a fiery vermilion through pinks to
pure white, the saucer-shaped flowers being produced in quantity
during early spring. In autumn there is an additional bonus from
the crops of large, yellowish-green, quince-like fruits which
can be used to make a pleasant preserve similar to crab-apple jelly.
The low-growing Simonii is one of the finest varieties for small
gardens, with semi-double blood-red flowers about an inch and
a half across, and its habit makes it an excellent plant to grow
under windows or against low walls. Rowallane is another deep
red variety which becomes massed with flower in March and
April and is rather taller and more vigorous than Simonii.
Knaphill Scarlet, slow growing at first, will reach five feet in
height when grown in the open and the two-inch flowers are
of salmon-scarlet. This variety flowers abundantly once established.
If a paler colour is required, the apple-blossom pink of Moerloosei
is hard to beat. Most Japonicas may be trained as wall plants and
will fill quite happily the awkward north or east facing position
on the house, although they should not be planted too close to
the wall itself where the soil is often dry. Nor, for that matter,
any wall plant.

Pruning need consist only of thinning out weak shoots after
flowering, and on walls outward-growing shoots should be
spurred back at the same time. Flowers are produced on short
spurs, one or more years old, rather like the apple, and eventually
it is possible to obtain a neatly-trained wall-covering which in
early spring should be a sheet of bloom. Remember, however,
that brick red buildings are not the best background for red and
crimson flowers—the paler-hued varieties are better.

Forsythias, harbingers of spring for many people, are such tolerant and commonly-grown plants that they tend to be looked down on, but their uses are many and few plants could stand such neglect and yet still provide a shower of golden bells in March—bullfinches and sparrows permitting.

Forsythia suspensa, with long trailing branches, is ideal for a north wall or fence, easily trained and very acceptable in this most difficult of garden positions to fill satisfactorily. A proportion of the old wood needs to be cut out after flowering and resulting young shoots trained in, otherwise it is more or less trouble-free. And to brighten the position in summer one of the clematis of the *Jackmanii* group can be allowed to ramble through the forsythia to flower in late summer. The clematis of this group can be cut to within 2–3 feet of ground level each February so leaving the forsythia a free field to bloom in March and April.

Other forsythias tend to become overlarge for the small garden and the popular *F.* × *intermedia* Spectabilis and its rich yellow sport, Lynwood, will quickly make large spreading bushes 8–10 feet through if not severely pruned after flowering each year—the renewal system advocated earlier suits them well. If space permits they are colourful and trouble-free but remarkably dull at other times of year. Do not be tempted by offers of a dwarf forsythia called Arnold Dwarf—a misery which seldom produces its yellowish-green flowers.

Very acceptable substitutes for forsythia and ideal for the small garden are *Corylopsis pauciflora* and *C. spicata*, both from Japan. *C. pauciflora* seldom exceeds 3–4 feet and is a densely-branched shrub covered with small clusters of cowslip-scented primrose-yellow flowers in early spring, the unfolding young leaves being pinkish-bronze. The taller *C. spicata* is similar with rather longer, pendant flower spikes and will reach six feet or more in height and width. Both are relatively slow growing and best on acid or neutral soils but not in cold draughty positions. *C. spicata* will tolerate lime to some extent but is not at its elegant best under such conditions.

Camellias are seldom seen in small gardens, their unfounded reputation for tenderness evidently still held against them. But few plants give a more magnificent display in April than the

many forms of *Camellia japonica* and its superb hybrid *C.* ×
williamsii. Acid conditions are essential and at present no really
satisfactory method has been found for growing them on limy
soils, but they make very good tub plants for a small patio or
even for outside the front door, and the gardener on lime can
grow them in this way using an acid, peaty compost in the tubs.
Use rainwater, not tap-water, if possible and make sure they
are never dry, particularly in midsummer when the flowerbuds
form, and they will reward you amply for your little extra
trouble.

The gardener on an acid soil has a bewildering choice of
camellias to try. The outstanding variety in my view is Donation,
with masses of large, semi-double soft pink flowers for some six
weeks in March and April. Young plants a foot or so high will
produce flower and, even if frost takes one crop of flowers,
there are usually many undamaged buds ready to replace them.
A moist, reasonably drained soil, sheltered from wind either in
an open position or against a west or north wall is ideal. Mulching
each season is normally the only cultural requirement, pruning
being restricted to slight shaping and cutting for the house.
All are evergreens which may reach 10 or 15 feet in height but
are easily kept within bounds. There are literally hundreds of
varieties to choose from and it is worth going to a nursery to
pick out the ones you like best. Don't just buy any old unnamed
camellia—it may be good, but it is worth paying a little bit extra
for named varieties of *C. japonica* like the large scarlet Adolphe
Audusson, Elegans, a deep peach-pink, and the formal double
crimson Mathotiana.

Rhododendrons require the same acid soil as camellias and
again it is seldom worth bothering to grow them if your soil is
limy or chalky. If it is acid or neutral then the choice is staggering.
One must forget for the small garden the great mound-forming
hardy hybrids and the magnificent large-leaved species and
concentrate on the recently-developed range of dwarf hybrids
and the evergreen and deciduous azaleas (which are botanically
rhododendrons) and on some of the beautiful dwarf species,
which are easy and trouble-free.

Basically their requirements are those outlined for camellias, an acid soil which does not dry out, particularly in summer when the following year's buds are forming, and an annual mulch of peat and leafmould. Feeding with a magnesium-rich granular fertilizer may sometimes be needed if the leaves become chlorotic, and pruning of unsightly branches is occasionally necessary. Otherwise nothing is required apart from some deadheading and perhaps a warning not to dig or hoe too near their fibrous surface roots—mulch instead.

Let us forget some of the early flowering rhododendrons like *R.* × *praecox* and Tessa. They are very lovely, but the flowers are so often frosted it is best to use the space for plants which are almost certain to give a fine display a little later in the season. Several of the hardy hybrids, the ironclads, which grow perfectly well in full sun, remain manageable in size for the small garden. The bright red Doncaster, flowering in May-June, and Britannia, slightly earlier, with ruby-red flowers, seldom reach more than six feet and are slow growing. More spreading and spectacular with its large bright red, orange-tinted blooms is Elizabeth, May flowering and an ideal small garden plant. Purple Splendour is taller, but again slow and a marvellous sight in June when covered with the royal purple, black-flexed flowers. The lovely Bow Bells, a neatly rounded bush of 3–4 feet with pale foliage and bell-shaped rosy-pink blooms, flowers in April and May, accompanied by blue or violet relatively small-flowered hybrids like Blue Diamond, Blue Tit and Blue Bird, bushy dwarfs seldom reaching five feet in height. Moerheim Pink, very free-flowering, is an acceptable dwarf substitute for the well-known strong-growing Pink Pearl, whilst in the yellow range the old Unique is available still, large-flowered with yellow, apricot-tinted blooms on a 6–7 foot plant, preferring a little shade.

The Japanese *R. yakusimanum* is a superb and easy dwarf shrub with silvery young growths and May-produced blush-pink flowerbuds opening to pure white. It is compact in habit, free flowering even on young specimens, and, if it passes on its characteristics to its hybrids and other colours can be bred in, will prove invaluable. There are many other dwarf species which can be tried including the pink. *R. williamsianum*, the low-mounded rosy-purple *R. keleticum*, and the violet *R. russatum*, and none is really difficult provided the basic cultivation details are observed.

The evergreen and Japanese azaleas, small-leaved, dense-growing shrubs smothered with brightly-coloured small blooms in May, appeal to most gardeners and, although some are slightly tender in the colder counties, they give unbeatable value and are not very expensive. They prefer slight dappled shade and the conditions outlined for rhododendrons generally, but are so little trouble otherwise it is surprising every garden on acid soil is not well stocked with them. Colours range from the bright pink of Hinomayo through the crimson Hinodergiri to the magenta Hatsugiri—not everyone's colour—and the delicate 'Takasago' in pale lilac. A medley of other larger-flowered hardy, more or less evergreen azaleas is also available, known as Malvaticas, Malvatica-Kaempferi, or Vuykiana hybrids. The colour range is similar to the Japanese hybrids and again personal choice must play a large part in selection. They are excellent for the small garden, May or June flowering; a few reliable varieties are the white Palestrina, Vuyks Rosyred, Purple Triumph, the orange-scarlet John Cairns, and the deep rose Vida Brown.

We cannot leave the great rhododendron tribe without mention of the deciduous azaleas, brilliantly coloured and often fragrant, which are at their best in late May. Open or slightly shaded positions and the usual acid soil, plus annual mulch, suit them best. They are of course stronger growing than the ever-green azaleas, eventually six to eight or more feet depending on variety, but if one or two can be included in the smaller garden their gaily coloured flowers and often attractively tinted autumn foliage give good account of the space taken up. Named varieties are available but are more expensive than seedlings of the Knap Hill and Exbury groups. Unless one is set on a particular variety I suggest a few seedlings, which can be obtained to colour—red, orange, yellow, pink or white—from one of these groups as the best value.

Magnolias, sumptuous and large, often dominate front gardens but mature plants of the popular *M.* × *soulangiana* leave little room grow anything else. Smaller, if less spectacular in flower, is *M. stellata* a slow-growing Japanese shrub with white, many-

petalled flowers in March and April. Both the white form and the
pink flushed forms known as Rosea and Rubra make fine
rounded specimens not often more than five or six feet high and
so ideal for our purpose. They respond well to rich living and
some protection from wind, usually requiring a lime-free, humus-
containing soil and a good annual mulch—much the same
treatment as rhododendrons. Magnolias have fleshy roots and
once planted are best not disturbed, sometimes taking a little time
to settle. Recently an upright form of *M. X soulangiana* called
Picture has been introduced, with large, deep purple flowers,
white inside, and producing blooms at an early age. This looks
to be a very good plant for reasonably small gardens growing
upwards instead of outwards and so less space-consuming.
M. liliiflora Nigra is again very suitable for small gardens, with a
flowering season from May on and off until September, deep
purple-red large flowers on a rounded shrub slowly reaching
six or eight feet. It flowers when young and thrives in all but
chalky soils, a well tried, beautiful small garden plant.

Flowering cherries, like the large magnolias, unfortunately grow
too large for many gardens as they spread often twenty or more
feet. Three shrubby cherries are very useful small garden plants
for April, particularly *Prunus triloba* Multiplex, to four feet in
height, with double rosettes of peach pink; *P. glandulosa* Albi-
plena, rather similar but in double white; and *P. tenella* Fire
Hill, a dwarf almond with brilliant rose-red single flowers.

All cherries and their relations grow well on acid, neutral, or
limy soils and, if possible, prefer an open, sunny position.
Pruning should be avoided except in the case of *P. glandulosa* and
P. triloba, which can be cut back after flowering to encourage
vigorous young wood to flower the following year and can also be
trained in this way against low walls. They are particularly useful to
cover the brickwork under bay windows. On poor soils some
feeding may be necessary, but an annual compost or manure
mulch is normally sufficient to keep them in good condition.

Some of the dwarf brooms are very rewarding plants, taking
up little space and requiring virtually no attention after planting.
Cytisus × kewensis in April and May covers itself in creamy-
yellow flowers and forms a spreading shrub only 12–15 inches

high and 2–3 feet across, whilst the brilliant yellow *C.* × *beanii* is usually even lower, often not more than nine inches high and spreading similarly. Slightly taller and more upright in habit is the rose and white Peter Pan which achieves two feet in height. It is also possible to grow many of the hybrid brooms in yellow, rose, red, and purple in restricted spaces if the shoots which have flowered are cut back after blooming. This encourages sprays of young growths to appear, and these will flower the following season, after which the pruning process is repeated. These hybrid brooms are extremely free flowering and grow, like all their tribe, in poor soil conditions, providing ample recompense for the small trouble of pruning once a year. Of similar aspect is the double-flowered gorse, *Ulex europaeus* Plenus, very compact in habit and smothered in April and May with long-lasting golden blooms. As easy plant, best on poor dry soils.

Associating well with these brooms is *Daphne cneorum* Eximia, a beautiful, spreading, low evergreen shrub, seldom a foot high, slowly forming mounds 2–3 feet across, covered during May with deliciously scented, deep pink flowers. Full sun and plenty of humus are its requirements. It shows a welcome indifference to lime and is certainly not a difficult plant, as many Daphnes are reputed to be. Try also the equally easy *D. retusa*, a dense-growing small evergreen shrub to 2 or 3 feet, with leathery leaves and rose-purple, inwardly white, sweetly perfumed flowers, and Somerset, narrow-leaved and with pale pink blooms, equally scented.

Good neighbours for the brooms and Daphnes are Berberis, of which several species and hybrids can be thoroughly recommended. *B. darwinii*, a tough, glossy evergreen with small, three-pointed leaves, comes from southern Chile and Argentina, producing a mass of brilliant orange flowers in April and May. It slowly reaches 8–9 feet and as much through, but it takes many years to do so. Smaller in stature are Corallina Compacta, Gracilis, and Prostrata, forms of *B.* × *stenophylla*, which has *B. darwinii* as a parent. All are of easy cultivation, even on heavy soils, have evergreen narrow leaves, and vary slightly in habit and in the depth of colour of their orange-yellow flowers. For some shade *B. candidula* can be used, with dark shiny leaves, silver beneath, and bright yellow flowers, a shrub to about 2½ feet in height and 5–6 feet across, dense and labour-saving as a handsome ground cover.

Apart from the winter *Viburnums*, there are several spring-blooming species and hybrids, tolerant of most soils, which remain compact bushes not often over five feet in height and from April to May produce rounded bunches of pink-tinted white flowers which scent the air for several yards around. *V.* × *juddii* should be planted in all gardens, large or small. Of good constitution and unlike the more frequently recommended *V. carlesii* it does not suffer greatly from aphid attack. Fulbrook and Anne Russell are two excellent hybrids of this latter species, slightly more open in habit and equally sweetly-scented. Beware, however, grafted plants of these Viburnums which are apt to sucker from the base. Any suckers must be removed right to the point of origin. Don't merely cut them off at ground level—this leaves part of the sucker underground and this will proceed to produce several further growths.

SUMMER

During the summer months of June, July and August roses, in particular, are the main source of colour in many gardens. It is not possible in this relatively short chapter to consider the many rose varieties in their different groups, but there are numerous other small shrubs worth planting. The mock oranges, or *Philadelphus*, sometimes known incorrectly as syringas, produce white, sometimes purple-suffused, scented white blooms in June and July. Most will quickly outgrow the average garden, but there are several very attractive small varieties, like Silver Showers, with single sweet-scented, cup-shaped flowers; the purple-centred Sybille, also beautifully fragrant; and the double white, bushy Manteau d'Hermine. They reach 4–5 feet in height and thrive even on the poorest of chalky soils, benefiting by a thinning of the old wood after blooming.

Deutzias, often confused with *Philadelphus*, are beautiful white- or pink-flowered shrubs thriving on any reasonable soil, acid or limy, and blooming profusely in June and July. Some form large ten-foot high spreading shrubs, and are not suitable for the small garden, but others, like the rose-pink Mont Rose and the deep carmine Rosealind, can be maintained at 4–5 feet with annual removal of old shoots after flowering, and produce large sprays of the star-shaped blooms regularly each season. The flowers of the white *D. gracilis*, an attractive shrub only three feet high, are prone to frost damage (although the plant itself is quite hardy) so it should not be grown in areas subject to late frosts. The hybrid *D. × rosea* is available in a number of forms varying from white to pink, all compact shrubs with arching branches and all excellent value for the small garden.

For sunny, dry places the Jerusalem Sage (*Phlomis fruticosa*), which we have had in gardens since the early seventeenth century, provides grey-felted foliage and dumpy spikes of yellow-hooded flowers on a broad-spreading shrub 2–3 feet in height. Requiring a slightly warmer position is *P. chrysophylla*, rather similar in habit and flower, but with neater yellow-tinted foliage, a beautiful shrub at all times of year.

In the same colour range are the finger-bushes, or shrubby Potentillas, which start to flower in June and continue more or less without stopping until October. A great number have been named, differing in small details, but basically all have small yellow, less often white, flowers like miniature single roses and divided leaves similar to fingers on a hand. Absolutely hardy and vigorous on any soil, they require only the pruning out of the oldest wood in spring to remain in condition for many years. Reliable varieties are: Elizabeth, a spreader of dense growth to about three feet in height with bright primrose blooms; the bright yellow, slightly taller Jackman's Variety; Beesii or Nana Argentea, silver-leafed and only 1½ feet high; and Tangerine, the flowers coppery-orange or yellow, depending on season.

Rather similar in their flower shape are the rock-roses or Helianthemums, which are excellent dwarf shrubs for dry, sunny positions on any soil, producing multitudes of single or double flowers during June, from pale yellow to pink, orange, red, and white. Most shrub or alpine catalogues list up to a dozen or more varieties. The young growth may be trimmed back after flowering to prevent their becoming too straggly, but apart from this no other attention is required. Their larger relatives, the *Cistus*, are equally as accommodating, although they do not always with-stand severe winters. Hot dry open sites suit *Cistus* best. Most are small shrubs 3–5 feet tall (with a few exceptions) covered with white or pink flowers, sometimes marked with yellow, purple, or maroon in the centre. They are beautiful shrubs during June and July, when their blooms with the texture of tissue-paper open, and at other times of the year their neat evergreen foliage, often aromatic, is very pleasing. One must expect to replace them after very severe winters, but, as cuttings root readily in July, this is no great hardship and well worth it for the colour they provide with virtually no maintenance. Very large-flowered are the maroon-centred, white-flowered Pat and the sticky-leaved, compact-growing *C. palhinhae* with five-inch white flowers, whilst the rather tall and somewhat hardier *C. laurifolius* has white, yellow-centred blooms. Silver Pat, a name aptly descriptive of this grey-leaved small shrub, and the deeper purplish-pink Sunset are the hardiest in this colour, whilst *C. salviifolius* Prostratus, sage-leaved with white, yellow-based flowers and *C. X lusitanicus* Decumbens, a large-flowered, crimson-centred white, provide wide-spreading low shrubs for banks or ground cover.

The Genistas are closely related to the brooms (*Cytisus*) and require similar garden treatment. *G. tinctoria*, our native Dyer's Greenweed, a variable plant, has given us several dwarf and beautiful garden shrubs. One, named Royal Gold, forms a small rounded bush 2½–3 feet tall and rather wider, bearing during July and later thickly massed spikes of bright yellow flowers. A double-flowered form of *G. tinctoria*, known as Plena, is equally free flowering, but of almost prostrate habit, six inches or so in height, and spreading to 5–6 feet eventually. The Spanish gorse, *Genista hispanica*, forms a spiny mound which reaches three feet in height and in May and June is a mass of rich golden flowers. Like many of its family it should not be given too generous soil treatment. From the Balkans, and flowering at the same time, comes *G. lydia*, a lovely plant for a bank or wall with slender pendulous branchlets of soft green and bright yellow flowers. If you have an ugly piece of concrete or walling to cover, try the ground-hugging form of G. *pilosa* known as *procumbens*. The whip-like shoots make a thick mat, moulding themselves to the contours of the ground, and provide an abundance of bright yellow flowers in May and June.

We tend to forget that some Fuchsias can be grown successfully outdoors, and although in severe winters they will be cut to the ground, they quickly shoot again most seasons, are in flower by midsummer, and continue until the frosts. When first planting, particularly in cold gardens, put them in a slight depression a few inches deep and gradually fill the depression to normal soil level once the fuchsia has become established. This leaves the rootstock several inches further away from frost when winter comes and with a slight covering of dried bracken at the crown in autumn they will usually grow away vigorously the following spring. Be careful to fill the depression gradually as the young plant will resent immediate deep planting before its root system is fully established. The well-known Riccartonii, scarlet with purple 'skirts', and the rather more graceful Gracilis are two very reliable fuchsias; and a form known as Versicolor, with leaves variegated creamy-white and grey-green, has scarlet and violet flowers. All grow to 4–5 feet. Tom Thumb is a very fine dwarf, 1½–2 feet, with a succession of violet and carmine blooms. The larger-flowered fuchsias are generally tender, but quite a number have proved reasonably hardy. Mrs. Popple in scarlet and violet, the red and white Mme. Cornelissen, and Chillerton Beauty with white, pink-flushed sepals and soft violet petals, are all well worth trying.

The Rose of Sharon, *Hypericum calycinum*, has long been recommended to cover the awkward bank or shady corner. Some of its relatives are valuable and easily grown, long-flowering plants, of which *Hypericum* Elstead, a shrub to about three feet with masses of small yellow flowers followed by bright salmon-red fruits, is to be recommended. Its one drawback is that it is prone to a leaf rust disease, and if this occurs, cut the stems to the base and burn the leaves and top growth. Fresh shoots will normally be produced from the base the next spring. 'Hidcote' will grow 4–5 feet and is hardy and trouble-free with myriads of golden cup-shaped blooms from July until October. Similar are *H. patulum*

forrestii and Gold Cup, both hardy and long flowering. Smaller in
stature is *H.* × *moseranum*, 12–18 inches, first-class ground cover
with a beautiful variegated form in white, pink, and green. All
these Hypericums are excellent value and if pruning is required it
simply consists of cutting any unwanted growths out to the base in
early spring. Virtually any soil, acid or chalky, except one which
is badly-drained, will suit them.

Hydrangeas often grow into huge shrubs and fill up small
gardens rapidly, but good smaller varieties can be obtained. They
grow well on limy soils, unless very alkaline, but the flowers are
then pink or red and they cannot, without a lot of trouble, be
made to produce blue flowers unless the soil is acid or neutral.
If you wish to try 'blueing' hydrangeas, use a preparatory
aluminium-based colourant—don't waste time with bags of old
nails and similar junk as sometimes recommended. On very
limy soils a good mulch may be needed annually to help prevent
chlorosis of the foliage. Hard pruning is quite unnecessary and
indeed undesirable. Cases where hydrangeas fail to flower are
often attributable to indiscriminate pruning, and it is normally
only necessary to cut off the old flower heads in early April after
they have served their purpose of protecting the dormant buds,
which produce the next crop of flowers, from frost damage.
On mature bushes some thinning of very old shoots may be
needed, otherwise leave well alone. Ami Pasquier, a purplish-
crimson of 3–4 feet; Vibraye, soft pink or intense blue, depending
on soil, to five feet, and valuable as, even should the terminal bud
be killed, it produces blooms from the side shoots, unlike many
varieties; and the compact Westfalen in crimson or deep violet
blue are all good 'mop-head' varieties. The 'lace-caps', with
flatter flower heads and an outer ring of large infertile flowers
surrounding the clusters of small fertile flowers in the centre, are
vigorous, but can be maintained in the small garden at 4–5 feet
with a rather wider spread. Blue Wave (pink on alkaline soils)
is a common and very beautiful variety; Lanarth White, more
compact to three feet, having white florets. Relatively new and
exceedingly good is Preziosa, not a lace-cap, but of similar
character, with more rounded flower heads of a warm rosy-red,
and of more upright habit to four feet. A suitable companion of

comparable size is Bluebird, clear blue or soft pink, and of lace-cap habit.

Valuable late summer plants are the forms of *Hibiscus syriacus*, quite hardy and very late in producing their foliage. They are of stiff, upright growth, and relatively slowly will reach 6–8 feet in height and as much through, but can be pruned back hard in March if required. The double varieties are messy plants, but the singles, with lovely cup-shaped blooms, are most effective in July and August. Four excellent varieties are Woodbridge, a rich rose-red with a deeper centre; William R. Smith, with large, crinkled white blooms; the deep violet-blue, dark-centred Blue Bird, and Red Heart, white-flowered with a striking maroon centre. Any soil, in full sun.

And, finally, in this summer list Lavender cannot be omitted. Again there are many garden forms, but none is better for small gardens than Hidcote, deep purple-blue in colour, silvery in foliage, and only eighteen inches high. It makes an admirable scented dwarf hedge for bordering paths and, given full sun in any well-drained soil, will thrive for years. The old flower stalks should be cut back in early autumn, and a slight clipping in early spring, avoiding cutting into the old wood, will keep it trim and neat as a hedging plant.

Autumn

At a period of the year when most plants are fading in flower, quite a range of dwarf shrubs have still to bloom or, in some cases, having begun their season in late summer, carry on until frost and cold intervene. Our common heather, *Calluna vulgaris*, is one of the longest-flowering shrubs, the first varieties flowering in July and August, other as late as October and November. There is extraordinary variation in habit, flower colour, and even foliage colour in these heathers, and to select a few varieties to recommend is very difficult. They do not, however, tolerate any lime or chalk in the soil, and thrive best in a well-drained leafy soil, benefiting from a compost mulch until the plants join up and make this impracticable. White heather can be provided by the free-flowering double Alba Plena and the long-spiked single Mair's

Variety; crimson-purple by Alportii and the double Tib; and pink by the semi-prostrate double J. H. Hamilton, the taller and rather similar Elsie Purnell and H. E. Beale, both doubles, and by the dwarf, hummocky County Wicklow in double shell pink. Golden, orange, and grey foliage is also a feature of modern varieties and amongst those which can be strongly recommended are Gold Haze, white-flowered with bright yellow foliage, particularly in summer; Golden Feather, its long sprays of yellow foliage a blend of yellow, gold, and orange; Sister Anne, dwarf and grey in leaf with pink blooms; and the taller Silver Queen, silver-grey with pale mauve flowers.

Many others are offered, and, if you become enthused with heathers, go to see well-known heather gardens where many varieties are grown and choose those you like—in the north and Scotland: Edinburgh Botanic Garden; Harlow Car, Harrogate; and the Liverpool Botanic Garden at Ness; in the south: Windsor Great Park and Wisley. Planting in groups of 3–5, with fifteen inches (or less for smaller growers) between plants, gives a good display and the ground-covering effect and consequent labour saving increases from year to year. Pruning should be carried out immediately after flowering, and consists merely of clipping the flower-spikes back to a point just under the lower flower. The plants become less floriferous after a few years and groups may need replacing gradually, but for all-year beauty with the minimum of maintenance heathers are very hard to equal.

Erica cinerea, the bell-heather, blooms from July to September but is more touchy and on wet, cold soils is best avoided. If it likes you, few dwarf shrubs are as colourful, and such varieties as the compact white Alba Minor, the intense scarlet Atrosanguinea, the glowing deep pink C. D. Eason, and the lilac-pink Eden Valley are reliable. The normal height is 12–15 inches for these varieties and a sunny open position is essential.

The Cornish heath, *Erica vagans*, is a dwarf spreading shrub seldom over a foot in height, agreeably easy to grow on average garden soils, and colourful in August and September, the spent russet flowerspikes remaining attractive throughout winter. In this case, removal of the flower heads may be left until February.

The colour range is white to deep pink, the flowers being produced in long, fairly compact spikes. Lyonesse, a white; Mrs. D. F. Maxwell, cerise-pink; the rose-pink St. Keverne; and the aptly-named Cream are all free-flowering varieties.

The very long-flowering *Daboecia cantabrica*, the Irish Heath, blooms from June to November, and is ideal for growing with heathers, requiring the same cultural conditions. The urn-shaped, pendant flowers are produced continuously during summer, well-spaced on long spikes, giving a delicate hazy effect useful for interspersing with the more solid colour masses of the other heathers. The hardy Atropurpurea in deep rose-purple, and the white Alba are excellent; the lovely rich pink Praegerae is a touch tender and best left out of plantings in cold gardens. Once established, a mild clip-over with shears after flowering is all that is required.

With the same long flowering period as *Daboecia* is *Abelia* × *grandiflora*, a semi-evergreen with gently arching branches and dainty pink and purple flowers borne continuously in summer and autumn over neat, glossy foliage. Never spectacular, but always attractive, it is very useful as a 'backbone' shrub, reaching five or so feet high and as much through. Pruning is scarcely needed and it will grow on any type of soil.

Many dwarf Hebes, the shrubby Veronicas, come into the same category, providing good evergreen foliage and white, lavender, blue, or violet flowers right through summer and autumn, thriving on all soils. A number are not hardy, unfortunately, particularly the beautiful red or pink-flowered varieties like Simon Delaux, but many are much tougher than their reputation allows. Autumn Glory, a two-foot rounded shrub with bluish-green foliage and bright violet flower spikes begins to flower in June or July, a little earlier than its name suggests, whilst Margery Fish in lavender, and the slightly paler Bowles Variety, will often continue in bloom until Christmas. Both are small 2–3-foot shrubs, only requiring an open, well-drained site and a slight haircut to remove spent flower-spikes once flowering has finished. Midsummer Beauty is rather taller, and may reach four feet, providing long spikes of lavender-purple from July to September. Compact, small-leaved, and excellent ground cover in sun, is the violet-flowered Carl Teschner, a nine-inch shrublet, quite hardy and blooming in late summer.

The late-flowering blue Spiraea, *Caryopteris × clandonensis*, with aromatic grey-green foliage and tufts of rich blue flowers in September and October, is valuable, particularly on chalky soils. It may be trained against a low wall or several plants grouped in the open garden, where they form a haze of blue in autumn. Growth starts late, not usually until April, and pruning should not take place until then, shoots being cut back almost to the base of the previous year's growth. In the same category culturally and for pruning are the hardy Plumbago, *Ceratostigma will-mottianum* and the Russian or Afghan Sage, *Perovskia*. The former plant may reach 2–3 feet, massed with bright blue flowers from July until October, when the foliage becomes red-tinted and adds to its beauty. *Perovskia*, with tall upright growths with grey-green aromatic leaves, will reach four feet, with long sprays of lavender-blue in September. Blue Spire and Blue Haze are two varieties currently offered, both at home on any soil if well drained, and requiring pruning as for *Caryopteris*.

An evergreen which does not flower until October is the handsome-leaved *Fatsia japonica*, with bold, shining dark green leaves and large ivory-white flower heads. It forms a large shrub 8–10 feet high in time, but can be pruned to keep it within bounds, and is ideal for filling the awkward corner in the semi-shade once occupied by spotted laurels in suburban gardens.

Berrying shrubs of small stature are few but good. *Pernettya* has already been mentioned for winter use, but the berries are well coloured by October so it fits into the autumn scene as well. Low growing Cotoneasters like the creeping evergreen *C. dammeri* are sprinkled with red berries in autumn, and the well-known fishbone Cotoneaster, *C. horizontalis*, provides bright orange-red autumn leaf tints and a multitude of red fruits as well. It is equally at home trained up a north or east wall as on the flat, where it forms mounds two or three feet high. Longer lasting in fruit is the evergreen, hummock-forming *C. conspicuus* Decorus, its interlaced branches covered in bright red berries, often the winter through, as birds generally leave them till little else remains to eat. Lime or acid conditions suit Cotoneasters equally well.

The spindles of *Eunymus* can be disappointing, as they do not all fruit as regularly as one would like, with the exception of Red Cascade, a six-foot shrub with arching branches laden with rosy-red and orange capsules in autumn. This is certainly worth planting on any soil, perhaps amongst small groups of heathers to provide a little height. Again they are perfectly happy on chalk soils, as are most Viburnums, of which *V. opulus* Compactum is ideal in a small garden, neat and compact in habit, massed with juicy red fruits in autumn, and with bright rosy-pink autumn leaf tints. Other Viburnums, such as *V. betulifolium*, are very lovely when covered with fruit, but unless space is available to grow two or three individuals, they do not fruit regularly so must be excluded if room for only one plant of the species can be found.

THE YEAR ROUND

This seasonal selection of shrubs for the small garden has made only brief mention of plants grown mainly for foliage effect which provides colour, interest, and sometimes scent the whole year. Some foliage heathers have been recommended and there are many more, perhaps equally as good, which can be chosen to suit an individual's preference.

Few plants are as effective throughout the season as *Ruta graveolens* Jackman's Blue, a form of the common rue, with striking blue-green foliage and a compact busy habit, usually not more than 2–3 feet high. Light soil and sun is preferable, but it will grow well on heavy clay or chalk, given reasonable drainage. On hot sites the purple-leaved and gold-variegated forms of common sage are excellent foliage plants, and cotton lavender, *Santolina chamaecyparissus* (*S. incana*), seldom over two feet, is a very fine mound-forming subshrub with bright, silver-white woolly foliage. Any trimming or pruning can be carried out in April. A bright green-foliaged version, *S. virens*, is equally good, and both make excellent dwarf hedges, thriving on any average soil in full sun.

Hebes have been mentioned as flowering shrubs, but many are also valuable for foliage. *H. albincans* makes a hard, dense, rounded, almost white-leaved shrub, reaches two feet in height, and produces a mass of pearly-white flower spikes in summer. *H. pinguifolia* 'Pagei' is similar, but on a smaller scale, again quite hardy, whilst of entirely different aspect is the shrub offered as *H. armstrongii*, with whipcord-like growths of copper-gold, reaching eventually about three feet. Deep glossy green foliage is characteristic of the dense two-foot *H. vernicosa*, free with its lavender flower-spikes in June and July, whilst of similar growth but with neat apple-green leaves and white flowers is *H. subalpina*. All these Hebes are New Zealand shrubs, quite hardy in all but the very severest winters, when some damage may occur, but otherwise easy in any well-drained soil.

Grey and silver foliage, usually aromatic, is the contribution of the curry plant and its relatives. Small shrubs to two or three feet, they look to be tender but in fact are surprisingly hardy. *Helichrysum angustifolium*, with grey-green narrow leaves, smelling strongly of curry, is yellow-flowered, as are the silver-foliaged *H. plicatum* and *H. italicum*. Given open positions in sun and good drainage, and they are indifferent to soil; most useful to plant near patios or stonework, where they immediately seem at home. *Senecio laxifolius*, grey-leaved and daisy-flowered, three feet high, is also suited by a similar position. The foliage is very fine throughout the year, the sprays of bright yellow flowers contrasting well with the grey-textured leaves in June and July.

Dwarf Berberis, like the deciduous *B. thunbergii* Atropurpurea Nana, with red-purple foliage, and the recently-introduced Aurea, equally striking in bright gold, are ideal for small gardens—and so the list can go on. In a relatively short discourse one cannot hope to include all the worthwhile shrubs—dwarf conifers, climbers, and roses have had no space at all. But those plants mentioned are all available in the horticultural trade and, given the conditions mentioned, are easily-grown shrubs, all offering beauty of flower or foliage with which to create a garden attractive throughout the year, which with careful initial planning will require only limited maintenance for years to come.

4 *Fruit in Smaller Gardens*

FRED LOADS

Fred Loads has been a colleague of mine for more than twenty-five years and I have, therefore, had every chance to observe his gardening knowledge at first hand for a long time. He is one of the most knowledgeable people I know and he constantly surprises me by the wisdom he can dredge from the depths of his vast store of gardening lore. He has been in gardening all his life, having started out as a gardener's boy in Norfolk. Since then he has progressed up the ladder until now he is a horticultural consultant and adviser to a large number of eminent gardening firms. He has contributed books and articles to gardening magazines over many years. He is particularly well-known on the radio, not only on Gardeners' Question Time, but also in Gardening for Children and Gardening for the Handicapped.

There are reasons galore why fruit should be grown and one of the most important is the pleasure one can get from gathering one's own fresh fruit and having it in the peak of condition. If by any chance there should be a surplus, the deep freezer will take care of it so that it can be enjoyed out of season.

The designation 'small garden' is very ambiguous, but even if it only consists of an area of concrete, fruit trees may be grown in a practical manner in large tubs. If the garden is only the width of the house and has no great depth from back to front, various fruits can be grown, depending on the training and choice of types.

For example, fruits of all kinds lend themselves to training on walls and wooden fencing, and these can include gooseberries and currants as well as the more exotic peaches, nectarines, apricots, choice apples, pears, and plums.

SOIL

Fruit trees and bushes will grown in any soil which will sustain a decent crop of weeds, provided it is well drained and not waterlogged. Not waterlogged means that surface water disappears twenty-four hours after heavy rain and that when a hole is dug water does not seep in.

In fact, very rich soil is to be avoided. A well-maintained vegetable garden being turned over to fruit, or poultry-runs, or similar soil conditions will produce rapid growth, lots of foliage, but very little fruit.

In soils which are rather hungry the root system will develop vigorously in search of plant food and as fruit trees are permanent and semi-permanent crops, food can be added in a solid form such as farmyard manure, compost, or chemical fertilizers.

As apples and pears belong to the hawthorn family, any area in which the common hawthorn will grow well will suit these fruits.

Fruit such as apples, plums, cherries, and pears which grow on trees are known as top fruit, whilst currants, gooseberries, raspberries are referred to as soft or bush fruits.

It is essential for all fruit trees that good preparation is made, but this does not necessarily mean adding large quantities of manure or fertilizer but refers more to the breaking up of the soil and taking out a hole considerably larger than the roots of the tree.

Special care in the preparation of a site is essential if you intend to plant a tree near a wall on which it is to be trained on horizontal wires spaced at 9–12-inch intervals, either as an espalier, where the branches are at right angles to the trunk, or in the form of a fan.

Fruit trees are literally made up of two parts, the root stock and the top part or scion. Apples and pears are grafted, plums and cherries are budded. The lower portion which goes into the ground, is known as the root stock. Root stocks are carefully selected, are given names and numbers, and may have the effect of dwarfing or reducing the size of the tree or increasing its vigour. This means that, if you want a small tree for a small garden, you should order a variety on a dwarfing stock.

As a further illustration, a variety such as Blenheim Orange on a vigorous root stock would make a tree ultimately thirty feet high and possibly a 30-foot spread, whereas if it had been grafted on a dwarfing stock it would make a tree at the very most 10–12 feet high, with a 6–8-foot spread after twenty years.

The effect too of the dwarfing stock is to make the tree produce fruit more quickly. A tree on a vigorous or free stock may take anything up to fifteen years to come into fruit, whereas a tree grafted on a dwarfing stock will fruit in the third or fourth year. The vigorous tree may have a life from eighty to 100 years, whilst the dwarf may last only thirty years.

Fruit trees are not happy in dense shade particularly from over-hanging trees so try to give all fruit trees a position as open to sunlight and air as possible. All training and pruning techniques are directed to admitting the maximum amount of air and light into the centre of the tree so as to assist in ripening the young growths.

Most catalogues will give you illustrations of the different forms of training, and from the diagrams you should be able to select the form which suits your own particular garden.

It is better to buy a tree which has been partially and initially trained by the nurseryman, as this not only acts as a guide for further training and pruning but also means that you have very little to do for the first year or two after planting, as it will continue to grow along the guidelines set by the nurseryman.

The diagrams at the end of the chapter will give an indication of the main forms of training.

POLLINATION

Although fruit trees may bloom regularly every year, it does not necessarily follow that they will set fruit. There are several reasons for this, two of the main ones being: (a) that it needs another variety to provide the pollen to fertilize the blossoms or (b) the weather at the time of flowering may be so wet, cold, and windy that there are few or no pollinating insects. This is equally important in the case of virtually all top fruits. At the end of the chapter will be found a short list of varieties suitable for pollinating standard varieties.

In the catalogue these requirements are usually indicated by letters such as SF, which means 'self-fertile'; PSF, 'partially self-fertile'; S, which indicates that the flowers are sterile without the assistance of pollen from another type of variety. This is particularly so in the case of sweet cherries, which in almost every case need the pollen of the bitter or cooking varieties. If this is all Greek to you, when ordering by post or from a garden centre, ask for 'compatible varieties'.

Wall fruit, such as peaches, nectarines, and apricots, even when self-fertilizing, can often be assisted in pollination by dusting the open flowers with a rabbit's tail on the end of a cane. This little attention may make all the difference between a good set and a poor or non-set.

When you are debating whether to plant fruit trees, remember that, if there is room for one or more ornamental trees such as a flowering cherry and a crab-apple, you might as well grow the edible variety as the blossom is just as ornamental, but the tree will provide you with edible fruit instead of sour crabs and no cherries.

Stone-fruits, which include plums, cherries, peaches, nectarines, damsons, and greengages, need more lime in the soil than do apples and pears and this should be added at planting time or as a top dressing in the form of crushed limestone. As lime has a habit of disappearing in the soil, this dressing should be renewed about every third year at the rate of $\frac{1}{2}$ lb. to the square yard over the root area. In fact, many older trees would benefit from this especially if you have trouble from the stones cracking in the fruit.

Obviously, in a small garden there will not be room for many top fruits but conditions may lend themselves to utilizing either the walls of the house, boundary walls, or even fences, and along these some very choice fruits may be grown.

Even if the wall is in complete shade, it will suit the Morella cherry which would provide the pollen for a sweet cherry. In northern districts, indeed, a wall may be the only place on which choice apples or pears can be grown.

PRUNING

The pruning of trees is a precise art and the owner of a small garden has neither the time nor even the inclination to learn all its finer points, particularly as it would involve the study of bud formation and development.

Very briefly, a tree such as an apple produces two types of bud, a long thin one which is a growth bud from which nothing but another shoot will come, and the fruit buds which are plump and roundish and will carry clusters of blossom and, with luck, fruit. The object is to induce the tree to produce as much fruiting wood as possible. The harder the pruning the more likely the tree is to produce growth. Gardeners have a saying that 'growth follows the knife', meaning that the harder you cut the more growth you will get. This may seem contradictory when you want to prune to shape the tree.

A standard tree, or one with a head, should be pruned as near as possible to a goblet shape, with no growth in the centre and as open as possible with a framework of branches. The object of this is to allow air and light into the centre of the tree.

Obviously, in fan, espalier, and cordon trees it is impossible to produce such a shape, as all the branches are aligned in one plane. Here the first few years are more complex, and the efforts of the pruner should be directed to producing a framework of branches to the desired shape.

After this, when the tree starts fruiting, there is a strain on the vigour of the tree and growth is restricted. Very often then no pruning is necessary except the removal of dead branches and branches which cross and chafe one another.

All cuts should be sloping and done with sharp secateurs, about ¼ in. above a bud. Avoid making any cuts too far away from a bud or just between two buds, as this portion will almost certainly die off; and a fungus may attack the dead snag and work back into living wood, so that ultimately the whole branch may die.

At the risk of making the job appear complicated, I must point out that certain varieties, such as Beauty of Bath, Bramley's Seedling, Grenadier, Irish Peach, and Worcester Pearmain, are known as tip-bearers, which means that the fruit is produced on the tips of the shoots. Here the method of pruning is to cut some of the lateral shoots hard back, leaving about half merely tipped or left unpruned.

TYPES OF TREES TO PLANT

Bushes (Fig 5). These have a main stem varying in height from 2–3 feet, with the branches spreading from an open centre and are the most suitable types for small gardens.

Fig. 5.

Dwarf Pyramids. Have a main stem 4–8 feet high, from which short side branches are trained to maintain the shape of the traditional Christmas tree, with the branches starting about two feet from the ground. These require more skilful pruning than bush trees but they have the merit of producing heavy crops and may be planted more closely together.

Cordons (Fig. 6). Usually have one main stem, but they can be trained to produce two, three, or four. With a single-stemmed cordon, the side growths are pruned to develop fruit spurs along the whole length. No lateral growths are allowed to produce branches. The best way is to train them on a long cane fixed to wires at an angle of 45°. Cordons need supporting for the whole of their life as this is a very unnatural but profitable way of growing apples in a confined space.

Fig. 6: Cordon.

Standards. As these usually make very big-headed trees, they are unsuitable for a small garden.

Espalier (Fig. 7). These can be trained along fences or walls, or grown in the open trained to wires spaced 10–12 in. apart and fixed to strong posts.

The diagrams indicate the shapes of the trees mentioned.

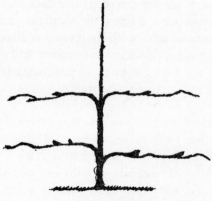

Fig. 7: Espalier.

FEEDING

In a confined area, small fruit trees are likely to benefit from fertilizer applied to other plants, but where the trees are in an isolated position such as near a wall, then they should receive at least one application in the spring, just about the time of bud-burst. This may consist of a general fertilizer, such as National Growmore. If the weather is dry, this should be generously hosed in.

Isolated positions are usually dry in any case and adequate water must be given throughout the growing season; otherwise the tree will not only suffer from lack of water and be unable to make sufficient replacement growth, but in such a sheltered and often sun-baked position, may attract to it all sorts of insect pests, in particular red spider.

In a confined area, too, there will be the temptation to grow other plants over the root system of the tree. This temptation should be resisted as both the tree and the plants will suffer from root competition. No deep cultivation such as forking or digging should take place immediately over the root system of the tree as this not only breaks the roots and reduces the root system, but may cause suckering.

PLANTING IN LAWNS

In a small garden which may consist partly of lawn and partly of flower borders, the odd specimen tree may well be planted in the lawn. If so, the soil should be particularly well broken up, especially if the lawn is an established one.

Remove an area of turf about a yard in diameter. Dig out this to a depth of two feet, breaking up the bottom of the hole and returning some of the top soil to come into contact with the roots of the tree, leaving some of the lower soil to fill to the top. Do not replace the turf, but leave the area bare so that the roots can be watered and fed.

Short-lived annuals or even permanent bulbs such as crocuses and snowdrops may be planted in this area without detriment.

Top Fruit

Although your small garden cannot accommodate many trees or fruit bushes, it pays in the long run to take as much care as if you were planting ten acres.

First of all, therefore, get a good catalogue and study the varieties offered, or go along to your garden centre and discuss the matter with some knowledgeable person there. Then select what you want, bearing in mind the need for compatibility to ensure full pollination and fertilization. A point to remember here is that, if there are no other trees in the vicinity, the compatible varieties should bloom at the same time, otherwise you will have little success.

When planting, take out a generous hole, break up the bottom, do not add any manure and certainly never place any manure so that it touches the roots. On very poor soils you could well work in some well-decayed manure, a bit of leaf mould, peat, or compost to provide an organic content, and you could mix in with some of the soil a handful or two of bonemeal. This is harmless and long lasting and provides mainly phosphates. Thereafter mulch and add a complete fertilizer at 1 oz. per square yard to the surface annually. In the case of stone-fruit, give a dressing of lime as well.

If you have selected cordon-trained trees, espaliers, or anything with a long stem which needs support, put in a good stake at the time of planting so as not to damage roots when driving it in afterwards. See that the ties are adequate and renewed occasionally so that they do not cut into the tree.

Generally the trees will come to you already shaped and pruned, so try to follow this pattern.

Plant your trees if possible in November or before Christmas whilst the soil is still comparatively warm, so that the newly planted trees get away to a good start.

It is quite possible that from an early planting quite a considerable amount of blossom may be produced the first year, but it is not advisable to allow the tree or bush to carry a crop the first season. This is a big temptation to the beginner, but it should be resisted as your object should be to build up a good root system and a good top before imposing the strain of fruit-bearing on a newly-planted tree.

An overabundance of plant food either in the soil or applied to the surface will not do the tree any good, as the more the roots have to search around the better will be the root system, and only after it has a good root system can the tree make use of any applied fertilizer. One exception to this is to give a spray once or twice during the growing season with a foliar feed, a soluble fertilizer which can be mixed with water and sprayed over the foliage to assist in developing both top and root. The amount absorbed is very small but is adequate.

If the soil is at all dry at planting time, whether it be autumn or spring, see that there is plenty of water at the roots, not only to settle the soil around the roots, but to provide a moist root run, as the root system of a newly-planted tree is often inadequate.

If the trees arrive during frosty weather, leave the package in a shed or other frostproof place, but do not store in a heated garage. Avoid planting when the soil is frozen or very sticky, and, if there is a period of prolonged snow or frost, damp the roots.

If for some reason you are unable to plant them directly in their permanent position when they arrive, dig a hole and just lay the roots in it, covering them with soil and, of course, removing the covering, especially if it is a plastic bag.

The correct depth to plant will be indicated by the original soil mark on the main stem and will, of course, be the same depth as the original depth in the nursery. If yours is a very light soil, plant the trees just a little deeper, but don't cover the graft or union, especially with pears. Otherwise there is a chance of the variety producing roots as well as the rootstock and so unbalancing the tree.

Bush apples should be planted not less than 12 ft. apart and dwarf pyramids 4½–5 ft. apart. Cordons may be planted much more closely together at 2 ft., and at an angle of 45° instead of upright.

PEST AND DISEASES

There are scores of pests and diseases which can attack the apple tree alone, but this should not deter anyone from growing apples. These pests and diseases are unlikely to attack a tree all at once. All the same, when one sees a list of all the things that can happen, it is a bit off-putting; but remember the same applies to our bodies. If we brood over every disease that flesh is heir to, we might as well give up living!

As with all other plants, if a tree or bush is kept growing with a good root system and well-spaced-out branches, its very health is its greatest protection against both pests and diseases.

Simple tips are not to let damaged or diseased parts of the tree fall on the ground when pruning. Either hold them in your hand or put a plastic sheet under the tree. Never allow dead wood or fallen fruits to remain on the ground, as these may carry in them the grubs of such things as weevils and moths. Similarly, do not allow brown mummified fruits to remain on the branches. Use precautionary sprays such as lime sulphur against scab, and use a proprietary winter wash against insects during the dormant period.

Literature about pests is readily available in any horticultural shop or garden centre. Remember that one thing very often follows another, so don't let any pest or disease get out of hand.

Here are a selection of the more readily available varieties of fruit:

Apples (*Eaters*)

Laxton's Epicure: This is an early variety and in most districts ready at the end of August. A variety which must be eaten soon after picking as it will not store. Pollinators required would be Cox's Orange Pippin or Laxton's Superb.

Worcester Pearmain: A popular variety ready early to mid-September, again not suitable for storing. A good variety for northern gardens as it blooms late. The same pollinators as Epicure.

James Grieve: This together with Red Grieve is an ideal apple for the amateur and has the advantage of being a variety which will pollinate Cox's Orange Pippin. This latter is probably the most popular of all dessert apples and one which will keep for several months. In fact it may be kept, with care, until January and may be had in most forms of training.

Cookers

The ideal apple for growing in the small garden for cooking is Lane's Prince Albert. This has a naturally dwarf habit and can be kept well under control. It crops prolifically and keeps well; in fact, after Christmas they make quite good eating. Fortunately one of the pollinators required is Cox's Orange Pippin and if there is only room for two then these would make good companions.

Nectarines: Early Rivers is one of the best of the early varieties, ready in most districts late July. In a district of early frosts the variety Pineapple is very suitable as it flowers after the danger of frost is past and is ready in early to mid-September.

Peaches: Peregrine is probably the hardiest and most reliable, it is very prolific, of excellent flavour and is ready mid to end of August.

Pears: In a small garden Conference commends itself, as this has an erect habit and may be pruned to become even more erect, and has the additional merit of being self-fertile and so does not require a pollinator.

Plums: The Victoria is first choice as this can be trained as a bush or on a wall and has the merit of being self-fertile.

Cherries: The variety Morello is ideal for a north wall. It is a cooking variety but will act as a pollinator to a sweet cherry such as White Heart. Remember that a sweet cherry will take up quite a lot of room and will eventually make a large tree, and unless the situation is such where half of it could hang over a hedge, such large trees are best avoided.

BUSH OR SOFT FRUITS

Even in a small garden, especially where there are children in

4*

the household, every effort should be made to grow a few bush fruits, as nothing is more exciting to the child than to go out and gather fruit. Certainly it is a childhood memory which I shall always treasure. Except in very exposed sites, bush fruits are as hardy as a privet hedge and require much less attention. Indeed, blackcurrants may be used as a screen or a wind break, whilst gooseberries will produce enormous crops trained as cordons, espaliers, and even fans, on a wall.

Fig. 8. (see p. 105)

Gooseberries trained as espaliers are most ornamental, can be trained along the sides of paths and are extremely easy to gather. Even exhibition fruit may be produced on such trained bushes. Gooseberries also make excellent hedges and may be clipped in exactly the same manner as any other hedge. They will produce excellent crops.

Blackcurrants will tolerate much damper ground than other soft fruits, although the soil should never be waterlogged. Lime is not essential but they must have plenty of organic matter and will even take fresh hen manure if applied on the surface and not too near the stem. Their need is for plenty of nitrogen and even a mulch of farmyard manure should be supplemented with a handful of sulphate of ammonia.

White and red currants are perhaps less valuable and, where space is limited, these should be omitted and the fruit bushes confined to blackcurrants, gooseberries, and raspberries.

One advantage of the raspberry is that it may be grown in partial shade as it is in fact a woodland plant. Blackcurrant bushes have a useful fruiting life of about twelve years and need spacing at about 5-foot intervals. Gooseberries on the other hand, have an almost indefinite life.

BLACKCURRANTS

Blackcurrants like all other soft fruits are grown on their own roots, which means that any suckering growth which appears from the ground attached to or close to the parent plant is exactly the same variety as the bush itself.

Blackcurrants are always grown as bushes so they do not lend themselves to training in the same way as red currants or goose-berries. Branches spring from below ground ('stool'), as distinct from the method of growing gooseberries and red currants which are grown from a main stem known as a 'leg'.

Incidentally, nurseries are allowed only to sell bushes which are produced from stock certified by the Ministry of Agriculture. They can be bought at varying stages, but two-year-old is perhaps the best for the small garden and these should be drastically cut down to within 4 in. of the soil after planting.

Although blackcurrants will produce fair crops on almost any soil, even on thin sand, they will never give of their best without a good root system which needs good rich soil and generous treatment with fertilizers. They are very appreciative of heavy dressing of animal manure and the best way to apply this is in the form of a mulch in spring, after the soil has warmed up. The application of a mulch of manure or compost in autumn and winter is not recommended as this soggy mass keeps the ground cold by not allowing the suns rays to reach it.

They also appreciate inorganic fertilizers which may be applied about the bushes and over an area equal to the spread of the tops. This may be in the form of sulphate of ammonia or nitro-chalk but these additional dressings of fertilizer should not be applied until the bushes are bearing.

As blackcurrants flower early in the season almost as soon as the leaves are formed, they are liable to be damaged by cold winds or frost, and in a small garden it is easy to protect them by draping over them fine-meshed netting. The whole row may be draped or portions cut off the net for individual bushes. As there should be from five to six feet between the bushes and between the rows, it is perhaps an economy to drape individual bushes.

The same netting which is used for this protection may be used again when bushes are in fruit to protect them from the ravages of birds which are very fond of blackcurrants.

Pruning: All cuts should be made with a pair of sharp secateurs. In a small garden there is little need for the removal of thick branches, but if by any chance old spurs have to be cut off, do this with a saw. The cut ends of any open wound thicker than one's little finger should be dabbed over with paint, to prevent the entry of any fungus disease.

The best time for pruning is after the berries have been gathered and before leaf fall, as the removal of the surplus wood enables air and sunlight to get into the bushes to ripen off the new growths.

The whole aim of pruning blackcurrants is to encourage as much strong growth to spring from the base as possible. Old bushes, especially on poor soils produce young growths only on top and, as these are very short, the crop will be light and the berries small. Where bushes have been allowed to get out of hand and are not cropping very well, every other bush can be sawn to within 3–4 inches of the ground, well manured. These will produce fruit two years after cutting back severely.

Propagation. Hard wood cuttings are usually taken in early autumn from well-ripened one-year-old shoots about 10 inches long and about as thick as a pencil. All the buds on the shoot are left.

Prepare a trench 4–5 inches deep by sticking in a spade and pulling it towards you so that you have one straight and one sloping side. Place in the bottom about two inches of sharp sand and stand the cuttings 2–3 inches apart back to the straight side of the trench. Fill in the trench, firming with the foot. They should be left there for twelve months and then transferred to their permanent quarters.

An alternative method of propagation is by using soft wood cuttings, obtained by removing the soft growing tips from the branches. These should be about four inches long and the lower leaves removed. Trim the cutting just below a leaf joint and insert in sand-covered soil in a cold frame about three inches apart. Water and replace the frame light. The advantage of propagating in this way is that the young shoots are invariably free from the blackcurrant mite which causes big bud.

Pests of Blackcurrants. By far the most serious pest of black-currants is big bud. This is caused by the blackcurrant mite, which is only about one hundredth of an inch long. During the spring and early summer it lives on the leaves, and is virtually invisible to the naked eye. In early July it enters the developing buds and lays eggs. As they hatch the young mites feed on the inside tissue of the buds which start to swell until about the end of August they are twice the usual size.

During the autumn and winter the mites continue to grow inside the buds which become big and knobbly and as the leaves fall the buds are easily visible. These should be picked off and destroyed, and not thrown to the ground.

The best way of controlling big bud, apart from picking off the buds containing the mites, is to spray with lime sulphur just before the blossom opens. Unfortunately, certain varieties such as Davison's Eight, Goliath, and Wellington XXX are sulphur-shy, and the application of lime sulphur may burn the foliage. For sulphur-shy varieties, reduce the concentration by half or spray with Malathion.

A number of biting insects as well as greenfly may attack the foliage of blackcurrants and these should be controlled by spraying particularly on the undersides of the leaves with an insecticide such as Malathion. A bad attack of green or black fly may distort and crinkle the foliage badly and, although it will not kill the bush, it does reduce the feeding area of the leaves and consequently fruit buds are not built up as they would be with clean, healthy leaves.

Perhaps the most mysterious disease is reversion which often follows from an attack of big bud. Reversion is a virus disorder and the common names, nettle head or nettle leaf, are very descriptive of what happens. The affected leaves are much smaller and often contain fewer veins to the leaf but more points. Comparison with a large healthy leaf will readily show up the disorder. Plants sometimes revert branch by branch and produce a number of side shoots with pointed narrow leaves not unlike a clump of nettles, hence the names.

Unfortunately there is no known cure and even cutting out affected branches is useless because the disease will appear later elsewhere. As the blackcurrant mite appears to be a carrier of the virus, every effort should be made to eliminate big bud. Greenfly is also suspected of carrying the virus so even a light attack of aphis should not be neglected. Do not propagate from infected bushes, even if only part of the bush is attacked. The best protection against infection is strong, healthy, vigorous bushes.

Varieties. An excellent variety for the small garden is Laxton's Giant. The name refers to the size of the berries and not to the size of the bushes. This is an early variety and the individual berries are very large and carried on short double branches so that the bush can be kept well under control. It is sweet and juicy.

Laxton's Blacksmith is a vigorous bush and the fruit is excellent for making blackcurrant syrup and wines. If the sides of the bushes are tied or pruned back, you can produce a loose hedge about three feet wide.

Boscop Giant is an early variety with large sweet berries.

Cotswold Cross is a vigorous grower but of compact habit and is ideal for the small garden. This, in conjunction with the early varieties will produce a succession, for it is a late variety and, as it also flowers later, escapes frosts and cold winds. It can be used on the outer edge of the garden to act as a wind-break to more tender subjects.

GOOSEBERRIES

An ancient writer once wrote that the Lord made the gooseberry to flourish where the grape could not, it will thrive anywhere in the British Isles. A hundred years ago there were as many as 600 varieties available but many of these, because they were of local origin, have disappeared, although there are still some gooseberry societies who nurture varieties which will produce berries the size of large bantam's eggs.

The good varieties will produce dessert berries of large size and of exquisite flavour and colour. They can be eaten immature, small and green, long before other fruits are available, into jam, and as dessert.

The gooseberry bush lends itself to every conceivable sort of training and no garden is too small to accommodate a few bushes. The bushes can be trained as single, double, triple, or any other form of cordon, as fans (Fig. 8, p. 100) on a south or north wall, and as bushes. When grown as bushes it is essential that they be grown on a single stem rising from the ground, better known as 'on a leg'. This leg or single stem is produced at the 'cutting' stage.

When preparing blackcurrant cuttings, you leave all the buds on, but when preparing cuttings for gooseberries, remove the bottom four or five buds. So, when buying a bush make sure that it is grown on a leg as otherwise it will throw up growths from the ground and no amount of pruning or trimming will turn it into a shapely and manageable bush.

The term 'manageable bush' is very important because an untidy bush takes up a lot of room and produces a lot of useless growth. Gooseberries are usually sold as bushes but a specialist firm may also supply partially-trained cordons or espaliers. Even if they are not readily available, once you have a bush or some cuttings you can easily make your own espaliers and cordons. Starting from the cutting, root this as already described and, when a year old, transfer it to its permanent position. If a single stemmed cordon is desired, allow only one shoot to grow vertically and tie this to a cane. It is most unlikely that a single shoot will reach the desired height, so take it up as far as it will go the first year and cut off about four inches during the dormant period and train the topmost bud vertically up the cane, pruning back any side growths which appear, to three buds. Continue this treatment until the desired height is reached. Such a bush will occupy only about one square foot.

Espaliers can be trained on canes or wire merely by combining the upright training of the cordon with the horizontal training required for the branches of the espalier. Wait for a suitable side growth to emerge and treat this in the same way as the vertical growth, that is, cutting back the end and training along the next suitable shoot, until it has reached the distance you require. All side growths should be pruned to three buds.

The training of the bush is virtually the same, the bush goblet should be trained into a shape, centre open, with main branches treated very much the same as single cordon. In fact, a properly-trained gooseberry bush is really 7–8 cordons radiating from a single central stem or trunk.

Soil and Cultivation. Gooseberries will grow in virtually any soil and their need of nitrogen is not nearly so heavy as that of the blackcurrant. Their main requirement is potash, so give each bush a handful of National Growmore fertilizer in February each year and a light mulch in early April. This treatment may be given to all forms of trained bushes.

Pests and Diseases. The main pest of the gooseberry is the gooseberry sawfly which lays its eggs on the undersides of the leaves. The eggs turn into caterpillars which, if not dealt with straight away, will quickly denude the bush of leaves. Fortunately, they are easily controlled by spraying with Malathion or B.H.C., and this should be done as soon as detected. If the caterpillars are left to eat away the foliage, they will gorge themselves and lower themselves to the ground on silken threads. They will then burrow into the ground, change into chrysalises and stay there until the following spring when they emerge to eat your bushes once again.

The main diseases are mildew, European and American, but the latter is comparatively rare. To control them spray with any good fungicide such as you would use for roses. Do this as soon as it is observed on the tips of the shoots.

In some seasons greenfly or even black fly will attack the young foliage and this should be dealt with by spraying with derris, pyrethrum, or any good aphicide.

Varieties. The gooseberry is very adaptable for the same varieties may either be used for culinary purposes in the early stage (and in fact are best used at this stage for pies and tarts), almost ripe for preserves, and fully ripe for dessert.

Careless is a midseason variety with large, pale green, almost white, berries which are excellent for bottling or freezing.

Lancashire Lad is a mid-season red variety and the young green berries are excellent for pies and tarts.

Whinham's Industry is a fine mid-season red variety of excellent flavour and makes a very good dessert berry. Unfortunately in some districts this is liable to American mildew.

Leveller is a late variety with attractive very large, yellowish-green berries which crops very heavily. It produces very large berries suitable for exhibition and is excellent for dessert. So large are the berries that I have recorded twelve of these to the pound.

RASPBERRIES

Raspberries generally require a soil with a good moisture-holding capacity and, if this is not naturally available, it should be created by adding leaf mould, compost, or rotted farmyard manure, well mixed into the soil before planting.

In a small garden raspberries could be grown in rows as a screen for the compost heap, or close to a hedge, or near but not under the shade of trees as they will tolerate a certain amount of shade and grow freely in open woodland.

If planted in rows, strong posts approximately 6 feet high are required, with two or three strands of wire at equal distances joined to the posts. Canes should be planted 2 feet apart with at least 5 feet between the rows. In a small garden, however, I prefer a different technique. Because planting in rows is so often recommended, one often forgets that they can be planted as individual clumps, each with its own supporting stake and the clump encircled by a single strand of wire attached to the post. There is no reason why such clumps should not be placed at the back of a border or in proximity to and mixed in with shrubs, provided they have sufficient room.

After planting, the canes should be cut down to about twelve inches. This may seem a waste of time and canes, but it is unlikely that the canes you buy will produce any fruit and, if left unpruned, the roots may not throw up the necessary young canes for fruiting the following season.

Raspberries produce a large number of surface roots and care must be taken to avoid damaging these with the hoe, and forking over the ground should be avoided. In districts of low rainfall or light soil, a mulch should be applied in early spring, as they are surface rooters and liable to suffer from drought which inhibits the production of the young canes essential for the following season's crop.

The object in the first year is to produce both a good root system and young canes, so resist the temptation to leave the old canes uncut. Subsequent pruning consists of the complete removal, after picking the fruit, of all fruiting canes. The new canes should be tied in at the same time and after the clump has developed. Allow about six canes to each plant and remove the weaklings.

In late February the canes should be tipped by taking off the top six or eight inches to more or less uniform height to remove any unripened wood. This thin immature wood will probably die in any case and fungus may infect the dead tips and work back down the hollow canes.

Established raspberries will produce lots of young growth or suckers and these can spread to a considerable distance. Formerly you were advised to hoe these off as they appeared, but, if you spray with Paraquat between rows and plants to kill weeds, you may safely spray the suckers without harming the parent plant. If you want to make a new planting, the strongest of these suckers may be used, as raspberries are not grafted.

Pests and Diseases. Perhaps the worst of the raspberry is the raspberry beetle, because of the young larvae or maggots which appear in the fruit. The beetles, which are only about $\frac{1}{6}$ in. long, appear in May and feed on the blossom buds and the young foliage. Later on the eggs are laid in the open blossoms hatching out in about 10–12 days.

To control the raspberry beetle, correct timing is of great importance. Probably the best way to control the beetle is to apply derris dust when the flowers begin to open, repeating this about ten days later, a third application in a further ten days. Dusting, however, leaves an unsightly deposit on the fruit and the derris spray may be used as an alternative. Because raspberry flowers are visited in great numbers by honeybees, any spraying or dusting should be done in the evening after the bees have stopped working.

Greenfly often attack raspberries and any spraying done should be directed to the underside of the leaves where the greenfly are most likely to congregate. It is important that these aphids should be controlled as it is suspected that these carry virus disease which makes it impossible to produce worthwhile fruit. The canes take on a burnt-looking appearance, the leaves are small, the fruit small and withered.

Such plants initially produce vigorous-looking young growths so there is the temptation to give the canes one more chance. The virus disease can be transmitted by secateurs when pruning, and by simply rubbing the juice from an infected plant on to a healthy plant when gathering. There is no cure for this disease and the only thing that can be done is to dig up the canes and burn them. Don't plant raspberries in the same position again for several years.

Another disease is raspberry mosaic. The leaves are mottled with yellow spots and sometimes curled, and the vigour of the canes is greatly reduced. The infection spreads very rapidly, often by the same agency as other raspberry viruses. Again there is no cure and the affected plants should be dug up and burned.

Varieties. The Malling strains such as Malling Exploit, Malling Jewel, and Malling Promise are good disease-resistant strains, but are not of the same high quality as Lloyd George. The strains of this variety now available have been produced from improved New Zealand stock to produce heavy crops of fine flavour. As it crops on the young growths and laterals it is quite a good autumn fruiting variety as well as a summer cropper.

The variety September is a new autumn fruiting variety which extends the raspberry season well into the autumn. The berries are medium large, juicy, firm, richly coloured, and of good flavour.

Yellow varieties are available and are generally of a good flavour, but the crop is not as heavy as the better known red varieties.

If you can find it, Pynes Royal, a dwarf type often not more than 2 ft. 6 in. high, is one of the best for the small garden. It produces heavy crops of excellent fruit, especially if generously treated and not allowed to go short of moisture.

5 *Growing Flowers*

S. B. WHITEHEAD, D.Sc.

Dr. Stanley B. Whitehead is one of the best known names in gardening. He is the author of Everyman's Encyclopedia of Gardening, In Your Kitchen Garden, In Your Flower Garden, The Winter Garden, *etc. As a doctor of science, combines training with a wide down-to-earth experience of his subject. He writes very lucidly and clearly, with a care and a precision which make his work a joy to read. Although the tables he provides in this chapter may, at first sight, seem complicated, they are, nevertheless, the concentration of a great deal of gardening wisdom and will repay close study.*

In their diversity of form, texture, colour, and fragrance, flowers make the supreme contribution to the beauty and appeal of our gardens. The botanist sees them simply as evolved and modified leaves, no matter how exquisite and radiant their arrangements of petals, florets, stamens, styles, and so forth, and tells us that they are but the erotic parade and sexual prelude to a plant's own pinnacle of achievement—the production of its progeny in seeds. But for most of us, it is on the flowers that our eyes are focused, and, fortunately, growing flowers is a skill we can all master from the outset of our gardening lives.

All flowering plants may be grown from seeds; most of them easily, since it is their natural way of reproduction. Among the easiest to raise are those which we call annuals—plants which grow from seeds, flower, fruit or form seeds of their own, and die within a year. They are invaluable in providing gay colour quickly and for long periods in the warm weather months; a godsend to those making a new garden, filling in the spaces between young, forlorn-looking newly-planted shrubs, trees, and perennials economically and giving a show while the permanent planting scheme is properly worked out.

Correctly chosen, annuals can be used almost anywhere, in beds, borders, or the rock garden, as edgings and plant cover to bulbs, shrubs, and the wilder parts of a garden, even to clothe walls and fences, or in experimental colour schemes. Their performance gives clues to the characteristics and limitations of soil, site, and aspect. When their course is run, their remains can be converted to humus via the compost heap.

Horticulturally, annuals are classed as hardy (HA, for short); half-hardy (HHA), or tender (TA), according to the range of temperatures and climatic conditions under which they will grow and thrive.

The Hardy Annuals

Hardy annuals are plants largely native to cool temperate climes like our own. They are the easiest of plants to raise since they do best when sown out of doors where they are to flower, and may be sown from March to early May. The more quickly and strongly the seeds germinate and the seedlings develop, the finer the mature plant and the longer they will flower. Consequently, soil preparation and the choice of conditions for sowing are highly important.

A seed is a plant in dormant embyonic form, usually provided with a reserve of food to sustain it throughout germination, imperviously encapsuled in a tough seed coat (testa), which is breached by a small hole (micropyle), just above the scar (hilum), where the seed was originally attached to the mother plant. A seed begins to germinate when oxygen (air) and water seep through the micropyle to the embryo, which then begins to grow, breaking through the testa with its first root (radicle), and then the embryonic shoot (plumule), carrying its seed leaves (cotyledons) and growing point that seeks the light. The speed with which all takes place is governed by the temperature, though the seed itself must be viable or capable of coming actively to life.

Seeds diminish in viability with age. Although their decline in germinating power varies according to their kind, it is usually wise to use fresh seeds, not more than one or two years old, for raising such short-lived plants as annuals, particularly where the seeds are very small. The trend among seedsmen is to ensure the harvest freshness of seeds under dry-air, cool conditions, and packet the seeds in moisture-excluding sealed packets.

To germinate, seeds need only air and moisture, with sufficient warmth. You can check the germination percentage of a seed sample by placing, say, ten on damp blotting-paper or flannel in a warm room and observing how many germinate in a given time.

When a seed has germinated it is not long before the seedling plant exhausts the food reserves in the seed and must seek further nutrition from its environment, particularly the soil. There is a widespread but mistaken belief that annuals do best on poorish dry soils. In truth, many do adapt themselves to such conditions, but plants and flowers tend to be small and quick to seed. They give of their best only in soil properly prepared for them, sufficiently well-drained and porous enough to permit good air circulation, containing enough organic matter and humus to retain moisture, and enriched with fertilizers in proper balance.

The top soil should be dug or cultivated well ahead of sowing time and weeds and roots removed. Heavy soils with a sticky clay content can be made more crumbly by dressing with gypsum ($\frac{1}{2}$ lb. per sq. yd.). Strongly acid soils benefit if dressed with hydrated lime (4–6 oz. per sq. yd.). All soils should have a liberal top dressing of sifted, well-rotted manure or compost, or moist peat worked into the top few inches, and on light soils the addition of seaweed meal will help moisture retention. After firming well, work in a light dressing of fertilizer as the surface is raked to a well-broken crumbly finish, what traditionalists call a friable tilth.

Strong nitrogenous fertilizers may actually retard germination and later promote vegetative growth. For flower production, phosphates are a primary need, so a mixture of 2 parts by weight of bone flour, 2 parts superphosphate, and 1 part sulphate of potash at 1 oz. per sq. yd., or a general fertilizer at half the normal recommended rate, is suggested; to be followed by a feeding with a liquid fertilizer or a little dried blood or Chilean potash nitrate when the seedlings have formed true leaves and are growing away.

Sowing Techniques

Having regard to the diversity of soil, climate, and conditions under which seeds are sown in the length and breadth of Britain, it is better to be guided by soil conditions and temperature than by the calendar. It may be safe to sow in late February in a mild locality and on a light soil in the south, but not until three to six weeks later in the colder midlands or farther north.

The old tag runs 'sow dry, plant wet'. In other words, soil conditions are right for sowing when the ground is drying out and workable and unlikely to cake. The soil should also be warm. Seeds will only lie dormant, or rot, in wet or cold ground, and nothing is gained by sowing too early. Happily, soils tend to warm quite quickly in spring. You can often detect this by handling it, though the best guide is an inexpensive soil thermometer thrust into the top inch or so for a reading. When this reaches above 15°C. (58°F.) the soil is warm enough for sowing, as it will get warmer thereafter.

The depth of sowing can be critical, and it is important that the seeds be well spaced so as to avoid the overcrowding of seedlings which engenders weakly specimens and encourages fungus disease or parasites. A good rule of thumb for the larger seeds that can be sown singly is to place them at a depth of about twice their diameter. Smaller seeds can be mixed with an equal bulk of fine sand and sown in tiny pinches, or through a seed-sower. A simple one can be made by rolling a piece of flexible clear plastic sheeting into a cone, fastened with sellotape; cutting a small aperture at the point through which the seeds can trickle and be regulated with a finger over the end. This works well for seeds sown in line.

To sow larger areas, a large perspex specimen-box can be pierced with a needle to give seed-size holes in the bottom, through which seeds can be sifted to fall reasonably well spaced. After such sowings, the seeds should be lightly covered with sifted sand. It helps to reduce possible losses from soil pests and parasitic fungi if the seeds are lightly coated with an insecticidal/fungicidal seed-dressing prior to sowing, and weed competition can be inhibited by the application of a pre-emergent herbicide immediately after sowing. Slugs and snails can take a tremendous toil of young seedlings overnight but bait pellets, based on methiocarb or metaldehyde, sprinkled a day or two before seedlings break through, can prevent this, and is particularly advisable in damp weather and on limy soils.

An increasing number of seeds is being prepared pelleted, or coated with fertilizer and this makes them easier to sow with accurate spacing.

As soon as the seedlings can be easily handled they should be thinned to leave robust specimens spaced at distances of at least two-thirds their expected full height, and the soil stirred to prevent caking. Tall annuals can be given twiggy peasticks for support. Once in flower, it helps to keep them blooming by removing spent flower heads regularly.

In planning annual borders, it is most effective to grow the plants in somewhat irregular groups or drifts rather than in regimented line or geometrical division, and while a gradation from tall plants at the rear to dwarf at the front is the rule, it can be broken by taller plants out of line here and there for contrast. A border of annuals is likely to be more colourful and longer in flower than one of herbaceous perennials.

Deservedly popular, the hardy annuals are chiefly grown as varieties rather than as species, and such is the spate of breeding and hybridization that it would be an injustice to try and list them here. Better to consult the latest seedsmen's cataolgues. The taller-growing kinds will be found among the sunflowers (*Helianthus annus*), larkspurs (*Delphinium ajacis*), rose mallow (*Lavatera rosea*), double-flowering godetia, *Clarkia elegans*, hybrid tickseeds (*Coreopsis tinctoria*), and cornflowers (*Centaurea cyanus*).

For annuals that grow to 12–18 in. without staking, the star of the veldt (*Dimorphotheca aurantiaca*), Californian poppies (*Eschscholtzia californica*), night-scented stocks (*Mattihola bicornis*), Shirley poppies (*Papaver rhoeas*, etc.), love-in-a-mist (*Nigella damascena*), Mignonette (*Reseda ordorata*), chrysanthemums (*Chrysanthemum carinatum*), marigolds (*Calendula officinalis*), Clary (*Salvia horminium*), sweet scabious (*Scabiosa atropurpurea*), *Phacelia campanularia*, *Ursinia anethoides*, and again godetia and corn-flowers offer varieties in many colours.

Dwarf annuals for border fronts, rock gardens and carpeting can be drawn from sweet alyssum (*Lobularia maritima*), toad-flax (*Linaria maroccana*), candytuft (*Iberis amara*), flax (*Linum grandiflorum*), baby-blue-eyes (*Nemophila insignis*), stardust (*Leptosiphon* or *Gilia* spp.) and dwarf forms of nasturtium (*Tropaeolum* sp.).

The climbing or trailing annuals are excellent for hiding rough banks, heaps of stones or rubble, tree stumps, trellis, or fences for a season while more permanent plants are getting established, and will be found in the tall single nasturtiums and the pretty silvery-leafed Japanese hop, *Humulus japonicus variegatus*.

But the queen of climbing annuals to be sown where it is to flower is the sweet pea, *Lathyrus odoratus*, in its many varied colour forms. Although its culture for exhibition or perfection in long-stemmed, large blooms is highly specialized, the sweet pea can be grown very simply from seeds sown ½ in. deep, 3–4 in. apart, to clamber naturally up netting supports, peastick hedges, or tripods of slender posts, starting in March, provided the soil has been well prepared by bastard-trenching, liberally laced with rotted organic matter, generously fed with bonemeal (4 oz. per sq. yd.) and a little sulphate of potash (1 oz. per sq. yd.) in the winter. A good dusting of lime helps if the soil is acid, and during growth the plants must not suffer from any water shortage at any time. The semi-dwarf Knee Hi strain is splendid for hedges or mounds of blooms, 4 ft. high, but the new very dwarf sweet peas have fewer flowers to foliage.

Some of the hardy annuals are tough enough to survive our milder winters, and may be sown in late summer, preferably in well-drained and sheltered quarters, to bloom in late spring or early summer the following year. Marigolds (*Calendula*), Love-in-a-mist, Baby-blue-eyes, Shirley poppies, *Saponaria vaccaria*, and *Phacelia campanularia* usually succeed.

THE HALF-HARDY ANNUALS

Originating in warm temperate climes or sub-tropical highlands, the half-hardy annuals differ from the hardy in their greater sensitivity to low temperatures and frost and do not normally thrive from early sowings out of doors nor fully ripen their seeds before winter. The seeds need somewhat higher soil temperatures to germinate well and the seedlings need protection against the radiation frosts so common in our spring. While it is possible to grow many half-hardy annuals from seeds sown in the open in May or early June, flowering is thereby delayed, and except in southern and favoured gardens is apt to be cut short as summer gives way to autumn.

Consequently, the half-hardy annuals are best started under glass, in a frame, greenhouse, or propagating-unit, with a modicum of heat, and grown on until they can be planted out of doors where they are to flower without any danger from a night frost, perhaps in late April in the mildest localities, usually in May, though in cold areas you may have to wait until June. Included with the half-hardy annuals for growing under similar treatment are the half-hardy perennials such as Antirrhinum, *Cobaea scandens*, *Begonia semperflorens*, Dahlia, Geranium (*Pelargonium*), Heliotropium, *Impatiens holstii*, Lantana, and *Statice sinuata*.

These half-hardy plants are most popular for bedding and infilling borders or temporarily empty spaces, and are excellent for window boxes, vases, patio troughs, and tubs, and provide gay summer colour abundantly. The choice of plants offered in catalogues is often bewildering and will be governed by personal fancy, but as well as considering floral colour and its power for the effects you want to produce, some thought should be given to the size of plants and their height for their growing positions.

Few of these annuals top 3 ft., but where robust plants growing 2–3 ft. tall are needed, you can find them in the Rocket strain of antirrhinums, the Climax strain of African marigolds (*Tagetes* sp.), the single-flowered Cosmos, Nicotiana, equally fine for fragrance, Asters, Salpiglossis, and the giant Zinnia; all well fitted to take their place in the border or the middle of an island bed.

A PIC

Botanical name	Common name	Height (inches)	Spa (in
Adonis aestivalis	Pheasant's eye	12	6
Agrostemma g. v *milas*	Corn cockle	30	12
Alyssum maritimum v.	Sweet Alyssum	3–4	4
Anchusa capensis v.	Alkanet	15	8
Asperula orientalis	Woodruff	12	6
Bartonia aurea (Mentzelia)	Blazing Star	15–18	6–
Calceolaria integrifolia†	Slipper flower	8–12	4–
Calendula officinalis	Marigold	18–24	9
Centaurea cyanus	Cornflower	12–30	6–
Chrysanthemum carinatum★	Chrysanthemum	18–24	9–
Clarkia elegans	Clarkia	24	9–
Convolvulus tricolor	Dwarf Convolvulus	12–18	6–
Coreopsis tinctoria	Tickseed	9–18	4–
Delphinium ajacis ★	Larkspur	30–36	12–
Dianthus × *heddewiggii*	Annual Pinks	9	4
Dimorphotheca aurantiaca★	Star of the Veldt	12	4
Echium plantagineum	Viper's Bugloss	12	4
Eschscholzia californica	Californian Poppy	6–9	3–
Euphorbia marginata	Snow on the Mountain	24	9–
Godetia grandiflora★	Godetia	6–24	3–
Gypsophila elegans	Baby's Breath	15–18	7–
Helianthus annus vs.	Sunflower	36–96	12–
Helichrysum monstrosum	Everlasting flower	30	12
Humulus japonicus†	Hop	Climber	18
Iberis umbellata★	Candytuft	9–12	3–
Lathyrus odoratus★	Sweet Pea	Climber	3–
Lavatera trimestris	Mallow	36	12
Linaria maroccana vs.	Toad-flax	9	3
Linum grandiflorum	Flax	18	8
Matthiola bicornis	Night-scented stock	12	4
Nemophila insignis	Baby Blue Eyes	6	3
Nicandra physaloides	Shoo Fly plant	36	12
Nigella damascena vs.	Love-in-a-mist	18	9
Papaver rhoeas	Corn poppy	24	9
Phacelia campanularia		6–8	3
Reseda odorata	Mignonette	12–15	4–
Saponaria, Vaccaria segetalis	Soapwort	24	8
Scabiosa atropurpurea	Sweet Scabious	36	12
Tagetes signata pumila	French marigold	5–7	2–
Tropaeolum majus★	Nasturtium	6–84	4–
Tropaeolum peregrinum	Canary Creeper	Climber	12–

† technically perennial.   ★ hybrid

)Y ANNUALS

Flower colours	*Notable forms*
n, yellow	v. *citrina*
nk	
pink, purple	Little Dorrit, Royal Carpet, etc.
	v. Blue Bird, sometimes biennial
ragrant	v. *setosa;* good for cutting
, fragrant	
	Sunshine F_1 hybrid; a sub-shrub
s	Orange King, Lemon Queen, Art Shades
rose, white	Blue Diadem, Polka Dot
aried	Monarch Court Jesters, hybrids
, pink, purple	Brilliant, Royal Bouquet
ellow, white	Crimson Monarch, Royal Marine
s, reds, brown	Crimson King, Dazzler, Tiger Star
inks, white etc.	Giant Imperial, Regal and Supreme
	Fireball, Gaiety, Peppermint strain
, salmon, white	Aurantiaca hybrids
inks, white etc.	Blue Bedder, Dwarf hybrids
ellow, orange	Orange King, Aurora, Mission Bells
beauty	(Milky sap can be irritating to skin)
reds, white etc.	Tall double vs. intermediate, Whitneyi vs.
pink	Covent Garden, Rosea
ellows	Excelsior hybrids, Autumn Beauty, etc.
, reds, pinks	Tall hybrids, Dwarf hybrids, for drying
h	Vs. *lutescens*, and *variegatus* for foliage
	Candy Pink, Dwarf Fairy, Rose Cardinal
aried	Spencer strains, Galaxy, Bijou, Knee-Hi
rhite	Alba splendens, Loveliness, Sunset
s, red, white	Excelsior hybrids, Fairy Bouquet
e, scarlet	Venice Red
h-lilac	
ue	Small apple-like seed pods for drying
rhite, rose pink	Miss Jekyll, Persian Rose, Persian Jewels
llow, etc.	Shirley, Ryburgh hybrids, Begonia-flowered
, white	Giant Machet, Red Monarch
	Very useful for cutting
pinks, rose	Azure Fairy, Cockade vs. Coral Moon
s, crimson	Golden Gem, Gnome, Paprika
	Gleam hybrids, single and double dwarfs

The popular bedding plants which top out at 9–12 in. include a riot of antirrhinums, dwarf forms of Aster, African and French marigolds, Nemesia, Petunia, *Phlox drummondii*, *Salvia splendens*, ten-week stocks, and Verbena in variety. Varieties of Ageratum, Celosia, *Lobelia erinus*, Mesembryanthemum, and *Portulaca grandiflora* provide the dwarf mats or hummocks of colour for edging and frontal border displays.

More and more frequently seedsmen offer varieties with the qualification F_1 Hybrid, sometimes F_2. This indicates that the seeds are the progeny of two true selected parent strains of exceptional qualities. They have to be raised afresh each year under carefully-controlled conditions of pollination, and are therefore more costly. Any seeds found set on the hybrid plants themselves, however, will not be worth propagating.

SEED SOWING UNDER GLASS

The key essentials in raising half-hardy annuals from seeds under glass are a rooting medium or compost that assures to the seeds air and moisture in good balance, and a balanced supply of nutrients to the seedlings, and enough warmth. You can make a start in February or March when you can assure seeds a soil temperature of 18–21°C. (65–70°F.), and an air temperature of at least 15.5°C. (60°F.).

Soil temperature is assured by providing what is termed bottom heat, which means placing the seed containers over a source of heat such as on slatted shelves above heating pipes, or on sand or grit in which electrical heating wires are buried, or in propagating-units equipped with heating elements. Air temperature calls for heating apparatus, which may be fired by solid fuel, gas, oil, or electricity. As the spring advances, however, dependence on artificial heat becomes less, and seeds, both of half-hardy and hardy annuals, can be sown later where little heat is available.

The traditional system is to sow seeds in standardized containers —wooden boxes or plastic trays, measuring $14 \times 8\frac{1}{2} \times 2$ inches inside—with a layer of drainage material such as gravel or broken crocks over the base, and then filled with the rooting medium, well moistened and firmed. If only a few plants are to be raised, a smaller container, such as a seed pan or pot, may be used. Sow seeds as thinly as possible so that the seedlings are easily differentiated, and lightly cover them with sand or sifted soil. Cover the container with a sheet of glass to conserve moisture, and wipe this free of condensation and turn it daily; and cover the glass with a sheet of opaque paper, as most seeds germinate best in darkness. Alternatively, put the container in a thin plastic bag fastened down with an elastic band, which has the advantages of being less affected by condensation (any water can be run off by tilting the container slightly to one side), unbreakable, and light in weight.

As soon as the first shoots show through, the coverings must be removed, and the seedlings given air, careful watering to keep the soil nicely moist, and moved nearer the source of light to to secure sturdy growth, but with temporary protection from direct hot sun that can be so scorching in spring.

When seedlings are making their first true leaves and are of a size that can be lifted with a forked wooden blade and a minimum of root breakage, they should be 'pricked out' (transplanted) into boxes or trays 3 in. deep, and spaced about 2½ in. apart, in a richer compost, and watered. Grown them on until late April or May, then move them to spend 2–3 weeks in unheated quarters, such as a cold frame, to 'harden off' by being increasingly exposed by day to outdoor conditions, but with the frame top replaced when temperatures fall at night. When the frost risk is past, the plants should be separated and planted out where they are to flower in May or June.

The Choice of Rooting Mediums

Plants do not later make good any deficiencies in their development at early stages. With short-lived annuals it is vital to ensure optimum germination and seedling development in order to have superb flowering performance, and a first-class rooting medium is essential to these ends.

Formerly, gardeners and nurserymen had to make up their own rooting mediums, usually varied mixtures of soil, sand, and organic matter. Since the late 1930s, however, as the result of researches by the John Innes Horticultural Institution, formulae for standardized soil composts have been available for seed-raising, pricking out, and potting, that give excellent results with all flowering plants. They are based on mixtures of sterilized loam, sand, and peat, plus precise amounts of nutrient materials so that plants can be raised pest-free and disease-free, and of high potential performance. We can make up these composts ourselves or buy them ready prepared, though it is important that they should be fresh. If kept more than a few weeks, the John Innes composts change in chemical balance and deteriorate.

In more recent years, difficulties in obtaining good loam soil and the expense of sterilizing and handling it, have led to the development of soilless composts, originally in California. These consist of mixtures of fine sand and sphagnum moss peat to which is added precise amounts of natural calcium carbonates (limestone) and fertilizers to provide plant nutrients. Again, formulae are available to enable the gardener to make them up, such as the UC composts, formulated at the University of California, or the GCRI composts, formulated by the Glasshouse Crops Research Institute at Ruddington, in Britain. Or you can buy factory-mixed soilless composts under various brand names (Arthur Bowers, EFF, Levington, Vermipeat, etc.). A further development is the formulation of soilless composts based solely on carefully-prepared peat, plus precise amounts of nutrient materials, and these are being increasingly offered commercially. And if you add a formulated nutrient organic compound (known as Bio Base) to well-moistened milled and prepared horticultural peat, you have a good rotting medium instantly to hand.

The soilless composts have great advantages for gardeners. They are light in weight, clean to handle, initially pest- and disease-free, and easily managed. They retain the growing qualities for at least a season, and allow us to improve on the traditional methods of propagation.

All well-formulated composts are of a sufficiently porous compost to allow us to omit drainage materials from seed and seedling containers. The plants themselves lift and transplant with less root breakage. The peat content gives good moisture retention, and time can be saved in watering, though it is highly

Crocus tomasinianus spreads happily in rough grass, on paths and even into the rubbish heap (*Harry Smith*).

Winter cyclamen (*Cyclamen coum*) make an early appearance in the New Year. Plant them so that the curved faces of the corms are downwards. They grow well among tree roots (*Harry Smith*).

Hypericum monogynum makes an attractive show, particularly as seen here against a wall (*Ken Lauder*).

Chives (*Allium schoenoprasum*) make an attractive display. They will thrive in most soils but need a sunny position (*Harry Smith*).

Aubretias enliven a garden with their Spring presence. Here they are supporting white Persian lilac (*Syringa persica*) and complementing the tulips (*Christopher Lloyd*).

A raised flower bed adds a new dimension, as this photograph shows taken in the garden of Mrs C. Mure. Among the plants visible are gazanias, *Ajuga reptans purpurea* and *Oenothera missouriensis* (*Harry Smith*).

One of the most attractive conifers is *Chamaecyparis obtusa* 'Cripsii' with its yellowy-gold tint. It reaches a maximum height of some twenty-five feet, but takes many years to achieve it (*Harry Smith*).

A delightful combination of the yellow poppy-like *Hunnemannia fumariifolia* and the brilliant purple of *Verbena rigida* (*Christopher Lloyd*).

A most effective display from these dwarf ageratum—a mixture called suitably Mosaique (*Christopher Lloyd*).

A splendid example of several *Lilium regale* raised by Miss Evelyn Organ from seed. She covered them with bracken through the winter and dressed them with peat and sharp sand in March and June (*Eileen Price*).

Rudbeckia 'Autumn Glow', growing to three feet, can make a delightful late summer and autumn splash (*Christopher Lloyd*).

Informal paving can be both attractive and labour-saving. Here
Linum arboreum and 'Warley Rose' (*Aethionema*) flourish between
the stone slabs (*M. E. Kitson*).

The value of a greenhouse: this photograph shows, on the right, Mrs Goold-
Adams' capillary bench on which pots stand on damp sand, drawing water
from below by capillary attraction (*D. Goold-Adams*).

Hosta crispula flowers deep purplish in late June, early July. One of the most common of garden *Hostas* (*J. E. Downward*).

This member of the *Hosta* family—*ventricosa*—is most attractive but comparatively rarely cultivated in Britain. It has bell-shaped, deep violet blooms which appear in late July and August (*J. E. Downward*).

Evergreens looking their best, among them *Picea pungens, Chamaecyparis pisifera* and *Tsuga canadensis (Harry Smith).*

The Publishers wish to acknowledge the assistance and co-operation of the Royal Horticultural Society in the compilation of the illustrations.

important that soilless composts should not be allowed to dry out, as they are difficult to re-wet. Whatever compost is used, it should be thoroughly mixed in advance, and when placed in the containers, gently firmed, evenly watered, and allowed to drain and warm up in the greenhouse or frame before sowing.

NEW TECHNIQUES

It used to be held that pricking out strengthened plants, since they formed more bushy root systems. So they do; but this is because severed or torn roots have to grow new ones, and these consist of two or more rootlets budded from behind the point of severance. Inevitably, this checks the onward growth of the plant, delaying its flowering, and is a time-consuming procedure.

It is recognized today that it is better to grow plants from seeds without any check or disturbance of the root system. Instead of growing the plants communally, sharing the same root space, the plants are raised separately, in various ways.

You can, of course, obtain dividers or make them of thin cardboard in lengths to fit the depth of a box or tray to form $2\frac{1}{4}$ in. squares, cut halfway through at the intersecting points, fill these with compost and sow 2 or 3 seeds per compartment, removing the weaker as soon as this is apparent. The single seedlings should then be grown on without pricking out, and can be later transplanted to their growing stations with a minimum disturbance of roots.

Or the paper-pot system can be used, whereby individual plants are grown in hexagonal paper pots, which are made joined together in lengths of collapsed strips. When opened out they can be placed within boxes or simply placed on a propagator-base or frame, filled with compost and subsequently sown. In the case of fine seeds, it may be simpler to raise seedlings in a seed pan, and then prick them out separately into individual containers at an early stage of growth. An economical alternative to the paper-pot system, is to use flexible-walled black polythene pots 2–3 in. in diameter.

A system that allows plants to be grown from seed to planting-out virtually without check is to use pressed peat-wood fibre

5

FORMULAE FOR COMPOSTS

John Innes Seed Composts: (JIS)
   2 parts by bulk sterilized medium loam
   2 parts by bulk horticultural peat
   1 part by bulk coarse sand
   Plus per bushel (8 gal.):

   1½ oz. single superphosphate

   ¾ oz. ground chalk or limestone

John Innes Potting Compost: (JIP1)
   For pricking out or first potting

   7 parts by bulk sterilized medium loam
   3 parts by bulk horticultural peat
   2 parts by bulk coarse sand
   Plus per bushel (8 gal.):

   4 oz. John Innes Base* (JIB)
   ¾ oz. ground chalk or limestone

John Innes Potting Compost No. 2 (JIP2)
   For potting on, and container growing

   As above, but with twice the amounts of
   JIB and ground chalk

John Innes Base (JIB)
   2 parts by weight hoof and horn (⅛ in. grist)
   2 parts by weight single superphosphate
   1 parts by weight sulphate of potash

John Innes Liquid Feed (JIL)
   15 parts by weight ammonium sulphate
   2·75 parts by weight potassium nitrate
   2·75 parts by weight mono-ammonium phosphate
   (½–1 oz. per gal. soft water, freshly dissolved)

FORMULAE FOR SOILLESS COMPOSTS

University of California Seed Compost: (UC Mix D)
   3 parts by bulk sphagnum moss peat
   1 part by bulk fine clean sand
   Plus per bushel (8 gal.)
   $\frac{1}{4}$ oz. potassium nitrate
   $\frac{1}{4}$ oz. sulphate of potash
   $1\frac{3}{8}$ oz. superphosphate
   4 oz. ground magnesian limestone
   3 oz. ground chalk or limestone

UC Potting Compost: (Mix D)
   For pricking out or first potting

   as above, plus 2 oz. hoof and horn meal

UC Potting Compost: (Mix D)
   For potting on, and container growing

   as for above seed compost, plus 4 oz. hoof and horn

Glasshouse Crops Research Institute Seed Compost: (GCRI S)
   1 part by bulk sphagnum moss peat
   1 part by bulk fine clean sand
   Plus per bushel (8 gal.):

   $\frac{1}{2}$ oz. ammonium sulphate
   1 oz. single superphosphate
   $\frac{1}{2}$ oz. sulphate of potash
   4 oz. ground chalk or limestone

GCRI Potting Compost: (GCRI P1)
   For pricking out or first potting

   $\frac{1}{2}$ oz. ammonium nitrate
   1 oz. potassium nitrate
   2 oz. single superphosphate
   3 oz. ground chalk or limestone
   3 oz. magnesian or Dolomitic limestone
   $\frac{1}{2}$ oz. Frit No 253A★

  ★ A trace elements mixture, available from Tennant Trading Ltd,
    9 Harp Lane, Great Tower Street, London EC3.

containers (Jiffy, Root-o-Pot, etc.), which are usually impregnated with nutrient salts and are porous in use. When the containers have been filled with a chosen compost, seeds may be sown in strips consisting of small square containers jointed together. It is important that the peat-fibre should be thoroughly wetted by soaking well before use. When the seedlings are making sufficient root for the root points to show through the walls of the containers, they may be transplanted as they are, into $2\frac{1}{2}$–3 in. peat-fibre pots to be grown on. Ultimately you simply place the plant with pot into the soil where it is to flower out of doors. The freedom with which the plants grow and roots develop enhances performance, while the cost of the pots is partially offset by the humus and nutrient contribution that the decomposed pot makes to the soil.

A further method of propagation that should commend itself to the modern gardener with limited time and effort to expend on tedious routines is to use specially prepared units of compressed sphagnum moss peat, impregnated with lime and nutrient salts, known as Jiffy 7s. When wetted, preferably by overhead watering for seeds, the units expand into small cylinders, encased in a thin plastic net, and are ready for sowing. With normal treatment as for more orthodox propagation, the single plants in their units can then be grown on until ready to plant out in the open complete. Units are obtainable with holes in them to be filled with compost if desired, and are supplied on tape, or in trays. They are particularly useful in raising plants from seeds which are expensive and few in number.

Seedling plants under glass are very vulnerable to mismanagement. Although the use of good composts assures freedom from trouble at the outset, such composts can readily become infected by green algae or lichen growth, and the fungi which cause the stem rots and wilts loosely termed 'damping-off'. The most likely source of contamination is the water supply. Rain or soft water is usefully advocated, and, if this has been collected and stored under light-tight conditions, it is usually safe; but clean tap-water is to be preferred to stagnant water from tubs or tanks open to the air and green with slime. It is helpful to use water at greenhouse temperature when possible, though this is not highly critical when watering is done through a fine-rosed watering-can or spray from overhead.

Many gardeners prefer to water by immersing containers in a water-bath and letting the compost take the moisture up by capillary action until the surface glistens, but this runs a risk of chilling the plant roots too much, unless allowed to drain freely afterwards. Watering is very important to plants but can easily be overdone. It is not something to do by rote, but according to light, humidity, and temperature. The aim is to keep the rooting medium nicely and uniformly moist without flooding pore space. Obviously, more water is needed on bright dry days than on dull overcast days. And, other things being equal, the higher the temperature, the greater the need for water and a maintenance of buoyant humidity. Watering is a skill that grows with practice and experience in your own local conditions, provided you observe your plants' reactions well.

In any case, it is always wise to water early in the day so that a house or frame is closed relatively dry at night. Similarly, ventilation to maintain a stimulating but draughtless circulating of air calls for opening the ventilators or starting the air-extracting fan as the temperature rises, but the reverse immediately it begins to fall.

Propagating on the lines suggested should give you freedom from parasitic insects and most pests, unless slugs or woodlice have invaded under glass. Both can wreak much damage among seedlings. If you cannot find the culprits for instant removal, put down a few pellets or methiocarb or metaldehyde bait. To deal with woodlice, dust crevices, benches, shelves, and under containers with a carbaryl dust (Sevin).

PLANTING OUT HALF-HARDY ANNUALS

We should never forget that the quickener of life is light, and it is its growing intensity and duration each day that speeds the half-hardy annuals to flowering. Almost without exception they prefer open sunny positions, and, as soon as frost dangers recede, they should be planted out, preferably in soil rendered moist by rain, or in a dry spell, by a soaking watering the previous day.

A PICK OF I

Botanical name	Common name	Height (inches)	Space (inch
Ageratum houstonianum	Floss-flower	4–9	6
Alonsoa warscewczii†	Mask-flower	9–12	8
Amaranthus tricolor vs.	Joseph's coat	24	9
Anthirrhinum majus†	Snapdragon	12–4	9
" "	"	15–18	12
" "	"	24–36	15
" "	"	15	9
Arctotis grandis★	African Daisy	30	9
Aster,★ various	Starwort, Asters	9–12	6
"	"	18–24	9
Begonia, tuberous†		8–10	9
Begonia semperflorens†		6–12	6
Celosia plumosa	Prince of Wales' Feathers	10–15	8
Celosia cristata	Cockscomb	12–36	6
Cleome spinosa vs.	Spider Flower	36–42	12
Cobaea scandens†	Mexican Ivy	Climber	24
Cosmos bipinnatus vs.	Mexican Aster	24–36	12
Dahlia variabilis vs.		12–60	8
Felicia bergeriana	Kingfisher daisy	6	4
Gaillardia pulchella vs.	Blanket flowers	12–24	6
Gazania hybrida	Treasure flower	9	4
Geranium (*Pelargonium*)		18	12
Gomphrena globosa	Globe Amaranth	12	6
Heliotropium peruvianum†	Cherry pie	15–24	8
Impatiens sultani: holstii†	Busy Lizzie	9–12	4
Ipomoea (*Pharbitis tricolor*)	Morning Glory	Climber	12
Kochia s. trichophila	Burning Bush	24–36	15
Lobelia erinus vs.†		4–6	4
Mesembryanthemum criniflorum	Livingstone daisy	4	3
Moluccella laevis	Shell-flower	12–18	9
Nemesia strumosa		8–12	6
Nicotiana affinis (*alata*)	Tobacco plants	15–36	8
Petunia★		8–12	4
Phlox drummondii	Annual phlox	12	8
Portulaca grandiflora	Sun plant	6	3
Salpiglossis sinuata	Tube tongue	24–30	12
Salvia splendens vs.	Red sage	12–15	8
Schizanthus pinnatus★	Butterfly flower	24	9
Statice sinuata (Limonium)†	Sea Lavender	12–18	9
Matthiola incana v. *annua*	10-week Stock	12–18	12
Tagetes erecta vs.	African marigold	18–36	9
Tagetes patula vs.	French marigold	6–12	4
Thunbergia alata	Black-eyed Susan	Climber	12
Ursinia anthemoidea★		9–15	6
Venidium fastuosum	Monarch of the Veld	24–30	12
Verbena × *hybrida*	Vervain	6–12	4
Zinnia elegans★	Youth and Age	6–30	4
Zea mays vs.	Maize, Sweet corn	24–36	12

† technically perennial.   ★ hybrid

ɔY ANNUALS

Flower colours	*Notable forms*
ɱauve, white	Blue Mink, Blazer F_1 hybrids
	compacta
ᴇ colour	*splendens,* Shoojoy
	Floral Cluster F_1, Little Gem
	Intermediate vs. Little Darling F_1
	Tall, Rocket, Mme Butterfly F_1
	Rust-resistant vs.
yellows, reds	
pinks, blues	Milady vs., Lilliput, Dwarf vs.
pinks, blues	Duchess, Ostrich Plume, single vs.
s	Bertini, Fiesta
pink, red	F_1 hybrids, Crimson Bedder
ʳ, gold, reds	Golden Triumph, Scarlet Plume
s, reds	*nana* vs. (dwarf); Kurume (tall)
pink	Helen Campbell, Pink Queen
, white	
orange, reds	Sensation, Bright Lights
	Collarette, Coltness hybrids, etc.
s, reds	Lollipops, Lorenziana
yellows, red	
pinks, reds	Carefree F_1 hybrids, etc.
red, purple	Everlasting flowers if cut
blue	Marine, Marguerite, Lemoine's
ʳange, white	General Guisan F_1
ɪcarlet, pink	Heavenly Blue, Scarlet O'Hara, etc.
beauty	*childsii* v.
ᴠhite	Cambridge Blue, Mrs. Clibran, Imp. etc.
ᴀried	Sparkles
ᴠ green	dries for winter use
	Vars. *suttoni*
pinks, etc.	Evening Fragrance, Lime Green
ᴀried	F_1 hybrids, in multiflora, grandiflora
salmon, blue	Sutton's Beauty, Twinkle
, red, purple	Double-flowering
ᴀried	Chelsea hybrids, Splash F_1
salmon	Fireball, Royal Mountie
	Danbury Park, Dr. Badger's hybrids, etc.
ᴇllow, white	valuable for drying
pinks, etc.	Hanson's strain, Mammoth
	F_1 Climax, Jubilee and Lady vs., Crackerjack, etc.
s to reds	'Petite' strains, 'Brocade', 'Marietta'
yellow	Gibsonii v.
, orange	Special hybrids
yellows	Hybrids
, pinks, etc.	Madame du Barry, compacta vs.
	Fruit Bowl F_1, Peter Pan F_1
effects	*gracillima, japonica, quadricolor*

The soil can be prepared beforehand as for hardy annuals, and a few days after being transplanted, a liquid feeding with one of the foliar nutrient solutions will be of the greatest benefit.

Because they are short-lived, pest trouble and infection among annuals are easily excused or forgotten. Sudden collapses are often the work of soil insect larvae such as chafer grubs, wireworms, cutworms or, in the case of cruciferous annuals, cabbage-fly maggots. Such plants should always be taken up promptly for examination and, if necessary, insecticidal treatment carried out against a build-up of infestation. Unhappily, some favourite annuals become subject to recurrent diseases in certain areas, and when they are grown in the same soil too often, as the soil becomes contaminated with the fungus responsible or its spores. Antirrhinums, for instance, are subject to the fungus infection known as rust; asters may collapse with wilt; and hollyhocks go down with a rust disease. It is now possible partially to sterilize outdoor soils of fungi with a granular sterilant based on dazomet, but where these diseases have been experienced, it is wise to grow resistant varieties only.

THE FLOWERING BIENNIALS

A biennial is a plant which develops roots, crown, and leaves from seed one year, and flowers and forms its own seed the next year, thus spanning two growing seasons and dying within two years. There are only a few true natural biennials, however, and in gardening we stretch the meaning to embrace plants, which, although in fact perennial, give us their best flowering performance when grown as biennials.

As such, biennials include some of the most profuse flowering plants we can grow both for garden ornamentation and for cutting and bringing indoors. We need more patience in growing biennials since they are slower to come to flower, but they are economically and easily raised from seeds, since they can be sown out of doors, and thrive in a wide range of soils and situations ranging from full sun to partial shade, and since they over-winter they are usually hardy enough for most gardens.

Biennials are to be treasured chiefly for their early bloom in

spring and before midsummer, lending their sparkle of rich colour
to the garden scene before the annuals are properly awake.
In this respect they complement the flowers of the spring bulbs,
or may be planted to create solid beds of welcome cheer as soon
as winter has retreated. Wallflowers (*Cheiranthus cheiri*) in their
multi-coloured variety; their relative, the vivid orange-flowering
Cheiranthus × allionii, often known as the Siberian Wallflower
though it is a hybrid; are biennial by culture, though perennial
by nature, but deservedly popular for spring bedding, for
brightening the foreground of mixed flower or shrub borders,
and gracing window-boxes, tubs and vases.

The golden-yellow *Erysimum arkansanum* v. Golden Gem may
be described as a small edition of a wallflower, and is a true
biennial, and, despite its Texan origins, hardy for all but very
cold gardens. Also truly biennial are the spring-flowering strains
of Brompton stock (*Matthiola incana ×*) to bring shades of pink,
carmine, blue, and white in double-flowering plants.

There is just one snag about all the above plants which should
be noted. They are all of the *Cruciferae* family and therefore
prone to fall victims to the clubroot fungus disease that assails the
brassica vegetables; they should not be planted on suspect soil.

Lunaria annua or Honesty, alas another crucifer, usually belies
its trivial name by being biennial, seeding itself when once
established, and as welcome for its mauve-purple flowers in
spring as for its silvery spent seed-pods in autumn when it may be
cut for winter decoration. There are white, deep purple, and
crimson forms for variety.

The bellflowers (*Campanula*) can contribute handsome bloom
to summer in the single and double-flowering white, rose, and
blue forms of Canterbury Bells (*Campanula medium*), and its
variety *calycanthema*, the cup-and-saucer form; and the tall stately
Chimney Bellflower, *C. pyramidalis*, in blue and white forms
which is a true biennial though young plants may need winter
protection against chilly damp.

Sweet William, *Dianthus barbaratus*, is a variable species with
many cultivated colourful forms which are grown as biennials,
though sometimes behaving perennially, and has a few types
that can be grown as hardy annuals to flower the same year from

Botanical name	*Common name*	*Height (inches)*	*Spac (inc*
Campanula medium vs.	Canterbury Bells	30	12–
Campanula pyramidalis	Chimney Bellflower	36	15
Cheiranthus × *allionii*	Siberian wallflower	12	4–
Cheiranthus cheiri	Wallflower	9–18	4–
Dianthus barbatus	Sweet William	12–18	6–
Digitalis purpurea★	Foxglove	60–72	12–
Echium rubrum		36	15
Erysimum arkansanum	Alpine wallflower	9	4
Euphorbia lathyrus	Caper spurge	36	12
Lunaria annua	Honesty, Moonwort	30	12
Matthiola incana vs.	Brompton Stock	18	9
Myosotis alpestris vs.	Forget-me-not	5–12	3–
Oenothera biennis	Evening Primrose	30	15
Oenothera fruiticosa★	Evening Primrose	18	9
Papaver nudicaule†	Iceland Poppy	18–24	6–
Salvia sclarea	Clary	24–36	12
Verbascum × *hybridum*	Mullein	36–120	15–

† technically perennial.   ★ hybrid

early sowings. The common foxglove, *Digitalis purpurea*, with its red, pink, yellow, and white varieties, including the Excelsior strain, bearing flowers all round the stem, is a true biennial, though strong plants may produce offset crowns that persist for another year after the parent plant has flowered, and all make good specimens for borders, shady places and woodland.

Low-growing spring-flowering plants, which make good carpeters for border foregrounds or underplanting roses and tulips, are technically perennial but flower best when grown as biennials. They include the meadow daisy, *Bellis perennis*, in its double-flowering forms, forget-me-not, *Myosotis scorpioides*, in its rich blue varieties, and the various cultivated forms of pansies and violas.

To ensure the development of sturdy plants with adequate root system and replete with food reserves to winter soundly and flower freely when active growing conditions return, the seeds of biennials are best sown in May or June on well-prepared seed-beds of good loam soil, free-draining, and cultivated with the addition of rotted organic matter or moist peat, and a dressing of a complete fertilizer. Sow seeds in rows, 4–6 in. apart, as thinly as possible, and thin the seedlings thinned to 4 in. apart as soon as they are large enough to be easily removed. Thinned-out

NIALS

Flower colour	Notable forms and remarks
rose, white, lilac	Dean's hybrids, calycanthema vs.
white	
v, orange	Golden Bedder, Orange Queen
vs, red, orange, etc.	Giant-flowered vs., regular and dwarf
on, pink, red, white, etc.	Auricula-eyed, Messenger vs., Indian Carpet
, cream, pink, yellow	Excelsior hybrids, Foxy (3 ft.)
red	Burgundy
1-yellow	Golden Gem
sh	sometimes held to repel moles
e, white	v. *alba;* Munstead Purple
carmine, pink, white	varieties by colour
carmine	Royal Blue, Carmine King, Blue Ball
v	
vs	Fireworks, Highlight, Yellow River
v, pink, white, red, etc.	Kelmscott, Champagne Bubbles F_1
h-white, white-pink	v. *turkestanica*
v, white	Harkness' Hybrids, Miss Willmott

seedlings, lifted with care, can be transplanted if there is room for them in the plant nursery. Shelter from strong winds and hot scorching sun.

By September–October the plants will be ready for lifting and planting out in their flowering quarters. Weakly plants should be rejected. If each plant is lifted with its roots in a large soil ball, planted a little deeper, well firmed and watered, it will winter well, provided the new ground is reasonably well-drained. It does not need to be particularly rich. During periods of frost, the soil may lift, carrying the plants with it. When this is seen to happen, the plants should be refirmed in the soil at once. In March or early April, a light application of a liquid fertilizer as the plants are swelling their buds will give them a boost for full flowering.

In cold, exposed districts, biennials such as the Canterbury Bells and Chimney Bellflower which may be lost in hard winters, can be planted in cold frames or covered with cloches, and then planted out for flowering in late March.

FLOWERING PERENNIALS FROM SEED

Perennial plants are those that go on living for several years.

As such, they include shrubs and trees to grasses and aquatic weeds. Their numbers are legion for they are the dominant types of plants in the vegetation of this world. Of them, the hardy flowering perennials of gardens form a group of plants, numerous in kind and variety, which are the backbone of our herbaceous borders, and provide ornamental interest and bright colour to several other features such as shrubberies, rockeries, bog-gardens, and water-gardens, and often make good inhabitants of the wilder garden parts.

Although there are several choice varieties and hybrids which must be sought in the flesh as plants, the range of flowering perennials which can be grown from seed is astonishingly large, but their raising is full of exciting interest. Not only are the plants likely to be the most vigorous of their kind, but constitute the most economical way of adding to the permanent furnishing of the garden.

Many perennials have exacting requirements and their culture requires study and knowledge, especially their soil and situation needs. This is true, for instance of many alpine, aquatic, and exotic perennials from climates very different from our own. But here we are largely concerned with the hardy flowering perennials which can be easily raised from seed and are likely to succeed in most ordinary soils and gardens throughout Britain.

There are two simple ways of raising them. Most of them can be sown out of doors in a prepared nursery bed. This should be in a fairly sheltered part of the garden, on good loam soil, well forked to remove any perennial weed-roots, with a liberal top dressing of sifted rotted compost, manure, or moist peat, and superphosphate (1 oz. per sq. yd.) raked in. Inch drills can then be made with the back of a rake, about 6 in. apart, and filled with sand, and in which seeds should be sown thinly as for hardy annuals, with similar protection against disease and pests.

Seeds may be sown from April onwards, and although May–June is commonly advocated, the earlier the sowing, the bigger and more robust the plants will be for planting out in October. During growth the nursery-bed should be kept free from seedling weeds, and watered in dry periods. You will get a surprisingly high percentage of germination and this allows a selection of the best plants for permanent inhabitants.

Alternatively, if only a few plants are required, the seeds may be sown in deep boxes or pans, using a good compost, and after covering in a plastic bag, placed in cool shade on the north side of a hedge or wall to germinate. As soon as the seedlings are through, give them air and light, and grow on to a size that permits them to be transplanted to a nursery-bed.

The second method is to sow the seeds under glass, utilizing the shelter of a cold greenhouse or frame, as heat is unnecessary, and with the same techniques as outlined for raising half-hardy annuals. The methods of growing individual plants in Jiffy 7s or peat-fibre pots, transplanting them without root disturbance into 3 in. pots, as growth merits, for eventual planting out, are most useful in raising choice varieties, and those of which the seeds are expensive or few. The young plants do not, however, need the high temperatures or intense light that often prevails under glass in summer, and should be grown on in rather cool and partially shaded conditions in open frames.

Germination of perennials is variable, and sowings should not be abandoned until the season has run its course. Seeds with hard coats, such as lupins, germinate more readily if a tiny flake of the testa is chipped off with a sharp knife or file, thus allowing moisture to enter quickly. In the case of some species, seeds may remain dormant for many months if not sown when freshly ripe. This is true of *Primula japonica*, and other perennials which ripen their seeds relatively early in summer. Such plants germinate more readily from fresh seeds sown as soon as available.

Most young hardy perennials can be planted out in their permanent quarters in late September–October, and will then show their quality when they flower the following year. Some knowledge of their origins is helpful as a guide to placing them, and their habit, height, and spread should be kept well in mind.

In borders, it is usually necessary to have the taller plants to the rear, the dwarf ones to the front, filling in the middle reaches with those of intermediate height with some informality. Even more important, plants with different flowering periods should be arranged so that the border has some interest and colour over a

A PICK OF HARDY PERENN

Botanical name	Common name	Height (inches)	Flowers i
Achillea filipendula	Milfoil	60	Jul.–A
Achillea millefolium	Yarrow	24–36	Jun.–A
Achillea ptarmica	Sneezewort	30	Jun.
Alstroemeria ★	Peruvian Lily	36–48	Jun.–Ju
Alyssum saxatile	Madwort, Gold-dust	9	Jun.–Ju
Anemone coronaria	Wind flower	12	Jun.–Ju
Aquilegia ★	Columbine	18–36	Jun.–Ju
Armeria maritima ★	Sea Pink, Thrift	6–15	Jun.–Ju
Aubrieta deltoides	Rock-cress	4	May–J
Campanula carpatica	Harebell	6	May–J
Campanula persicifolia	Bell-flower	24	Jun.–Ju
Delphinium ★	Perennial Larkspur	36–72	May–J
Dianthus alpinus ★	Pink	8	Jun.–Ju
Echinops ritro	Globe Thistle	36	Jun.–A
Erigeron speciosus	Midsummer daisy	18–24	Jun.–Ju
Eryngium amethystinum	Sea Holly	24	Jun.–A
Gaillardia aristata vs.	Blanket flower	18	Jul.–A
Geum chileoense ★	Avens	24	Jul.
Gypsophyla paniculata	Baby's Breath	30–36	Jul.–A
Helenium autumnale ★	Sneezewort	36–48	Jul.–A
Heliopsis laevis vs.	American Ox-eye	36	Jul.–Se
Heuchera sanguinea ★	Coral Bells	18	Jun.–Ju
Iberis sempervirens	Candytuft	9	May–J
Kentranthus ruber	Valerian	24	Jun.–A
Lobelia cardinalis ★	Cardinal flower	18–48	Aug.–
Lupinus polyphyllus ★	Lupin	24–36	Jun.–Ju
Lychnis chalcedonica	Jerusalem Cross	36	Jul.–A
Monardia didyma vs	Oswego tea, Bee-balm	36	Jul.–A
Nepeta ★ *faassenii*	Catmint	12	May–S
Physostegia virginiana	Obedient plants	24	Jul.–Se
Primula auricula	Auricula	6–9	May–J
Primula denticulata vs.	Drumstick primrose	12	Apl.–M
Primula polyanthus	Polyanthus	6–8	Apl.–J
Primula vulgaris vs.	Primrose	6–8	Apl.–M
Rudbeckia ★	Cone flower	30–36	Jul.–Se
Scabiosa caucasia	Pincushion flower	24–36	Jun.–O
Sedum spectabile vs.	Stonecrop	18	Aug.–O
Sidalcea malvaeflora ★		24–42	Jul.–A
Tritoma (Kniphofia) ★	Red Hot Poker	36	Jul.–A
Trollius ★ *cultorum*	Globe Flower	24	May–J
Viola hybrida ★	Heart's Ease, Pansy	4–6	Apl.–O

† technically perennial.   ★ hybrid

WN FROM SEEDS

Flower colour	*Notable forms and remarks*
n yellow	Cloth of Gold, Coronation Gold
yellow	Cerise Queen, Flowers of Sulphur
:	Perry's White, The Pearl
, yellows, pinks, etc.	Ligtu Hybrids; sometimes slow to flower
w	Golden Queen, Silver Queen
on, blue, mauve, etc.	de Caen, St. Brigid
blue, white, yellow	Dragonfly*, Long-spurred*, McKana's*
, pink, red	Bloodstone, Vindictive, Giant Pink
, pinks, blues, etc.	Large-flowered hybrids
white	Blue Chips, white chips
, white	Telham Beauty, Bluebell, Snowdrift
, white, purples	Connecticut Yankees, Pacific Giants
rose, white, red	Allwoodii hybrids, Fay, Mars, etc.
	Taplow blue
pink, rose, etc.	Azure Beauty, Quakeress, Rose Triumph
	Slow to germinate, may be dried
ws, reds, etc.	Monarch strain, not long-lived
w, orange, red	Mrs. J. Bradshaw, Lady Stratheden
, rose pink	Double vs.
ws, orange, red	Riverton Gem, Bruno*, bigelovii
ws	Summer Sun
pink, scarlet	H. sanguinea × H. brizoides hybrids
:	Little Gem, Snowflake
ose pink, white	Seeds itself a little too readily
pink	Queen Victoria*, vedrariensis
, red, pink, blue, etc.	Russell strain; Minaret
	L. arkwrightii, 18 in., alternative v.
pink, purple	Cambridge Scarlet, Croftway Pink
der blue	
white	Summer Snow
us, fine foliage	Douglas Prize vs.
white, rose	Monard hybrids
, yellow, blue, red, etc.	Pacific Giants, Triumph strain
pinks, yellow, white	Jewel strain, Biedermeier vs.
w, to mahogany	Gloriosa Daisy tetraploids
violet, mauve	Hybrid strains
carmine	Autumn Joy, Carmen, Brilliant
pinks, salmon	Elsie Heugh, Mrs. Galloway, Wm. Smith
ws, red, orange	Hybrid strains
w, orange	Golden Queen, Orange Globe
l colours	Majestic F_1, Roggli, Super Chalon, etc.

long time, and plants should also be planned to blend well in colour. On the other hand, hardy perennials may be grown at their best in beds, which may be square, rectangular, round, elliptical, or sinuous in shape, with the largest plants in the centre. These can be enjoyed from all sides, and give scope for plants to be well matched to various aspects, light, and shade.

For effectiveness, it is best to plant in groups of three or more of a kind, spaced 12–18 in. apart, with somewhat greater spacing between the groups. This ensures the free access of light and circulation of air essential to plant health. A light mulch of compost, peat, bark fibre, or weathered sawdust over the roots of the young plants will defeat most ground frosts and ensure that the plants break cleanly into new growth when spring returns.

6 The Small Greenhouse

FRED LOADS

So many houses are now having a lean-to or other kind of greenhouse attached to them that I thought it worth while to ask Fred Loads to write an introduction to the principles which underlie its use.

There is a wonderful range of small greenhouses available today made in wood or metal, and so wide is the choice that considerable thought must be given to durability and suitability for the plants which it is intended to grow. All require some form of foundation, if it is only concrete or breeze blocks, which are often supplied with the greenhouse. Due regard should also be had to the site and its proximity to the dwelling-house for the supply of water, and gas or electricity for heating.

Lean-tos are available which can also serve the purposes of acting as house extensions and small conservatories.

If you buy a greenhouse from a catalogue, read the specifications carefully and, if possible, see the house *in situ* so that you can assess whether it is suitable for your needs.

Designs vary from firm to firm, but generally greenhouses are obtainable glazed to the ground, glazed on one side to the ground and to bench height on the other, or glazed to bench height only, with the base either of wood or some other material. The cheaper range, which has a limited use, are virtually plastic tunnels which consist in the main of stout plastic sheeting over a metal frame.

To get the best out of even a small greenhouse, some form of heat is desirable, even if it is only an oil heater to be used during the coldest months of the year. Without some form of heating, one is dependent entirely on heat from the sun, which means that it cannot be relied upon to keep out frost. It should be remembered that greenhouses glazed to the ground can be colder and take more heating than those glazed only to bench height.

There should also be guttering to catch rainwater, as this is valuable for it is soft and free from lime or other sterilizing chemicals. Not only is this rainwater valuable when collected, but, if it is neglected and allowed to drip to the base of the greenhouse, it can do irreparable damage, causing the woodwork to rot and undermining the foundations.

Internally, greenhouses are usually provided with benches, invariably of the lathed type, along each side. These are unkind to pot plants and should be covered with a sheet of thick polythene or roofing felt, which in turn should be covered with coarse sand topped with gravel. The object of this is to create a moist micro-climate amongst the leaves of the plants, as hot, dry air passing through the leaves slows up growth. Extremely hot, dry conditions also encourage a very damaging insect, the red spider, which once established on plants or in the greenhouse is extremely difficult to eradicate.

Similarly, the floor should receive careful consideration. The object of a floor in a greenhouse is to provide a firm, reasonably dry place to walk on, but in a small greenhouse a concrete floor over the whole area can cause many more problems than it solves. Here again, it is atmospheric moisture which is important, for concrete floors absorb water and dry up the atmosphere. In a benched greenhouse, it is better to make a path confined by an edging, made of three or four inches of ashes, covered with about three or four inches of clean chippings. Alternatively, if the floor has already been cemented, then heavy duty coconut matting laid down the centre path and kept damp will provide sufficient atmospheric moisture.

This provision of atmospheric moisture is essential, for example, where tomatoes are grown, for if the floral organ on which the pollen drops becomes too dry and not sticky enough to hold and retain the pollen grains, it results in the non-setting of the fruit. At certain stages excessive dryness may also cause the unopened flowers to fall off.

Contrary to general belief, there is no merit in growing tomatoes in the ground in the greenhouse; indeed, in a small greenhouse this poses more problems than growing in containers. The reason is that no matter how carefully the old plants are removed, a great deal of the root is left in the ground. When this root decays, it may produce certain toxins and form a breeding-ground for fungi. After each crop, therefore, the soil must either be removed or sterilized and, as virtually all soil sterilants give off harmful vapours, all other plants must be removed from the greenhouse whilst this is being done. Even the apparently innocuous Jeyes Fluid, which is often used for sterilizing, may give off a vapour harmful to plants in a closed greenhouse. It is therefore better to grow tomatoes by the other methods which are detailed later.

At the outset you should decide whether you want to grow pot-plants, foliage or flowering, on benches, whether accommodation is to be provided for taller subjects such as tomatoes and later chrysanthemums, or whether you are going to attempt many things simultaneously.

If you want to grow tomatoes in the ground or at ground level, it is essential that the greenhouse is glazed to the ground, otherwise the plants will be 'drawn' by lack of light and the lower part of the plant will be unprofitable. The reason often advanced for growing tomatoes at ground level is that there would be insufficient height for them if they were grown on the bench. This is not necessarily so, because tomatoes can be trained up under the glass to the ridge and then down the other side, thus producing as many trusses as it is possible to ripen.

Remember, too, that, if you intend to raise bedding plants from seed in the greenhouse, it is often impossible to plant them out when they are ready because of weather conditions, so a most valuable adjunct to a greenhouse is a cold frame or—perhaps two. If the bedding plants are ready, but the weather is not, they can then be put in the cold frame to harden off, while you fill the greenhouse with pot-plants or tomatoes.

The understandable ambition of anyone with a greenhouse for the first time is to grow a multiplicity of plants. Unfortunately, plants, like people, often dislike their neighbours or the conditions under which they live. For example, cucumbers and tomatoes are not happy neighbours as each requires different conditions at different stages of their development. The cucumber likes it moist and very warm, whilst the tomato enjoys lots of fresh air with the windows and doors wide open in the summer. Furthermore, the tomatoes take no harm if the temperature drops at night, but cucumbers resent this and show it by producing fruit which is bitter and inedible.

Similarly, you might have a burning ambition to grow a grape-vine. But grape-vines grow very vigorously and can soon cover the whole top of the greenhouse, excluding light beneath, so that only a few plants such as begonias or gloxinias would be happy in its shade. And a fruit tree, such as a peach, whilst very adaptable in its younger stage, can grow to a spread of eighteen feet and leave no room for anything else beneath.

Furthermore, a small packet of seeds can produce an enormous number of plants and before you know where you are the sides of your greenhouse will be metaphorically bulging.

In a greenhouse, say 10–12 ft. long, you can erect a partition, made of strong plastic sheeting stapled to a light framework, with a curtain of the same material over the entry. This would give you *two* small greenhouses with no loss of light, and each could be kept at a different temperature or a different degree of humidity. One end, preferably that farthest away from the door, could be heated and a modest collection of orchids built up—or begonias, gloxinias, streptocarpus, and other rather exotic plants would grow quite happily. Heat can be conserved by lining the inside of the greenhouse with clear polythene sheeting which can be kept in position from November until April. This would not only conserve the heat, but, by keeping one end of the greenhouse warm, enable you to 'force' some bulbs and rhubarb.

Remember, too, that, unless you have a shed, potting, sowing seed, and pricking off seedlings into boxes, must be done in the greenhouse and this takes up a considerable amount of room. For this purpose I use a portable bench which straddles the path and rests on the benches on each side. It is fitted with 6-in. sides and a 12-in. back so that soil can be tipped on it for mixing and potting. After the various jobs have been done, the contraption can be taken out, or in an emergency, during the busy part of the year, used as an extra bench.

Where possible, space should be found for a small water tank which, for preference, should be above ground so that it takes on the temperature inside the greenhouse. This is important because, for seedlings and certain other plants, aired water at the same temperature as the greenhouse is highly desirable. Cold water from a tap or from a tank or tub outside would be far too cold in the early part of the year.

This may sound a formidable list of suggestions, recommendations and exceptions, but, believe me, they are merely common sense and will logically fit into the scheme of things. It is also very important that you should consider them right at the beginning.

Consider, too, whether the greenhouse is to be wired for electric light or heating. If the greenhouse is to be electrically lighted or heated, pay due consideration to safety, and perhaps have the job done by a trained electrician. In any case, make sure that suitable cable is used. Ordinary light-duty electric flex affixed to a bulb socket in the bathroom or kitchen is not good enough. It rots easily and is very dangerous as there is a lot of moisture in a greenhouse. Think also about the provision of wires stretching from end to end for the training of tall plants or climbers.

Fertilizers and hormone weedkillers which give off a vapour should not be stored in the greenhouse for the fertilizer will become damp and lumpy and the fumes from the weedkillers may cause damage to plants.

I have said that greenhouses fitted with benches on each side are most suitable for pot plants, and it may seem that the underneath part of the benches is so much waste space. This is not so, as these can be darkened for the forcing of rhubarb and chicory, or for forcing bulbs, which is best done in the dark and warmth. Furthermore, it is often necessary, at the end of the season, to rest such plants as fuchsias, hydrangeas, and begonias. These should be laid on their sides during the winter months, and the under-bench space is ideal for such storage.

CHRYSANTHEMUMS

It would be excusable if one were put off growing chrysanthemums by the tremendous volume of literature about them. In places where gardeners foregather, one hears all sorts of terms such as 'stopping', 'timing', and 'disbudding' bandied about and one could not be blamed for despairing of ever growing a few chrysanthemums to put in a vase. In point of fact, nothing could be easier. It is only necessary to put a piece of an old plant or a rooted cutting in the ground or in a pot and it will bloom with only regular watering and enough support to ensure that it does not blow over.

'Timing' and 'stopping' charts according to variety and district are precision guides to enable you to produce flowers at a given time, either for exhibition on a specified date or for the market. 'Break' is another mysterious word and simply means that the single stem of the rooted cutting can be induced to divide into two or more branching shoots, either naturally or by artificial means. The breaks referred to by growers are usually artificial ones, caused by pinching out the growing point which produces breaks, literally at the command of the grower. By this means a single shoot can be made to break into two, and they too will break if you pinch out the growing point again. The reason for this is that, if the chrysanthemum is left to its own devices, it may break naturally, but it could be too late in the season to get a worthwhile flower.

Chrysanthemums are influenced more by light or length of day than most other plants. The reduction in the number of hours of daylight in the autumn influences the formation of the buds, and advantage is taken of this by commercial growers who darken the greenhouses in which the plants are growing to create an artificial day-length. By this means blooms can be had during the long days of summer. In other words, the plant is deceived by the grower into producing buds.

This darkening technique is frequently used in the artificial dwarfing of chrysanthemum plants, so that growers can produce neat heads of blooms, one or three plants in a pot, in late summer. These plants are dwarfed artificially by the application of certain

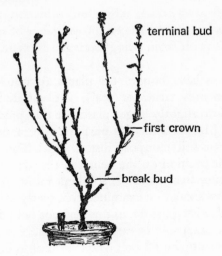

Fig. 9.

chemicals, but this is very much a professional job and considerable experience of chrysanthemum-growing and the varieties to use is needed before it can be undertaken by the home gardener.

To grow a few blooms for the house, however, one should start with 'cuttings'. These are portions of the young growths which are produced at the base of the old plant in the spring. The young growth is detached with a sharp knife, the end dipped in a hormone rooting-powder, and the cutting then inserted in a mixture of sand and peat in a cold frame where it will root.

You can purchase unrooted cuttings, but, as there is considerable risk in doing this, rooted cuttings are best, whether they are to be grown entirely outdoors or finished under the cover of glass. Chrysanthemums normally grown under glass are not hardy and will not stand severe frost. Similarly, hardy chrysanthemums which will winter outdoors do not take kindly to the warmth even of an unheated greenhouse. Each category can in turn be divided into singles, incurves and decoratives.

The expert chrysanthemum-grower divides chrysanthemums up into a number of sections, but the beginner can be content with three: early, midseason, and late. By and large, they present fewer problems.

For the small greenhouse, earlies and midseasons are perhaps the best buy, as late varieties need the assistance of some form of heat to prevent them from being damaged by frost or excessive damp.

Assuming you have bought the plants as rooted cuttings in small pots (generally made of peat), you should immediately transfer them into slightly larger plastic or clay pots, using a soil comparable to J.I. No. 2 for this purpose. Alternatively you can use one of the 'no soil' composts instead of J.I. The plants should be given a light position on the bench in the greenhouse (which must be free from frost), and the soil kept moist. As they grow, the young plants should be examined frequently to see that they are not infected with greenfly, as this pest not only debilitates the plant but is also suspected of carrying diseases.

The young plants should be grown on until the pot is full of roots and at this stage it is best that they be transferred to a larger-sized pot. This second pot must not be much larger than the first; for example, from a 3-in. pot to a 4½-in. pot is a big enough move. As the plant increases in size it should be transferred to a progressively bigger pot, until the final 9-in. pot is reached. It is usual to put only one plant in a 9-in. pot, filling the pot only to two thirds so that a top dressing can be applied later (Fig. 10).

To induce the initial 'break', which has already been referred to, pinch out the growing-point when you can count six leaves on one side of a single shoot. In about ten days the almost invisible buds in the axils of the leaves will be seen to be growing and these in turn will make strong growths.

By this time the weather outdoors should be good enough for the pots either to be stood outdoors or for the young plants to be planted in a prepared and manured piece of ground. The time at which they can be safely stood outdoors, will depend on the district, but is normally early June in the north and mid-May in more favoured districts.

By this time they will have made vigorous young plants and should be supported by a cane to which the plant is tied with some soft tying material. When the plant has made another six leaves, the tops of these new growths can also be pinched out and after this no more pinching or stopping is necessary.

(I would remind you that these are basic instructions for the beginner, who, if interested, will go on to study more detailed literature, and it is recommended that joining the Chrysanthemum Society will give considerable advantages.)

The soil should never be allowed to dry out at any time. As the plant grows, it needs additional plant food which can be given as dilute fertilizer, either dry or in liquid form, or by the addition of more and slightly richer compost. For this, J.I. No. 3 may well be used. The soil for chrysanthemums at all pottings should be made firm and in the final pots should be lightly rammed with a potting-stick. This need be nothing more than a piece of broom-shank, cut to about 15 in. long which is used to tamp the soil down firmly.

When stood outdoors, pots containing chrysanthemums should be tied to a wire to prevent them from being blown over, for the plants may become top heavy as the season advances.

Watering is one of the main problems and to cope with this the pots may be stood in a trench and the space between the pots filled with peat. Alternatively, boards can be placed on each side of the pot and again the space filled in with peat, which should be kept damp. The pots should be stood on a firm surface, —rolled ashes, concrete, or any other material through which worms cannot penetrate.

An alternative method of dealing with the young plants is to plant them out in the ground 18 in. to 2 ft. apart and supported with canes. You then lift them carefully when the buds have formed in the autumn and transfer them to beds in the greenhouse.

The two crops, tomatoes and chrysanthemums, do well together, because the space occupied by the tomatoes in the summer can be occupied by the chrysanthemums later in the year. This technique of planting and lifting can be carried out only if there is soil space available in the greenhouse. I mentioned earlier that it pays to have removable benches, otherwise, in a small greenhouse, there is insufficient headroom for most ordinary varieties of chrysanthemums.

As with tomatoes, the beginner is advised to use either a general purpose fertilizer, or one specially prepared for chrysanthemums; and here again it is good sense to follow closely the directions on the packet. Many experts have their own pet formulations but don't worry your head with these until you have mastered fundamentals of chrysanthemum-growing.

As strong winds and heavy rains can be expected towards autumn it is worth repeating that plants, whether in containers or growing in the ground, should be securely tied.

As soon as there is a likelihood of frost, the plants should be taken in to the greenhouse, or failing this a temporary erection of bamboo canes made so that fine plastic mesh or polythene sheeting or both can be thrown over when frost or heavy rain threatens.

When the chrysanthemums have been housed, it is essential that they receive all the fresh air possible. To this end, doors and ventilators should be kept open night and day until the weather becomes really severe. Even then a certain amount of ventilation should be given, otherwise damp may cause the blooms to rot in the centre.

As chrysanthemums are very prolific in bud formation, it is desirable to pinch out a number of buds and, if large blooms are wanted, leave only one bud. With some varieties you can leave the buds to produce what is known as a spray. This has a considerable attraction but only try it with certain varieties, for many of the modern ones have been bred to produce large flowers.

Considerable care is needed in disbudding, as the stems of the buds are short and extremely brittle. It is best done with the finger and thumb, the bud being rubbed out rather than pinched. They should never at any time be cut out with a knife or scissors. Reduce the number of buds gradually, starting from the lowest ones and reduce to about three, which can either be left to form sprays or finally reduced to one strong central bud to produce one bloom on a stem. Within reason, the earlier this is done the better so that the plant has less work to do sustaining unwanted buds.

Propagating: Care should always be taken to see that the plants for future propagation are correctly labelled because varieties differ in their requirements. After the plants have finished flowering, cut them down to within six inches of the ground and tie a label to the stem.

Whether the plants are pot-grown or lifted from the ground outside they will occupy considerable space, which, in a small greenhouse, is at a premium. So remove the plants from their pots and shake all the soil off them; you can assist this by beating gently with the palms of the hands. Put this soil on the compost heap to become revitalized; alternatively, sift it and use it as a lawn dressing. Never use it for seedlings or other plants.

Next, thoroughly wash the old stools (roots) in water, to which has been added a dessertspoonful of Jeyes Fluid to a 2-gallon bucket of water, leaving them in the water for about two minutes. The stools can then be packed together in a shallow box and the root system covered with a mixture of sand and peat, thoroughly watered. If these stools are kept free from frost, they will start to produce young growths from the base of the old stems. More cuttings will be produced in this way and the stools will certainly occupy a lot less space than if left in pots.

Cuttings can be taken from January onwards, rooting the largest-flowered varieties first. As soon as the cuttings are about three inches long, detach them cleanly with the point of a knife, remove one or two of the lower leaves, and insert them to about a third of their length in a mixture of equal parts sand, peat, and clean soil. Water them thoroughly, and stand in a light, not too warm place in the greenhouse. You should be able to strike ninety-nine per cent.

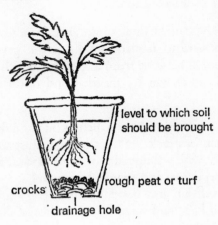

level to which soil should be brought

rough peat or turf

crocks

drainage hole

Fig. 10.

Pests and Diseases

Fortunately the chrysanthemum is a robust plant and will usually throw off attacks by pests. Nevertheless, it is far better to counter-attack as soon as any attacks are noted.

Greenfly: This can occur at any stage of the plant's growth both indoors and out. When not in flower, spray with Malathion; when in flower, fumigate.

Leaf Miner: This is a fly which lays its eggs on the leaves, the maggot disfiguring and destroying the leaves. Spray with a systemic insecticide.

Capsid Bug and Frog Hopper: These are larger insects which damage leaves and flower-buds. At first sign of damage, spray with Malathion or B.H.C.

Chrysanthemum Eelworm: Possibly the most devastating pest, it is a tiny, almost invisible creature which travels in a film of moisture on the foliage and stem, and works upwards from soil level. Affected leaves turn black, hang limp, and are of no further use to the plant. Strip off and burn the leaves at the first sign of infestation. Spraying with Malathion will go some way towards giving control, but it is safest to burn the infected plants. Do not put fresh plants in infected soil.

Virus diseases: These make their appearance from time to time and are not a very serious menace to the home gardener but no propagation should be done from any plants which have obvious signs of disease as shown by mottled and distorted leaves and flowers.

Mildews: At the cutting stage or when in bud and flower, various mildews sometimes attack. At the first sign, dust with flowers of sulphur or spray with a fungicide; or, if in bloom, fumigate with a combined insecticidal and fungicidal smoke.

Plenty of fresh air and good ventilation go a long way to hardening the foliage and warding off attacks of disease.

TOMATOES

Most people with greenhouses like to grow tomatoes and chrysanthemums, which is quite understandable as these two crops are profitable over a long period. It is not really a practical proposition to raise one's own tomato plants in an unheated or partially heated greenhouse because a temperature of 50° or more has to be maintained night and day. It is therefore advisable to buy plants from a reliable source.

Incidentally, when you order tomato plants state that they are for an unheated or a lightly heated greenhouse so that the nurseryman may 'harden them off' to suit your conditions. When fetching them from the nursery, see that each plant is individually wrapped in a sheet of newspaper as chilling can cause a check to growth for up to three weeks.

The next most important thing is to be sure that the soil is warm, and here the home gardener can score in that he has several ways of doing this. The best soil temperature for tomatoes is around 56°F. but it is extremely difficult to raise soil to this temperature when the surface is flat. It is useless trying to warm up the soil by pouring on hot water. A far better way is to ridge the soil and expose it to sun and artificial heat. Before planting the soil should be firmed and the plants planted on ridges approximately 20 in. apart.

Other methods which are available to the home gardener are the 'ring' culture; the bag, pillow or mattress; box, trough, or plastic bucket. The advantage of all these is that the medium in which the plants are grown is above the surface and air and warmth can circulate around it and warm the body of the soil to the average air temperature of the greenhouse in about forty-eight hours.

The rings which give their name to the 'ring culture method' are bottomless containers, plantpot-shaped and made of whale-hide or similar material. These are stood on a base of sand, aggregate, peat, or ashes about 3 in. deep. The base may be insulated from the soil underneath by a sheet of polythene. This is a worthwhile technique if the soil is wet, cold, or infected by diseases. The rings are set out 20 in. apart and half filled with a good soil mixture, such as J.I. No. 2 or its equivalent.[1] A bushel of soil will suffice for approximately nine rings, and to measure a bushel, fill a 2-gallon bucket four times. Plant with a trowel, sinking the plants about an inch lower than the top of the ball of soil. Firm but do not water for at least twenty-four hours after planting.

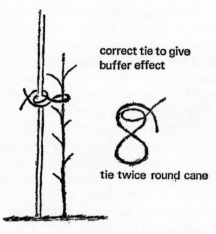

correct tie to give
buffer effect

tie twice round cane

Fig. 11.

Boxes, 10-inch pots and plastic buckets with holes in them for drainage, may also be used for growing tomatoes, and you can stand these on the benches, or on the floor if the glass goes right down to the ground. Troughs may be made of boards or even polythene sheeting and stood on the benches. As above, the containers should be filled with J.I. No. 2.

The pillow or mattress, which is comparatively new is a plastic container usually filled with a 'no soil' compost of the Levington type. It should be slit along the top and the plant inserted into the rooting medium. This method provides a sterile, rich volume of soil which is clean and easy to use.

Soon the plants will require support, by canes or more usually

---

[1] This is 7 parts by bulk of medium loam, 3 parts peat or leaf mould, and 2 parts coarse sand, to which should be added $\frac{1}{4}$ lb. J.I. Base Fertilizer, and $\frac{3}{4}$ oz. chalk to 1 bushel of soil.

by string. Tie the string to the stem of the plant with a non-slip knot and secure the other end to the overhead wires which I advised you to have stretched from one end of the greenhouse to the other. They and the frame of the greenhouse must be strong enough to take the weight of the plants, estimating a weight of about 10 lb. per plant. With a very light-framed greenhouse an internal stay may be necessary. If the plants are grown on the benches, however, and trained up under the sloping glass to the ridge and down the other side, little weight is imposed on any vulnerable part of the structure (Figs. 11 and 12).

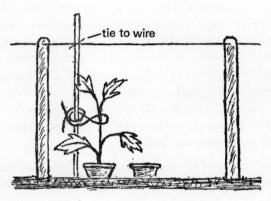

Fig. 12.

As the plants grow, they will require more and more air and the ventilators should never be tightly closed. Planting in an unheated greenhouse should not be done until the end of May or even the beginning of June, but where even moderate heat is available, planting can commence at the beginning of May. The most important thing is not to be too greedy and try to get too many trusses. Five is a good average for a moderately heated or unheated greenhouse.

Cultivation during the growing season consists of watering, feeding, ventilating, and maintaining a reasonably even temperature without wide fluctuations. Remember that a small greenhouse will heat up rapidly during the day and cool quickly at night. To avoid this, keep the door and ventilators open during the hottest part of the day, closing them as the temperature drops, but don't shut the ventilators down tight, otherwise the atmosphere will become wet and saturated and various fungus diseases can quickly develop.

Feeding: The initial compost used must not be too rich but should contain enough food to sustain the plant until the third flower truss has been formed and the bottom one set. The soil should be kept moist at all times and not allowed to fluctuate between very dry and very wet. Never apply fertilizer in dry or liquid form when the soil is dry—always water first.

Proprietary fertilizers are readily available and the beginner should use these rather than attempt to make his own. They should be applied exactly according to the directions. Occasionally, however, according to the season, slight variations may be adopted. For example, an extra feed of nitrogen may be given during very sunny weather in the form of dried blood or sulphate of ammonia; during dull, cloudy weather, the occasional extra feed of sulphate of potash will act as a substitute for sunshine. At the end of the season a single feed of superphosphate will help to ripen off the remaining fruit.

Training and Setting: Unless the flowers are fertilized, the embryo tomatoes will not swell, and setting can be encouraged by tapping the trusses gently to cause the pollen to fall. Tomato flowers are self-fertile, which means that the pollen within the flower will drop on to the stigma of the same flower and fertilization will result. Sometimes, however, the air can become too dry, resulting in a poor set, and an occasional spray with clear water will help it along.

A well-grown tomato plant will produce vigorous leaves, but these should not be removed until they are of no further use to the plant. The soil initially and subsequently should be firm, as this discourages excess leaf growth and encourages flower and fruit formation. As the fruit ripens the lower leaves may be removed, literally following up the removal of the fruit from the lower trusses. On no account cut leaves in half, but try to control the leaf growth by withholding fertilizer, remembering that excess nitrogen will produce large, brittle leaves. When a leaf has to be removed, do it by placing the hand beneath the leaf, pressing upwards until you hear a click, then bend it downwards and it will come away cleanly without leaving an open wound to exude sap and encourage the growth of various fungus diseases.

Healthy plants will produce side growths in the axils of the leaves and these should be removed by pressing out with the thumb when about 2 in. long. Never cut out side shoots as this too will leave open wounds. The removal of side shoots and leaves is best done during the day when it is warm and sunny, rather than at night when it is cool and damp. Removal during the day ensures that the wound will dry up quickly and form a scar which will keep out disease.

When the plant has reached its allotted height of four or five trusses, remove the growing point one leaf beyond the topmost truss and do not allow any more side growths to develop.

Varieties: When plants are bought in, the customer is usually at the mercy of the supplier, but if you have a choice, Eurocross, Ailsa Craig, Craigella, and Market King are all excellent varieties. If you wish to try an unusual one, Golden Boy is an excellent orange/yellow variety with large fruits of good shape and quality.

For growing outdoors or under cloches The Amateur is a dwarf variety growing only to about 15 in. and bearing good quality fruit of medium size. The growth in this variety as the fruits ripen stops so that no staking or pinching is required.

Pests and Diseases: Probably the biggest and worst pest in the ordinary greenhouse is the white fly and this must be controlled early by fumigation. Proprietary specifics are available for this pest and should be used according to directions.

The two diseases most likely to attack greenhouse tomatoes are sooty mould (*Cladosporium*) and Botrytis.

Cladosporium usually appears on the undersides of the leaves as a brown purplish dust and will quickly spread throughout the greenhouse. Watch out for this in July, remove any affected leaves and dust with sulphur or fumigate with a proprietary fungicide.

Botrytis usually starts on decaying leaves or stumps of leaves, hence the need to avoid cutting, and it is rampant where the atmosphere is damp and heavy, due to lack of ventilation.

6

The disease may attack old flowers and if spores drop on to the backs of the fruit beneath, the fruit becomes watery, takes on a glassy appearance and eventually drops off. This can happen to both ripe and unripe fruit. Botrytis prefers dead tissue, but it can invade living tissue when it gets hold. At the slightest sign of this disease, dust with flowers of sulphur.

One other disease which worries many people is Aucuba Mosaic which attacks most tomato plants and produces a yellow mottle on the leaves. This is virtually impossible to control and does little harm, in spite of the fact that the plants have a rather unhealthy appearance. This however can be improved by spraying either with a weak solution of sulphate of iron in water ($\frac{1}{4}$ oz. to 2 gal.) or with Epsom Salts, at the rate of a heaped teaspoonful to a gallon of water.

Greenfly attack tomato plants only in their early stages and can be controlled by fumigation, or spraying with derris.

Pests, Diseases and Weeds

A. BILLITT

Mr. Billitt started the Lenton Research Station in Nottingham in 1939 and was its controller until his retirement in 1967. The work of the station was to study pests and diseases, vegetables, fruit, and ornamental plants, and so his experience in this area is very wide. He was the first Chairman of the British Insecticide and Fungicide Council and is a member of the British Crop Protection Council. Since his retirement from Lenton he has been Technical Officer of the B.C.P.C., Chairman of its Publications Committee, and Secretary of its Conference Programmes Committee. Many readers will be interested to know that the garden frequently shown by Gardeners World on BBC Television is Arthur Billitt's garden at Clacks Farm in Worcestershire. This garden was specially laid out for BBC purposes and, as everyone who follows this programme will know, is a massive tribute to Arthur Billitt's gardening expertise.

Pests, diseases, and weeds have made problems for man ever since he began to isolate and develop plants for the production of fruit, vegetables, and flowers. The fight against them has been carried on for centuries, but only in the last fifty years or so, as the result of much research and subsequent development work, has the battle begun to be really effective. For instance, the real breakthrough in chemical weed control came with the discovery of 2, 4-D, and then MCPA towards the end of the Second World War.

As the result of the concentrated research work of recent years, we need no longer share the fruits of our labour in the garden with the caterpillar and the greenfly. If a simple but well-thought-out spray programme is maintained, gone are the days of scabby and maggoty apples. We need no longer accept as inevitable blighted plants reduced to near uselessness by fungus diseases. Even the professionals of the past had to be content with a low percentage of unblemished fruits and vegetables, as evidenced by the still-life artist's record of these subjects.

Now, with the availability of effective insecticides and fungicides, standards of quality are so high that a blemished product has little chance in the commercial market. Quite rightly this high quality is also required by the gardener and allotment-holder. Knowing what is possible, he must surely frown on crops spoiled in appearance by uncontrolled pests and diseases. In our gardens we want to grow quality produce, but we shall also probably choose quality varieties, which are not commercially grown because of lower yield, a hard-to-pack shape, or inability to withstand travelling, but possessing the excellent flavour and texture so much associated with home growing. We should certainly grow these varieties, but in some cases we shall find them more susceptible to disease than the hardy commercial varieties. The higher we raise gardening standards, including soil cultivation, the more important it is to give thought to the question of pest and disease control.

The basic gardening ingredient is the soil. Correct management of this, apart from establishing good practice and an orderly approach, can be the first line of defence against pest and disease. Cultivation of the soil in autumn and an early start to the preparation of open ground in spring will expose numerous pests, including wireworms and leatherjackets, to their predators, the crows and other insect-eating birds. If soil drainage problems are dealt with, the slug population will be reduced and a more healthy environment created for the root systems of our plants.

Although the addition of compost, and that now rare commodity farmyard manure, or any other bulky manure originating from once living material, will not make for immunity against disease, its regular use will provide conditions in which naturally beneficial organisms can work to the gardener's advantage. Illustrating this point is the fact that potato eelworm build-up is reduced considerably by the use of compost and farmyard manure **where potatoes** have featured too frequently in the cropping programme. The increased humus content of the soil supports the predacious fungi which in turn help to keep the eelworm at bay. Where chemical assistance is needed against this pest, Dazomet can be used fairly effectively provided that, as always, the manufacturer's directions are followed carefully. This chemical sterilizer has proved to be of great value in reclaiming tired greenhouse soils when tomatoes have been grown in the same medium for several years.

If possible, the soil should not be allowed to harbour trouble for the future. The early removal of diseased plants for burning, and the collection and burning of prunings, together with any unhealthy tree branches of leaves before they can lie on the soil, is well-rewarded effort. The harvesting of vegetable crops at maturity, rather than allowing them to remain a long while in the ground, will avoid the multiplication of their particular pests in the soil, at a time when their food supply is ideal, and also ensure that our own is stored away in its best condition.

Mineral deficiencies in the soil can lead to a higher susceptibility of crops to disease. A plant suffering from a mineral deficiency has a weakened tissue structure and is therefore more vulnerable to attack, so it is advisable to use a good general fertilizer, as directed by the suppliers, to ensure favourable conditions before planting.

Mulching with peat or lawn mowings on cultivated soil amongst established plants, leaving a few inches free around individuals, will reduce the spore release of fungi (for instance in roses to assist in the control of black spot) as well as conserving moisture during dry weather.

If lime is required in soil preparation for the vegetable-garden, this must not be applied where potatoes are to be grown as it encourages scab on the tubers. This illustrates a delicate relation-ship between soil condition and disease incidence and leads me to leave well alone when crops do well.

To ensure a fair start to plant-growing the introduction of new diseases into a garden must be avoided. A good insurance against this is to go to a really reputable supplier for fresh seed and plant material, being particularly careful over tricky subjects like the brassicas or cabbage family. Clubroot-infected plants of this group, given by a kindly neighbour, can result in a soil infected for twenty years. The source of all vegetable and other plants should be enquired into, but special care must be taken in respect of seed potatoes, raspberry canes, strawberry plants, and dahlia tubers.

Despite our adherence to the foregoing precautions there will still be problems in quality homegrown production. To beat opponents it is a good idea to study their method of play; in the garden our opponents are varied, but they attack according to form. Every season we are up against insect pests which provide quickly-seen evidence of their presence, and can usually be dealt with by direct action. We also encounter diseases which are not so easily seen until they have established themselves sufficiently to show characteristic symptoms for identification. Ideally these should be dealt with by preventive measures, but in both cases an understanding of the organisms involved and the weapons available is essential.

Insect pests can be divided into two groups very simply according to their way of feeding. One group, for example the greenfly, sucks sap from leaves or fruit; the other, for example the caterpillar, chews leaves or eats its way into plant tissue.

Sucking insects, with well-adapted mouthparts for taking up the sap, weaken plants very quickly. The objectionable sticky excreta deposited by aphids (which belong to this group) and the accumulation of shed skins from developing ones, make a high percentage of fruit and vegetables useless for human consumption and render flowering plants valueless for decoration. When it occurs on fruit such as tomatoes or more commonly on plums, the excretion forms a sweet nutrient to aid the growth of moulds. Aphids, once established in favourable conditions, can multiply at an alarming rate because, as well as breeding by an egg-laying process, they are also able to bear living young, thus increasing the number of generations produced in a season. A quick reaction is needed when aphids are detected to avoid the crop being over-run, and there is another potential danger in their presence: aphids can be the carriers of virus diseases. If a winged aphid feeds on a virus-infected plant and then moves to a healthy plant it will inject the second plant with the infection in the course of its continued feeding. Raspberry mosaic and virus diseases of potatoes and brassicas are spread this way, although not exclusively. Contact insecticides are used against the sucking insects.

Chewing insects can be divided again according to the part of the plant they attack. The leaf-eaters are those most easily seen, a very common example being the caterpillar of the cabbage white butterfly which bites its destructive pattern out of the leaves of any of the brassicas. With differently adapted mouthparts other chewing insects either bore into stems, chew roots, or in the case of the minute leaf-miners live and feed under the leaf surface, 'mining' or consuming plant tissue as they go. When chewing insects attack what I would call the main line of the plant, a main stem, root, or growing point, the loss resulting is obviously complete. For instance, larvae hatching from eggs laid near the growing point in the cauliflower will cause blindness, the single flower being the growing point and near at hand when the larvae start to feed. Wherever there is this type of damage to plant tissue, easy entry is possible for disease organisms. If the initial insect damage is limited and does not affect a vital part of the plant, a secondary occurrence, namely infection, may lead to a greater loss. The range of chemicals used against the chewing insects are, by activity, stomach poisons requiring effective application to the whole of the insect's feeding-area on the plant.

In order to tackle insect pests effectively in the garden, chemical substances must be used. The killing of insects is the objective of this, so, before going into the beneficial results and methods of chemical usage, we must realize that not all insects are enemies. Some are helpful and others essential. Insects which pollinate the flowers of fruit-bearing trees and bushes are essential, but their journeying from one flower to another, and more particularly from one species to another, makes their life hazardous where insecticides are used. Always keep chemical spraying under control, avoiding drift on to plants not in need of treatment and minimizing the effect on insects uninvolved in the current problem. Honeybees should always be protected and open flowers where they are working should not be sprayed or receive drift.

Those insects which act as the predators of harmful ones are helpful, keeping a natural balance in a situation difficult to organize artificially. Whenever possible selective insecticides, aimed at offenders only, should be used. The bad effect of using a non-selective insecticide, which kills *all* insects within its cover area, is highlighted by the phenomenal increase in the numbers of the once insignificant red spider mite on fruit trees following the introduction of DDT.

Although selectivity in spray material in relation to insects is necessary, human and animal safety must be of prime importance. The best methods of insect control are those based on substances poisonous to the insects but having no harmful effect on man or animals. Only insecticides and fungicides approved by the Ministry of Agriculture should be considered. Additionally the Ministry recommendations as to taint and soil residues in respect of approved substances are easily obtainable.

Long before the present-day insecticides were discovered soapy water was thrown over plants attacked by greenfly. This was not very effective, but the soapy liquid did penetrate the waxy protective covering of the aphids and seemed to reduce the build-up of aphid population. Modern insecticides are not based on soap, but do include synthetic wetting agents which add an increased power of penetration into the insects' armour. Because of this, less of the chemical is needed to obtain the desired result.

Although not as effective as some of the newer synthetic organic insecticides, those of vegetable origin, such as derris or pyrethrum, are probably the safest for the weekend gardener. Derris has the advantage of having contact activity as well as being a useful stomach poison. Neither derris nor pyrethrum kills 100%, but so far there have been no reports of resistance being built up following their continual use. These two have the added advantage of being harmless to birds.

Of the newer synthetic organic insecticides, Malathion, which was introduced in 1950, would be my choice for controlling greenfly and most other common sucking insects. Its danger level is low, but care is needed to prevent harm to bees and fish. It is available for application in either dust or liquid form.

Most plant diseases result from the presence of either fungi, bacteria, or viruses. Virus diseases are recognized by the gardener only by the changes they cause in plants, as the organisms responsible are of the most simple microscopic type. Colour variation or mottling and curling of the leaf, as seen in the mosaic diseases of raspberries and potatoes, is typical. When a virus is present the whole plant is affected and there is no hope of recovery. Prevention is the only recommendation to be made, bearing in mind the transmission risk from sucking insects and from the careless handling of ailing plants as may happen when tomato side-shooting is allowed to include a sick plant in a continuous operation. Here, virus-infected sap is carried on the knife blade. A reliable nurseryman for new stock, and a watchful eye to spot and destroy sick and degenerating plants is the answer.

Bacteria are small microscopic single cell organisms requiring food, heat, moisture, and oxygen for life. Welcome bacteria find these requirements in the soil and are responsible for the decay of organic material and the formation of humus. When this process occurs where it is *not* wanted, the few troublesome bacterial diseases result. Soft rotting, such as celery heart rot or carrot rot is of bacterial origin and is easily spread by contact, and is a great nuisance when storing vegetables. Subjects showing rot must be removed quickly to avoid greater loss. Canker or bacterial dieback in plums and cherries is self-explanatory and should be dealt with by the removal and burning of affected parts. Further spread can be limited by painting cut surfaces with a bitumen paint.

By far the worst group of plant diseases are those caused by fungi. These are spread by the production, under favourable conditions, of numerous spores usually airborne and all capable of starting their own destructive life. The fungi are plants themselves, but have no chlorophyll, unlike the usually recognizable green plants. In order to obtain supplies of carbon necessary for growth and energy, they live on the surface of leaves, on fruit and plant roots, or within the plant tissue itself, as parasites. Fungicide treatment of diseases in which the fungi are on the surface is very efficient as in the case of the powdery mildews. Where they are in the tissue itself, as they are in Black Spot on roses, the fungicide used will only protect plants not already affected and action should be taken long before the characteristic black blotches are seen. As with some other fungus diseases there

6*

is an over-wintering stage of Black Spot during which the spores rest in old fallen leaves ready to be released as weather conditions improve from February onwards. The infection of new buds takes place as soon as the bud scales open. The removal of dead leaves and mulching between plants upsets this sequence.

There are a great many different fungi causing a variety of diseases from gall formation and deformity to mildew, from scab to damping off or wilting amongst seedlings, but all are dependent on the release of spores from their spread. This stage and the conditions favouring it must be watched for by the gardener in order to achieve a good level of control.

One method of disease control is the growing of disease-resistant varieties where it is compatible with quality. Much work has been done by plant-breeders to select strains less likely to succumb to disease. It is less expensive to resist disease than to have to deal with it. These developments may lead to loss of flavour in edible crops, so one takes one's choice.

Correct control of the growing environment greatly affects the incidence of disease. The giving of as much space as possible between rows to crops out of doors will improve their health prospects. Avoidance of conditions known to be more conducive to specific diseases can be dealt with at planting time. This applies particularly to roses. In an enclosed situation the environment is under complete control, as in the glass house and the garden frame. Good ventilation with constant attention paid to the efficiency of any heating system used is essential if the troubles associated with damp, cold, stagnant conditions are to be avoided. Lack of air movement is ideal for the establishment of Botrytis Grey Mould, the plague of many a gardener afraid to leave a little air on at night in his greenhouse or frames.

To prevent the glasshouse and garden frame from harbouring disease, they need clearing out and washing down with household detergent every autumn. At the end of the season seed-boxes ought to be cleaned and painted with an approved wood preservative, or if made of plastic, well washed. Damping-off of seedlings should not arise in sterilized media such as John Innes or peat composts, but should it appear, the remedy is Chestnut Compound, used according to directions immediately the trouble is spotted. The use of the ring culture method, or of peat bags for growing indoor tomatoes will cut out the necessity of glasshouse soil sterilization against soil-borne disease.

Most chemicals for use by the gardener are in liquid or dust form. The liquids are usually concentrations to be made up in water, as instructed by the manufacturers. Many simple hand-sprayers to apply them are available. Dusts are generally sold in puffer drums; for quantities there are hand dusting-machines. Aerosol packs are handy for limited use, such as spot attacks on aphids, but expensive on a large scale, and there is a danger of damage to plants if held too near to them in operation. Insecticides and fungicides in the form of fumigant smokes may be useful in a confined space, for instance, ignited in a small glasshouse overnight with the ventilators closed. Whatever means are used, special care must be taken when spraying over or near seedlings, young plants potted on, or rooting cuttings, remembering that these are at a very tender stage.

FRUIT TREES

Apple, pear, and plum trees should receive a winter spray during November to January while the trees are completely dormant, the spray being applied through a coarse nozzle, on a still, frost-free day when the wood is dry. The product used should be based on tar oils. The use of tar winter sprays destroys the eggs of aphids, scale insects, and other sap-suckers, which have been laid in crevices in the bark. Lichen, which grows on trees in some districts, is also killed by these sprays, thus denying a safe egg-laying area to the insects. It may not be necessary to do much further spraying on plums. A derris insecticide application made in the spring when leaf growth is really going ahead and cater-pillars are seen to be chewing, should be sufficient. Apples and pears need more attention, starting as soon as the buds burst with an application of a mixed insecticide and fungicide spray, repeated again when the apple blossom is at the 'pink bud stage', and pears at the 'white bud' stage, followed by a further spray at 'petal fall'. In each instance the insecticide I select is derris and the fungicide Captan. The two will be purchased separately, but the manufacturer's recommended amount of each chemical may be combined in the single volume suggested. The object here is to prevent damage by insects and caterpillars which make their way from the blossom into the developing fruitlets, and secondly to prevent apple and pear scab. Both scabs are common fungus diseases, making fruit unsightly and stunted, large areas of the skin becoming covered with thick black patches. The tree spray applications should be generally effective, but to make quite sure the same mixed spray may be repeated once or twice while the fruitlets are still small.

Birds have not been mentioned, but just after Christmas they can become pests attacking fruit buds as they begin to swell, and later in the season when the fruit ripens. There is no need to trap or spray against them if the trees are covered with fine mesh nylon or plastic netting during each of the vulnerable periods. If deterred in this way the birds will stop trying after a few days and feed elsewhere. With careful handling the netting will last years.

Fruit Bushes

Blackcurrants, gooseberries, and raspberries should have a tar winter wash, but because their growth begins early it is wise to do the winter spraying before the New Year. Apart from the pests taken care of by this means, steps must be taken against big bud mites on blackcurrants. From March onwards, as the temperature increases, the mites emerge from already swollen buds, in which they have overwintered, to spread in increased numbers to other buds. Unchecked, the process snowballs into complete loss for the gardener. The safe treatment is two or three applications of lime sulphur starting when the leaves are the size of a ten-pence piece, allowing an interval of two weeks between treatments. A dilemma arises because several varieties of black-currant react badly to lime sulphur, their young growths showing quite a lot of damage after its use. As alternative substances are less safe, I choose to solve the problem by limiting my black-currant-growing to one variety only, namely Baldwin, on which the treatment can be used without any adverse effect.

Both blackcurrants and gooseberries can be attacked by

American gooseberry mildew. Fortunately Benlate, an effective systematic fungicide, is available for use against this and acts with success at the first sign of mildew on the growing tips. There is one caterpillar, that of the sawfly, which, if not stopped, can strip gooseberry foliage down to a collection of leaf skeletons in no time. One spraying with a derris insecticide when the caterpillars first appear will remove them.

Raspberries are not subject to many troubles, assuming that virus-free stock has been established, but the fruit can be spoiled for eating by the raspberry beetle which lays its eggs in the open blossom. Resultant larvae tunnel into the centre of the fruit. Again the safe insecticide is derris applied at flowering time, if possible in the evening, when honeybees have finished working.

STRAWBERRIES

On strawberries, sucking aphids, as transmitters of virus disease, can destroy the health of the plants and reduce the crop considerably. Malathion used as soon as aphids are seen will control them. Especially bad during spells of wet, cold weather at fruiting time is Botrytis, a fungus seen as grey mould, very furry in appearance. The trouble originates earlier in the year, so the mould formation can be prevented by spraying two or three times during the growing season with Benlate systemic fungicide. To avoid the risk of chemical residues in the eventually-formed fruits, spraying must not be done after flowering.

VEGETABLES

Brassicas: Members of the cabbage family are generally resistant to wireworm attack, so they are a good choice for planting after the breaking up of old turf, which may have a high wireworm population. Clubroot is the commonest disease in brassicas, and, once present, it has a long-lasting effect in the soil. Knobbly swellings form on the roots, leading to wilting, decay, and the death of the whole plant, and a residue of the organisms responsible, in the soil. A minimum of eight years is needed to free the ground of these before the crop is safe again after infection, and an even greater persistence is common. A heaped teaspoon of 4% calomel dust well mixed with the soil in each dibble hole at planting time, is the best precaution to be taken. Regular liming of the soil will reduce the risk of clubroot, creating a degree of alkalinity unfavourable to the organism's growth. Cabbage-root fly is a universal pest, the larvae eating the essential root structure and so causing the rest of the plant above ground to collapse and die. Control is gained here by applying BHC dust to the roots at planting time. It may be borne in mind that these larvae can also do damage to swedes, turnips, and radishes. The Cabbage White butterfly is identified by everyone, and derris insecticide should be used on brassica leaves to forestall the devastating eating habits of the Cabbage White caterpillar.

Potatoes: The use of virus-free seed potatoes removes much worry from growing this crop but it leaves the problem of potato blight. This disease occurs mostly in late-crop potatoes and susceptible varieties. Because of susceptibility to blight and also slugs it is best to grow King Edward. If blight breaks out at the end of the growing season, showing up as dark brown leaf-patches which turn mouldy in damp weather, the tops should be cut and destroyed. Any remaining diseased haulms will perpetuate the infection. Blight at a very early stage may be arrested with either Zineb or Maneb but, when advanced, spraying is useless.

Broad Beans have as their main pest, black fly, which can be controlled early in the season by a Malathion spray, or later by pinching out the growing tip when the plant is in full flower.

Peas will miss most soil-borne diseases if started in pots and then transplanted. This also prevents mice eating newly-sown peas. The pea moth is killed by a derris spray at flowering time, thus preventing maggots in the developing pods.

Carrots especially the early ones, need protection from carrot fly. BHC dust sprinkled along the drills when sowing will do this.

Onions benefit from this dressing too, against invasion by onion fly, and need a repeated dusting while the seedlings are small. The pulling of salad-sized onions from a row will attract the fly by the onion smell released, so onions intended for harvesting ripe should be sown thinly, to obviate thinning.

Tomatoes grown in the glasshouse must have adequate ventilation as still air encourages leaf mould fungi. For white fly there are either proprietary smokes or a Malathion spray, to be repeated every ten to fourteen days, but keeping strictly to the manufacturers' directions.

FLOWERING PLANTS

Chrysanthemums suffer leaf damage from aphids, capsids, and leaf-miners, the first two spoiling buds as well. BHC liquid is a useful insecticide against these. For powdery mildew, which is self-descriptive, Benlate is recommended. If eelworm build-up is detected, showing in loss of plant vigour, brown shrivelled leaves and poor flowers, the simple remedy is to remove and burn the sick plants, buying new healthy ones for planting in a different part of the garden.

Dahlias are prone to virus diseases, so BHC liquid spray is advisable for greenfly. It also checks earwigs, those insects which so deter the flower arranger. A reversed plant pot filled with straw and placed on a stake amongst the dahlia plants, makes a good earwig trap. The 'catch' can be destroyed each morning.

Roses grown in 'clear air' districts have an increased black spot problem because SO_2 (sulphur dioxide) in the air of industrial area helps to restrict it. To be effective, spraying with Captan must begin in February, before the leaf buds break, followed by repeats at fortnightly intervals. Winter pruning, removing dead leaves, and mulching all help. Against rose mildew spraying with Benlate must start immediately signs appear on growing leaves.

Beech is a hedging-plant which can benefit from inclusion when spraying. Severe aphid attack can shrivel the leaves, so Malathion sprayed in the spring when the buds burst is a good thing, especially to protect a newly-planted hedge. The treatment of large trees for either pests or disease is difficult because of size.

Usually the only practical course is to use a general fertilizer round the base to invigorate and so increase resistance.

WEED CONTROL

The control of weeds is closely linked to pest and disease control. Where weeds abound, diseases and pests lurk undisturbed; conversely, where there are ailing plants, weeds have a knack of germinating quickly and taking over. All weeds have a vulnerable seedling stage at which they can be destroyed easily by the hoe. A Dutch hoe used regularly throughout the growing season is the best weapon against annual weeds in herbaceous borders and in the vegetable garden. To be efficient, this tool must be used constantly, so to make the task acceptable, the hoe itself should be chosen carefully. Those having the metal part all in one piece, although maybe a little more expensive, are the best. For gardeners living near the countryside it is a good idea to find out which make is used by local piece-workers in field crops; they *have* to be effective. Also check the angle of the blade to make sure that it can be used with little back bending, to cut off seedling weeds just slightly below soil level. A lower action might simply transplant them, especially in damp weather.

Winter digging of cultivated areas is the starting point for good weed control. It is very important on heavy soils, where the help of frost is needed to obtain a good tilth, both for planting and the future use of the hoe. In spring, hoeing should be started before the seedling stage, where there is a workable tilth. Many weeds can be got rid of when only the white threadlike shoots from their seeds are visible in the soil, and there is still plenty of open working space. No plants, not even twitch, thistles, nettles, and docks can survive the loss of their green shoots above ground for a whole season. Deprived of access to energy-giving sunlight through emerging leaves, even weeds with masses of creeping underground roots are starved and eventually die. The greatest setback in the fight against weeds is when they are allowed to seed. Whatever methods are used, they must operate before the seed-shedding stage is reached. The old saying 'One year's seeding, seven years' weeding' is all too true.

As in so many other spheres, scientific research has given us chemical aids to use against weeds, and a sensible use of some of these, after priority has been given to good cultivation, is the best approach. A weed-free lawn is something to be proud of, and this is where selective weedkillers come into their own. Fortunately, the plants we want to keep in the lawn differ basically from the ones we want to get rid of, and their structural difference has made the formulation of chemical sprays, deadly to one and almost harmless to the other, possible. Desirable grasses are obviously quite unlike the common lawn weeds, such as daisies, dandelions, and clover. We can make use of selective 'herbicides' to eliminate all the more usual broad-leaved weeds. A spray based on 2, 4-D, or MCPA, with CMPP added to deal with clover, is a good recommendation. These sprays should be mixed according to the maker's directions and never used at any greater strength. A watering-can with a special boom, having small droplet holes along its length, provides the best means of application. The can should be kept for this job only, as the chemicals are hard to wash out. A large label on the can will prevent mistakes. A dressing with fertilizer a week or two before intended treatment will improve results. The spray should be applied during periods of active growth and when rainfall is unlikely. Mowing should not be done for at least a week afterwards and the first mowings after spraying must not be used for composing or mulching, bearing in mind the chemical content. A second treatment may be needed a month or so later. Newly-laid turf and newly-sown grass should not be treated during the first six months.

Chemical weedkillers have been developed for use in individual crops and it is hard to comply with the precise application requirements in the garden, especially relating to the residual type of weedkiller, such as Simazine. Once applied, this substance remains active in the soil for several months, restricting the planting of sensitive subjects. It is useful in controlling annual weeds in an established rose-bed if applied to weed-free soil in the spring. If the soil is undisturbed, it should remain weed-free for the season.

There is a role for Paraquat-based weedkillers for breaking in rough grass or very weedy areas, as their use makes digging easier a week or so later. The substance is active on leaves only, and breaks down immediately in the soil. Soft planting can take place at once. It has to be remembered that Paraquat is *not* selective and will kill the above-ground portions of all plants it touches. Weeds with strong underground root systems, such as nettles, thistles, docks, and twitch recover and, if they are to be killed by chemical means, 2, 4-D plus 2, 4, 5-T, available in combination as a 'nettle and brushwood killer', may be used.

For keeping down weeds in paths sodium chlorate or Simazine are suitable. Care must be taken if paths slope, in case the liquid runs where it is not wanted. Where trees and shrubs are likely to have roots underneath paths, there is a great danger to them, and physical removal of weeds above them would be safer.

All chemicals used in the garden, and most particularly weed-killers, *must* be kept out of reach of children and animals. If they are used sensibly they have their place with the other older tools of gardening, such as my favourite Dutch hoe.

8 Saving Labour the Organic Way

DR. W. E. SHEWELL-COOPER

This chapter is designed as an introduction for the many people who ask questions about organic gardening and its place in the world today. Dr. Shewell-Cooper is the Director of the International Horticultural Advisory Bureau at Arkley, in Hertfordshire, and is the author of over sixty books on gardening. His The Complete Gardener *has sold over 150,000 copies. He has broadcast on both television and radio in Bermuda, South Africa, Belgium, Tasmania, and Jamaica; his broadcasts in Australia in 1968 were voted the most popular of the year and as a result, were repeated in 1970. He is the most prolific horticultural writer of the century. He writes for forty newspapers and magazines, and answers gardening queries by letter by the hundred, and he travels all over Europe giving advice. For his report on Corsica he was made* Chevalier de Mérite Agricole; *and he has been similarly honoured in Austria, Italy, and Denmark. Dr. Shewell-Cooper lives in an English manor, with a beautiful eight-acre garden around it. Thousands of people visit the garden every year, and are amazed to find that there are never any weeds—but he never uses any chemical or artificial fertilizers, growing all his crops with organic manures and compost only. He is the founder and chairman of the Good Gardeners' Association which has thousands of members in Great Britain and abroad; he was founder and chairman of the British Association of Consultants in Agriculture and Horticulture. For many years he was also the honorary treasurer of the Horticultural Education Association. He is a freeman of the City of London and a liveryman of the Worshipful Company of Gardeners.*

To understand what has been described as the 'Muck-Magic'

school of gardening one must be a student of nature. Nature in the raw does no digging or forking—the leaves from the trees fall to the ground in the forest and they are pulled into the soil by the worms. This is the complete circle—i.e. the passing-back. Not only do the worms tunnel down sometimes even to six feet, but they chew up the soil and leaves, and the worm-casts they produce contain (according to Darwin) six times more nitrogen, seven times more phosphates, and even ten times more potash than the soil that has entered their bodies.

But it isn't only leaves that are pulled in. These are frequently covered with the manure of flies, gnats, bees, wasps, mice, rats, voles, badgers, foxes, and numerous other animals, plus, of course, birds. Organic gardeners call this manure the activator because it acts as food for the millions of living organisms in the soil which help to produce humus, which may be regarded as the blood of the soil. When a man has no blood in his body, he is dead—and a soil without humus is dead also and we call it a desert. The USA has been producing deserts galore in the last few years!

The basis of all organic gardening, therefore, is the compost heap, and this compost must be properly made. Eighty per cent of the compost heaps in Great Britain do not produce compost at all. Compost is a dark brown powder containing no weed seeds, no diseases, and no insect pests. It does, however, contain all the main plant foods (called macro-nutrients) and the minor plant foods like boron, molybdenum, lithium, manganese, magnesium, calcium, iron, and so on (called micro-nutrients). *But* in addition and just as important, properly-made powdery compost contains antibiotics, enzymes, and vitamins. Thus the plants grown with compost are largely free from pests and diseases and if they are edible, they taste far better.

There isn't space in this one chapter to give full details as to how proper composting is done—but those who are going to become enthusiastic organic gardeners, and thus be for anti-pollution and against dangerous chemicals—will read the *A.B.C. of Soils Humus and Health*.[1] The teaching must be: 'Everything

[1] Published by Hodder & Stoughton.

that has lived can live again in a plant'. So the keen gardener saves *all* his kitchen waste, including newspapers, coffee grounds, tea leaves, peelings of all kinds, crushed bones, and so on; and from the garden itself he collects leaves, the tops of carrots and beetroot, the stumps of cabbages and sprouts, potato haulm, lawn mowings, and any weeds there may be. The more varied the selection of waste matter, on the whole the better the compost.

For every six inches of waste when trodden down evenly, apply an organic activator—say, fish manure, seaweed manure, dried poultry manure, rabbit manure, at three ounces to the square yard. If the compost bin is made of wood—and it must be—if it is square—and this is vital—good compost can be made, especially if the floor is solid earth. The sides must have air spaces, so that the bacteria that are going to produce the perfect powdered compost can have a chance to breathe.

Those who cannot or will not make compost (those, in fact, who refuse to help prevent pollution, remembering that fifty per cent of what normally goes into the dustbin can be composted) should use sedge peat—not sphagnum peat. Sedge peat is the 'natural compost', and can be used whenever compost is necessary.

GETTING RID OF PERENNIAL WEEDS

In the flower-garden all that has to be done is to apply the compost one inch deep all over the soil where the plants are growing. Of course, before you start adopting this no-dig compost idea, you must get rid of the perennial weeds. I do this in two ways: (1) most of them can be killed by sprinkling dry powdered sodium chlorate on the leaves of the plants—not on the soil. This is taken in by the foliage down the stems to the roots and kills them; (2) plants such as bindweed can be killed by using a strong hormone like M.C.P.A., and painting this on the growing tips. Once again the hormone will be passed down to the roots and kill them.

Incidentally, at the Good Gardeners' Association trial grounds it has been discovered that there are plants that 'hate' one another and so it is possible to use some desirable specimens to drive away the perennial weeds that are not wanted. For example bindweed cannot live in the presence of *Tagetes minuta* and will be driven away by this little french marigold.

PLANTING

There is no need to do any digging at all when preparing the soil for roses, shrubs, or herbaceous borders. Worms dislike being disturbed, the soil bacteria hate being buried, and the soil itself dislikes having its natural up-and-down structure disturbed. So all that has to be done is to make the necessary holes for the roots of the plants that you want to put in, and then, having planted firmly and levelled the soil, to apply the properly-prepared, browny-black, powdery compost all over the soil one inch deep. It is no good arguing that it is impossible to do this on heavy clay soil, because, in the gardens of the Good Gardeners' Association which are on London clay, the shrubs, trees, and plants are thriving; and they were all planted without any preliminary digging.

Once the powdery compost has been applied evenly all over the levelled bed the worms start to do their work. Mind you, in gardens where deep digging has been done for years and where chemical fertilizers have been used liberally, there may be few or no worms, BUT (and I have put this word in capital letters deliberately) in the soil there will be worm capsules, i.e. worm eggs, and, when digging and the use of chemicals are stopped and when compost is applied liberally on the top of the soil, the worms will hatch out immediately and start doing their work. One good worm can produce nearly 100 young wormlings (to help dig your garden) in one year.

If the soil is low in humus, the worms will tunnel upwards and pull some of the compost into the soil, where it will be worked on by the millions of living organisms there. There can easily be 30 million living organisms in 5 cu. cm. of soil; so that, if the worms do pull in, say, a ¼-in. of compost or sedge peat, then, say in six months time, another ¼-in. layer must be added in its place. This pulling in of the compost may occur two years running, but at the end of this period the compost layer will usually lie on top of the soil, doing its job of suppressing annual weed seeds all the time, for many more years.

No Hoeing

It isn't sufficiently realized that annual weed-seeds, such as those of Shepherd's Purse, chickweed, annual meadow grass, annual nettle, and groundsel, can lie in the soil for very many years without germinating. When digging is done (bastard-trenching, for instance), the hundreds of weed-seeds that are dropped on the surface of the ground are buried, many of them not as much as a spade's depth, but just an inch or two deep. Whatever happens to the weed-seeds, we know that hoeing invariably brings them to the surface, where they germinate and grow, so regular hoeing means more weeds, and thus more regular hoeing.

Experiments have shown that there can easily be over 300 million weed-seeds in an acre garden. So, when digging and hoeing your $\frac{1}{4}$ acre of garden, you can easily bring near to the surface of the soil some 70 million seeds of annual weeds which can give a lot of trouble. And, of course, if the weeds are left even for a short time they in turn may seed and so perpetuate the trouble.

The Subsequent Planting

Once the layer of compost has been put on the soil there is little or nothing to be done. It is easy to tweak out the very few weeds that do appear, as I know from twenty years' experience. However, if a plant should die it is an easy matter to scoop aside the layer of compost, make a hole, put in the new plant, tread down level, and rake back the layer of compost again.

Special Hints and Tips

In the case of heathers, azaleas, hydrangeas, rhododendrons, and the like, the powdered bark of trees may be used effectively instead of compost. Sawdust causes denitrification, i.e. it causes nitrogen and valuable food to be taken from the soil by the bacteria as they try hard to rot it down. Powdered bark on the other hand does not have this effect, and I have beds at Arkley Manor that have been mulched with powdered bark for six years with excellent results and, of course, no weeds.

The layer of compost or sedge peat on the soil is not only a weed-preventer and an organic food, but, because it acts as a mulch, it keeps the moisture in the soil and in dry summers this is particularly valuable. It helps to prevent mildew and black spot on roses. Mildew commonly attacks plants suffering from water shortage. But the mulching of the compost conserves the moisture in the ground by reducing evaporation. The spores of black spot blow up from the soil, and covering the earth with compost prevents this from happening; and the antibiotics in the compost help to control diseases.

If you are sowing the seeds of annual flowers the compost may be put all over the soil. You take out the drills by simply drawing the compost aside. When the little plants are through, just rake the powdery compost back again to leave it level. The alternative is to sow the seeds in the normal way and, when the little plants are 3 in. or so high, apply 1 in. of the mulching material all over the ground.

LIME AND COMPOSTING

When taking over a new garden, test the soil to see whether it is acid or not. In the case of the vegetable-garden—the acidity may be corrected by adding hydrated lime at, say, 7 oz. per sq. yd. Fellows of the Good Gardeners' Association may have the soil analysed free and the soil chemist will advise exactly the amount of lime to use. After the first year, however, it is usually unnecessary to add any more lime, as the waste from the vegetable-garden should contain enough calcium, so that, when the compost is applied the lime is, so to speak, given back again.

In cases where the acidity is really serious I have known it necessary to lime for two years running, and after that to rely on the compost to keep the pH (as it is called) level. Those who need further instruction in this matter can always consult *The A.B.C. of Soil, Humus and Health*. Incidentally, the author of that book has never found it necessary, during the last twenty years, to add lime to his compost heap.

SOILS THAT ARE TOO LIMY

The trouble invariably occurs because the soil of the garden lies on chalk or limestone. In such conditions rake plenty of powdery compost into the top inch or two of soil and in addition apply it as a dressing 1 in. deep on the surface as usual. The idea is to ensure that the roots keep up in the top few inches of soil and do not reach down too deeply to get into touch with the lime.

It is quite extraordinary how the roots of plants will adapt themselves to their position. I used to advise deep digging, for instance, for Brussels sprouts which I had found go down 3 ft. or more. When I changed over to no-digging, what interested me was that the roots of the Brussels sprouts now spread themselves out in a wide circle and proved to be just as good an anchorage as the deeper-growing roots of the old system. In fact, I feel that the widespread roots give better results than the deeper ones.

SHRUBS—NO-DIGGING

One of the simplest ways of having an attractive garden is by the use of flowering shrubs. They are comparatively easy to plant; they last for years and years; they take little or no looking after; and they make a good screen, providing privacy where necessary. Once they are planted at the right distance apart (i.e. allowing, say, half the distance of their final height on either side), the soil should be levelled and firmed and the compost applied all over the ground to the depth of 1 in. No hoeing will be necessary and annual weeds will be completely suppressed.

In a small garden, always plant smaller shrubs, i.e. those that grow to no more than 3–4 ft. Choose a spot where there is plenty of sun and if possible arrange to have a fence or a hedge at the back so that the cold winds may be kept off. In such a garden, the border need be no wider than 4–5 ft. and, say, 14–15 ft. long. Make holes 6–7 in. deep and 2–3 ft. square to accommodate the roots of the plants. Spread the roots out like the rays of the sun in the bottom of the hole, cutting back cleanly any that are too long with a sharp knife so that they fit into the hole. Such pruning will encourage new roots to develop.

Plant firmly so that there can be no wobbling about afterwards. As each spadeful of soil is put over the roots tread well, wearing heavy boots! When the hole is full, leave the centre slightly proud to allow for the sinkage which will invariably take place. If a slight mound is not left the centre will drop slightly and a concave top will be produced in which the rain will collect. For this reason it is better, in the case of shrubs, to wait for four weeks after planting before applying the top dressing of compost 1 in. deep.

Arrange to plant shrubs which will give flowers, coloured leaves, or berries for most months of the year. Consult a good catalogue or a book like the *A.B.C. of Flowering Shrubs*, and choose shrubs such as Veronica, Rosemary, Olearia, Phlomis, Kalmia, Hypericum, Cistus, Berberis, Cotoneaster, and Escallonia. All of these have a number of species and varieties to choose from and are easy to grow.

HEATHERS

A heather bed is easy to manage and does very well under composting conditions. The general aim is to plant out the various varieties at, say, 18 in.–2 ft. apart, and to allow them to spread all over the ground. The plants will soon settle in if the soil is fed with sedge peat or powdery compost at the rate of 2 bucketfuls to the sq. yd. and a very light forking is given. After the heathers are in position the usual 1-in. deep mulching of the compost is given all over the area.

There are many different kinds of heathers—pinks, whites, reds, mauves; those with large bells; many with tiny flowers. Some have golden foliage, others are dark green; some are tall, others are short.

The *Erica carnea* group will put up with limy soil, and varieties I can recommend are Ruby Glow, King George, Springwood Pink, Springwood White, Vivelli, and Winter Beauty, a rose-pink. All these flower in the winter. In the summer if you have normal soil you can grow H. Maxwell, a bright pink, C.D. Eason, a glowing pink, G.G. Best, a pine pink, Eden Valley, a blue, Francis, a cerise, Con Underwood, a red, and Blazeaway, a variety with golden foliage.

THE COMPOST SMOTHER BORDER

At Arkley the Good Gardeners' Association have what they call a smother-garden or smother-border. Plants are used which spread quickly all over the ground and so cover it up completely and prevent weeds from growing. The plan is to level the bed or bank, i.e. to keep the soil free from lumps and hollows, and then, having covered the area with compost, to plant the desired specimens. For this purpose I can recommend the Rose of Sharon, with its lovely large, golden-yellow, cushion-like flowers; Periwinkle, the spreading plant with beautiful blue flowers; the Spanish gorse, with tiny sweet pea-like blooms; a horizontal-growing Cotoneaster; Berberis candidula; and one or two creeping ivies. All of these, other than the Cotoneaster and Berberis may be planted 2 ft. square; the others need 3 ft. square. Leave them, and in two or three years the border will be completely covered.

A LITTLE-WORK ROSE-GARDEN

The modern H.T. and floribunda roses are easy to grow, particularly under first-class compost conditions. The H.T.s produce biggish blooms somewhat pointed and with many petals. The bushes bloom in June and July and again in September. The leaves are bronzy-green or green. The floribundas are nearly ever-blooming. They produce a number of roses on one head and are generally regarded as impressive.

When the bushes arrive in their sack or plastic bag, unpack them and put the roots into a bucket half-filled with water for at least two hours. Don't of course attempt to plant if the weather is frosty; keep the bunches in their containers in a frost-proof place until it thaws. When it is possible to plant, make a hole for each bush 15 in. square and, say, 6 in. deep. Make the bottom of the hole slightly convex so that the bottom of the rose bush may 'sit' on this. If your rose-bed is to be made in the lawn, the soil that has been dug out of the hole should be placed on some sacking, so that it won't harm the grass.

Spread out the roots evenly like the rays of the sun from the centre of the hole. Don't allow the roots to be doubled up. Cut back any that are damaged with a sharp knife so that the cut side is downwards. Sprinkle fine soil over the roots to the depth of 1 in. and tread down firmly; then put on another layer of soil and tread again. Continue until the hole is full and, as with shrubs (see pp. 179–80), see that the centre is slightly higher. It is important when planting to ensure that the point at which the rose was budded is just below the surface of the ground. The soil mark on the base of the bush will indicate where the bud is placed.

Plant 30 in. apart either way, preferably in the late autumn or winter or in the very early spring, i.e. mid-March. If however, roses are bought in containers from a garden centre, planting may be done even in the late spring or early summer. In early May cover the bed with the powdery compost you have made yourself in the garden or use medium-grade sedge peat. Put it on 1 in. deep after treading the soil in the bed level. Once a year, say in March, fish manure may be applied all over the compost at 3 oz. per sq. yd.

Varieties. Good roses to plant on this organic method are Super Star, Piccadilly, Peace, Ernest H. Morse, Bettina, and Mischief, all H.T.s; and Elizabeth of Glamis, Orange Sensation, Evelyn Fison, All Gold, Masquerade, and Sea Pearl, all floribundas.

VEGETABLES

The vegetable-garden is the one place where the compost should be lightly forked or raked in. It isn't possible to sow the seeds until a fine tilth is produced. Add the compost to the surface of the soil in the late autumn and allow it to lie there all the winter. In the spring, when sowing-time comes, do the light forking—or you can use a small rotovator for this purpose.

Once a nice level tilth has been produced the seeds may be sown. No special flat-bottomed drills need be made for peas and beans. No trenches need be dug for celery or summer beans, and the potatoes can be grown almost on the flat. No celery trenches are needed because we are growing the new green celery, which is just as delicious as the usual blanched white variety so beloved by our fathers!

Varieties

Trials have been carried out over the last six years and the following varieties, compost grown, have been discovered to be particularly delicious.

Potato—the best-flavoured is Home Guard, an excellent 'chip, potato, with shallow eyes; easy to peel; definitely at its best when compost-grown. Craig's Royal, a second early, is also shallow-eyed and of good quality. Dr. MacIntosh has shallow eyes and crops heavily, especially on heavy soils.

Peas: Recommended varieties are: Kelvedon Wonder (only 18 in. high. Sow it early and sow it late. Good flavour and almost immune to mildew). Lord Chancellor (3 ft. high. Excellent flavour. A robust main crop). Histon Kingside (3½ ft. high and a heavy cropper. Main crop. Delicious). Sugar Sweetgreen (3½ ft. high. The pods are eaten as well as the peas, just like French beans. Good flavour).

Broad Beans: Red Epicure is an extraordinary bean. It is a long pod whose chestnut-red beans turn a straw colour when cooked. Exhibition Green Windsor beans remain a beautiful greyish-green colour when cooked. The flavour is excellent.

Dwarf French Beans: Phoenix Claudia (a truly stringless French bean. Pick it and cook it—delicious!). Processor (pods are rounded rather than flat. Stringless. Good flavour and quality).

Runner Beans: Streamline (a supple, tender bean, but pick on the young side for flavour). Crusader (fine, fleshy pods of first-class quality and flavour).

Beetroot: Empire Globe is free from white rings and so is very tender. Spangsbjerg Cylinder is a cylindrical-shape beet of a deep red colour right through, with first-class table qualities.

Broccoli: Green Comet (deep green heads, the sprouting type, good coloured clusters of buds. Delicious!) Markanta (an April–May curding broccoli. The snow-white heads are most appetizing).

Brussels Sprouts: Aristocrat (medium-sized sprouts, but very solid. Flavour first-class). Sanda, a mid-season bean, is worth growing for picking and putting in the deep freeze.

Cabbage: Fillgap (a Primo type of cabbage. Round firm hearts, almost 'all-heart'). Emerald Cross (flat, solid-hearted cabbage of first-class flavour and quality).

Carrot: New Scarlet Intermediate (roots are uniform; the flesh is sweet and solid; a first-class quality). Early Nantes (a very early stump-rooted variety. Hardly any core).

Cauliflower: Snow King (solid ivory-white curded. Delicious. Turns in three months after sowing). Dominant (not so large as Snow King, but delicious).

Leeks: seem not to vary in flavour after cooking. Therefore, grow a large variety, such as Marble Pillar, which can produce stems longer than any other kind.

Lettuce: Wonderful (crinkled, crisp, tender, icy leaves; lovely firm solid hearts. Lasts well in droughty weather). Little Gem or Sugar Cos (a small, crisp, tender cos, almost 'all-heart'. Never bolts. Excellent flavour).

Onions: Unwin's Reliance. This has the mildest flavour of all the onions.

Parsnip: Avonresister (almost immune from parsnip canker. Uniform roots. Delicious when roasted).

Tomato: Outdoor Girl (an early outdoor variety. Good flavour). Histon Ideal (a fleshy variety. The fruits are perfectly shaped and the skin is thin). Easicrop has fleshy fruits, especially good for sandwiches. Firm texture; first-class flavour.

THE CABBAGE FAMILY

The members of the cabbage family—the cauliflowers, sprouts, and the like—should be sown in a seed-bed, i.e. a small square of ground say 6 ft. by 5 ft. Rake in plenty of compost and apply hydrated lime as a surface dressing at 6–7 oz. per sq. yd. Sow the seeds in the level and firmed bed in rows, 6 in. apart and about ½ in. deep. If the weather is dry, give a good watering afterwards. This must be done through the fine rose of a can or by means of a sprinkler. When the seedlings are 4–6 in. high, they can be 'planted out' where they are to grow in the vegetable-garden. Give the seed-bed a thorough soaking before forking up the plants. Make holes with a trowel to accommodate the roots of the little plants and fill them with water. It is a good idea to plant in the evening so as to give the plants a chance of getting on the move during the night.

There are three types of cabbages, named after the seasons— winter, summer, and spring. Sow the seeds of spring cabbage in July and the others in March. In the case of Brussels sprouts for winter and spring use, sow in March and April, but for late summer and autumn use, sow in early August of the previous year. With cauliflowers for cutting in summer, sow in gentle heat in February—but for the main crop, sow outdoors in April. For spring and early summer use, sow in late August.

Leeks are started in the seed bed also, by sowing the seed in early April, so that the plants are ready for planting out in June or July. Make holes 6 in. deep and 5 in. apart with a dibber and drop one plant into the middle of each hole. Pour in a cup of water, but do not fill in the hole with soil.

ROOT CROPS

The seed drills should be 12–15 in. apart. The seeds can be sown in April, May, and July, ½ in. deep. The carrot rows can be dusted with derris when the plants are 2 in. high to prevent maggots ruining the crop. Parsnips and swedes are the only root crops to be thinned—to 6 in. apart, unless you want large swedes when they should be thinned to 1 ft.

PEAS AND BEANS

Here the drill should be a little deeper, i.e. 2–3 in. and the sowing done in March in rows, which for broad beans should be 2 ft. apart. Under this system the beans hardly ever get black fly, but, if it does appear, spray with a natural product, i.e. derris. French beans should be sown at the end of April in the south, and the middle of May in the colder parts of the north. For succession sow half a row every three weeks from early May until the middle of July—that is, if you like French beans as much as I do. Runner beans may be allowed to climb up wire netting or string, or you can grow the Hammond dwarf variety and sow it like French beans. These beans like plenty of water at their roots while they grow and the compost helps greatly in moisture conservation. Some gardeners cut down their climbing runner beans each year in late October, and they live through the winter and start to grow the following spring. I know this to have been done for over ten years with great success.

ONIONS

Onions grow particularly well under the compost system. The fact that the land is NOT dry helps greatly. The easiest way is to buy little bulbs called sets and plant them out at the end of March —pushing the bases into the soil so that the sets are half buried. The rows should be 12 in. apart and the sets 6 in apart in the rows. If the sets come out of place in the early stages just push them back into the soil again.

SALADS

There are two main kinds of lettuce—the cabbage and the Cos— but there are sub-headings like 'baby Cos' and 'crinkly crisp cabbage'.

Prepare the ground by raking, adding at the same time, fish manure at 3 oz. per sq. yd. Peg down a taut line from one end of your plot to the other, preferably so that the rows run north to south. Along this line scratch out a shallow drill ½ in. deep with the edge of a draw-hoe. Mix the lettuce seed with an equal quantity of powdered compost as this will make it easier for you to sow thinly—aim to place the seeds ½ in. apart, with the idea of thinning out later if all the plants grow. Sometimes these thinnings can be transplanted. The big crisp crinkly Iceberg type of lettuce needs to be thinned to 9 in. apart, the small Cos to 4 in. apart. In a very dry summer, be prepared to water using a sprinkler. Leave this in position in the evening for ¾ hr. so as to give a thorough soaking. Cut the lettuces early in the morning before the sun has got on them and put them in a cool place until you use them at lunch or tea.

Radishes can be sown as for lettuces from the middle of March onwards, unless you live in a colder part of the north, when you have to delay a week or two. It is an excellent plan to sow mixed seed, Saxa, Red Turnip, French Breakfast, and Icicle and it helps if you sprinkle more sedge peat down the drill at some time. The quicker radishes grow the more delicious they are—so be prepared to use a sprinkler to supply artificial rain in dry weather.

Tomatoes do very well on this compost system. Lightly fork the land adding powdery brown compost at 2 bucketfuls per sq. yd.—plus fish manure at 4 oz. per sq. yd. It helps, especially in light land, if wood-ash can be applied at ½ lb. per sq. yd. at the same time. Grow a variety such as Outdoor Girl. Small, dark green, sturdy plants, about 8 in. tall, should be chosen. These should be planted out in May or early June in holes made with a trowel 15 in. apart. The ball and a compost containing roots should be put in this hole and, after replacing the original soil, it should be well trodden down.

Provide each plant with a 6-foot bamboo cane, pushing it into the ground about 18 in. Tie up the stems of the plants 'loosely' as they grow so as to allow the stems to swell. As the plants grow, pinch out the little side shoots found in the axils of the leaves, the idea being to keep the plant to one stem. (Don't of course pinch off the shoots bearing the flowers!) Late in June apply compost or sedge peat 1 in. deep all round the plants at least 1 ft. wide. Feed the plants as each truss of flowers starts to set with a liquid seaweed plant-food. Water as the plants need the moisture— usually a good soaking every three days or so.

7

APPLES, PEARS, PLUMS

These do best when planted in grass; but this grass must be cut like a lawn and the clippings allowed to lie on the surface so that the worms can pull them in. It is advisable to apply a fish manure at 4 oz. per sq. yd. evenly all over the sward, in January and again in June. Sometimes if the trees are not growing well enough, compost or sedge peat can be given as a top dressing at 2 bucketfulls per sq. yd. in May.

After twenty-one years of research and experiment at Thaxted and Arkley, I am convinced that all kinds and types of crops can be grown successfully without digging or forking. The secret is the correct making of compost, plus the rotting down with the help of millions of bacteria and hundreds of worms. Once the compost is in position on the soil the worms do the digging and aeration together with the manufacturing of plant foods, and the living organisms in the soil produce the organic colloid called humus which is the 'blood' of the soil.

Organic gardening during the last twenty-one years has ensured (a) heavier crops (b) more delicious fruits and vegetables (c) less work (d) greater freedom from pests and diseases (e) more scent.

9   *House Plants*

W. DAVIDSON

I don't think there is any need to apologise for including a chapter on House Plants in a book designed to help the weekend gardener, more especially when it is written by such a distinguished plant-grower as Mr. Davidson. He comes from Wick in the far north of Scotland, whence he went to serve in the RAF mostly in India and Ceylon. As he says, on leaving the forces he wandered into house plants and nursery work with no thought of making a career of it. But it happened that he wandered into Rochfords, one of the biggest house-plant producers in Britain. Gradually, working his way up the ladder, he eventually became their Show Manager. The title 'Show Manager', is not very clear, but it means that he does a great deal of lecturing on house plants, much advisory work, and is continually in touch with the practical side of growing. Some years ago he wrote the Woman's Own Book of House Plants, *which, now in a third edition, is one of the most successful plant books of recent years. He has been involved in a television series entitled 'The Garden Indoors'. He writes with evident love and authority that carry complete and utter conviction.*

Whatever else we may have discovered about house plants over the years there is little doubt that we have learned that the majority die, not from neglect, but from a surfeit of attention. Most house plants do better indoors if they have to work for their living and are not mollycoddled. So they may well come within the scope of the weekend gardener who is much too busy to cope with more than the passing needs of his plants between Monday and Friday. The result of continual fussing in the way of watering, feeding, cleaning, and repotting is frequently a dull plant that lacks crispness. The reason for this is often that roots become inactive because they have little work to do. One can, therefore, assume that one does not require unlimited time in order to care for a collection of plants.

Obviously an important initial step for the beginner will be to ensure that the plants purchased at the outset are of the best possible quality. These will obviously cost a little more but the extra cost will be more than justified as the months go by. Frequently, the poor-quality plant will have come from a greenhouse that has been inadequately heated, and where plants have been crowded together in order to get the maximum number into the minimum amount of space.

For the beginner, presented with a wide range of plants, it is not easy to make a suitable choice; and it would be impossible to explain here all the various things one should look for in the way of defects or advantages. However, in general terms, crisp clean foliage is important, and signs of active growth at the tips of plants such as ivies should be looked for. The undersides of leaves and the tips of growing shoots require inspection as these are the places where pests are most likely to be found. Eradication of pests can present problems, so it is well not to get off to a bad start by setting up a collection with the beasties already in residence.

Dry, limp leaves will also present problems later, for leaves begin to fall from the plant as a direct result of the drought experienced earlier. Also, the shop or greenhouse that is cold and unfeeling is not a particularly good, even if only temporary home for plants. If it is cold during opening hours, you can be sure that it is very much colder and less pleasant during the night. So it is important that one should not only purchase plants that are pest-free and healthy, but also that they should be bought from a supplier who shows at least a little consideration for his plants.

Having purchased or acquired one's plant by way of a gift there are a few fundamental requirements that will help it to adjust and settle successfully into its new environment. On being unwrapped it will probably need watering, but the compost should first be checked for moistness, as excessive watering is the major problem where house plants, or almost any form of pot plant, is concerned.

The best way of checking moistness is to feel the compost with finger or thumb. If the soil is excessively wet, you can detect the condition by the simple process of lifting the pot to see if it is unusually heavy; but this means of detecting wetness is something which one learns with experience.

Providing perfect growing conditions indoors is well nigh impossible, so most of one's efforts are towards a compromise that will get as near the ideal as possible. In growing plants indoors the home of today, with its large windows and adequate interior lighting, gives us a tremendous advantage over the house plant-grower at the turn of the century who had to contend with very trying conditions. That is why we are able to grow a much wider range of plants. In the past the real toughies of the plant world were in the front line—such plants as the parlour palm (*Kentia belmoriana*), ferns in many varieties and, of course, the indispensable and all but indestructible *Aspidistra lurida*. This last had the apt and amusing common name of 'cast-iron plant', which gives some indication of its tenacious qualities.

From what we have said, it is clear that another step in the right direction will be the provision of a reasonable amount of light in which to grow the plant. The majority of plants offered for sale will object to being exposed to full sunlight, although a few, which include sansevieria, chlorophytum, crotons, and the ivies will revel in the sunlight provided it is not too fiercely hot. As a rough guide, you will find that plants with green leaves prefer more shaded conditions and those with variegated leaves will do better and retain their variegation if placed in good light, though not necessarily full sunlight.

Fresh air on hot days can be a blessing to almost all plants, particularly in rooms where there is central heating of some kind. This is one reason why they do so well on the kitchen window-sill where the window is open most days to admit fresh air and relieve the humid atmosphere (in itself a benefit to plant life). Fresh air is fine, but, contrary though it may seem, draughts can be particularly damaging, so keep plants away from cold, draughty areas.

Any gardener with an elementary knowledge of plants realizes that in order to do well they require feeding with a balanced fertilizer at regular intervals once they have become established. This principle applies equally indoors, and almost all plants that you buy will be well established and in need of fertilizing from the time of purchase, provided it is not in mid-winter (when most plants are resting). Generally speaking, feeding is necessary only during the spring and summer months when plants are producing new leaves. Avoid overfeeding plants, as this practice is likely to do more harm than good—it is far better to adopt a policy of little and often. It is also wise to follow the maker's directions on the fertilizer packet. A final point on feeding: after potting-on into fresh compost, plants should not require any form of fertilizer for at least three months; most plants will go for much longer.

Pests are not too troublesome as far as house plants are concerned but, in common with almost all plant life they do not go unnoticed by greenfly, mealy bug, red spider, and such like. To keep plants clean a practice of prevention is the best policy, which will mean giving the plants a precautionary spray with one of the many insecticides available at regular intervals. Twice or three times annually is usually sufficient. A most important precaution is not to spray or treat plants in the house, as unpleasant smells and unnecessary dangers will result. Take them out of doors on a still, warm day, and wear rubber gloves. Place the plant out of direct sunlight, raise it on a box of some kind and pay particular attention to the undersides of leaves when applying the spray. In common with fertilizer, use the insecticide as recommended by the manufacturer—extra heavy doses may well be more destructive as far as the pests are concerned, but the plant will, in all probability, not go unscathed.

As mentioned earlier, indoor plants are not very demanding in their requirements, and this is certainly true in respect of potting plants on into larger containers. Not all, but the majority will go for some two years between each potting operation. There are a few exceptions to this rule and the chlorophytum, which produces masses of thick fleshy roots, is one of them. Plants that do fill their pots quickly with roots, and those that are growing particularly well, will have to be potted on annually.

Knowing when to pot on a plant can be a difficult problem for the inexperienced indoor gardener, and it is not easy for the better informed to put the information into simple terms. One thing is sure and that is that one should never repot a sick plant, but there is an unfortunate tendency for the beginner to do this in the misguided belief that fresh compost must give the plant a new lease of life. Alas, disturbing roots that are, in all probability already damaged from over-watering, will only cause the plant a further setback. Plants should be potted when the soil is well filled with roots, or when the plant is growing vigorously. It is also an indication that plants need fresh soil when they lose some of their fresh green appearance and take on a slightly hard look.

In good growing conditions, a warm greenhouse for example, or a room where plants grow well, plants may be transferred to larger pots at almost any time of the year provided they have sufficient roots. In good conditions the roots will quickly get on the move in the fresh compost, which is an important consideration, as a sluggish root condition can be troublesome. However, where conditions are typical of the average living-room, it is better to postpone any potting-on operations until the spring of the year, April or May being the months preferred.

The compost to use is the subject of controversy and there are many different concoctions that one may prepare or purchase ready for use, and I am old-fashioned enough to think that the John Innes mixes take a lot of beating. For the majority of house plants, however, I feel that they need varying a little from the original formula. My experience suggests that two parts J.I. No. 2 or 3 (depending on pot size; larger pots will require the No. 3) and one part fresh sphagnum peat gives good results for most of the plants you are likely to encounter. Anyway, as you gather more unusual plants into your collection, it is inevitable that you will also acquire a fair amount of knowledge concerning different composts and plant requirements.

Simple rules concerning potting are that the plant should be potted into a new container that is only slightly larger than the one it was in, a further illustration that it is wise to do things in moderation. To avoid undue root damage, the compost should be watered before the plant is removed from its pot and the compost for most plants should be gently firmed with the fingers and not on any account rammed very hard. The compost in the new pot should be well watered to encourage the old and new compost to bind more closely together. The plant will then go for ten to fourteen days before further water is needed; if you keep the soil a little on the dry side to begin with, roots will be much more active than in a wet, sluggish mixture.

The hot, dry atmosphere created by central heating is blamed for many plant failures indoors and, indeed, one must agree that prolonged temperatures in the eighties can be fatal to all but the hardiest of plants. The majority of indoor plants will, nevertheless, approve of temperatures that are maintained evenly in the region of 65°F. Whether you have central heating or not, but more so if you have, it will be beneficial to the plant pot to be placed on moist gravel (never allow the pots to stand in water for any length of time), or if plant pots can be plunged to their rims in peat or moss. These media will retain a considerable amount of moisture if they are regularly damped, which will provide much more agreeable growing conditions immediately around the plant. By grouping a collection of plants together in a larger container they will grow very much better and will also provide an interesting focal point in the room. At all costs remember that plants should be well away from the damaging effects of heaters and radiators of all kinds, otherwise scorched and shrivelled leaves will be the inevitable result.

Aechmea rhodocyanea (Bromeliaceae): Commonly named the urn plant, it, along with many other plants in this family, has overlapping leaves that form a natural reservoir for water, so it could well be the ideal plant for the weekend gardener, as it will go for many days without attention. Keep the compost in the pot moist, on the dry side in fact, but it is important that the urn should be kept topped up. Changing the water occasionally will prevent it from becoming stagnant. Feeding is not essential, but the odd feed with a weak liquid fertilizer will do no harm. Cleaning of leaves will only ruin the plant's appearance as it has a natural grey 'bloom' that resents disturbance. These plants are costly as it may take anything up to six years to produce a flowering-size specimen from seed. However, they are among the most exotic of all pot plants and flowers go on for many months from the time they first appear in the water reservoir.

The main rosette flowers once only. When no longer attractive the bract should be cut away from the plant, and when the rosette itself subsequently dies back it should also be cut away. As the old plant dies back, from one to five new young plantlets will develop at the base of the parent stump. At all costs avoid damaging these when the old rosette is being removed as they will provide new plants for growing on. Either leave them attached to grow and develop in the same compost, or remove them carefully with a sharp knife when they have made five or six leaves. Plant up individually in peaty compost and keep in an even temperature of at least 70°F. until established, when the temperature can be reduced to a growing temperature between 60–65°F., which is just about room temperature with central heating.

Aphelandra Brockefeld (*Acanthaceae*): Of the available aphelandras this one is undoubtedly the best, as it has attractive foliage as well as colourful yellow flower bracts. Keep compost moist at all times, as any drying out will inevitably result in loss of leaves. Complete and permanent saturation should be guarded against as this sort of soil condition is harmful to the vast majority of pot plants. Having a very active root system, it must be fed regularly.

Potting on into larger containers will only be necessary on one occasion, from a 5- to 7-inch pot, as plants tend to become unwieldy in very large pots and older plants seldom look attractive. It is better to raise new plants from cuttings—cuttings taken with two pairs of leaves are not difficult to root in a peaty mixture if they are placed in a small heated propagator.

When yellow bracts have lost their attraction, the plant should be cut back to a sound pair of leaves; new growth (from which cuttings can be made) will subsequently appear in the axils of the topmost leaves. Brown scale insects on the undersides of leaves and on stems can sometimes be troublesome—these should be rubbed off with a sponge that has been saturated in a solution of Malathion. Use rubber gloves and perform the operation out of doors.

7*

Ananas bracteatus Var. (Bromeliaceae): The pineapple of commerce is produced from *A. commosus* which has plain green leaves and is much less attractive than the variegated form, but interesting if it can be purchased in fruit, or can be induced to produce fruit indoors. Though having overlapping leaves, it does not retain water, so the compost must be watered much more frequently than one would the compost of an Aechmea for example. The variegated pineapple has to be some four to five years old and growing in a 7-inch pot before it is likely to produce fruit. If grown in good light to improve the colouring, this plant when in fruit can be a very striking and beautiful plant. However, it would be expecting rather much to hope to accomplish this indoors; a greenhouse would be the more likely place. The Ananas has spiteful spines on the edges of its leaves which makes the task of potting on into larger pots a difficult operation. To simplify things it is advisable to draw a strong polythene bag, with the bottom slit across, up around the plant before attempting to do any potting. The compost for all Bromeliads must incorporate a good amount of peat and leaf mould to ensure that it is open and fibrous.

Azalea indica (Ericaceae): A traditional florists' plant that is available in late autumn, winter, and spring in many shades of pink and red. Purchase plants that have only a few blooms actually open and they will last very much longer indoors. Keep in a cool, light room and ensure that the compost at no time dries out—for preference rainwater should be used. After flowering, keep indoors until frosts are no longer a danger then place the plants out of doors. As it is important to prevent drying out during the summer months, build a bank of wet peat around the pot, or dig a trench and fill it with peat and sink the pot into it. It will also be beneficial if the foliage can be sprayed over regularly with rainwater. Bring indoors to a cool light room before frosts are likely. Patience is sometimes needed as plants flower better in the second year after purchase. Pot on every second or third year using ample peat and leaf mould in the mixture.

Begonia Fireglow (Begoniaceae): As there is such a vast range of begonias that make excellent house plants, it seemed best to select one of the most recent introductions to mention here. This one has made a tremendous impact all over Europe and is now grown annually by the million. For nurserymen to adopt a plant so willingly it must have many good qualities, not least that it must be reasonably easy to grow in their greenhouses. Equally well, it must appeal to the housewife as a colourful plant that she can cope with fairly easily indoors. This plant fulfils all these requirements and, along with the poinsettias of recent years must surely rate among the most successful of post-war plants. (The pot chrysanthemum would, naturally, also come into this reckoning.) Place this begonia on a light window-sill, water it only when the compost dries a little, feed it regularly, and it will be most rewarding. Mildew can be a bit of bother, but this is easily controlled by dusting with one of the many powders available for this purpose.

Begonia Rex (Begoniaceae): Much sought after by the lady with an interest in flower arranging; her husband with *B. rex* in his greenhouse will despair of ever growing good quality plants that have not had leaves snipped off at regular intervals for some special arrangement or other. It is good policy on purchasing plants of reasonable size in small pots to pot them up into larger containers without too much delay, as they remain much more compact and attractive when growing in 5-inch rather than the 3½-inch pots in which they are usually sold by the nurseryman. Grow in good light, but protect from full sun, and give the compost a thorough watering by plunging the pot in a bucket periodically rather than giving frequent small amounts. *B. rex* are available in many colours and are excellent subjects for planting in mixed bowl plantings. Once plants have become woody and leggy there is not much that can be done with them and they are better renewed.

Beloperone guttata (Acanthaceae): There is also the greenish yellow *B. lutea* which is really attractive as a larger plant. Both have the interesting common name of shrimp plant, on account of the flower bracts' resemblance to shrimps. Remove flowers from very young plants so that they have a better chance to become established. Keep them well fed, moist, and potted on annually and they will do very much better. The time to prune is often a problem; well, untidy plants can be trimmed to a better shape at almost any time, but autumn is advised. Non-flowering shoots propagate fairly easily at any time if a temperature in excess of 65°F. can be maintained. Potting compost: J.I.3 with a little extra peat added.

Croton codiaeum (Euphorbiaceae): Like Joseph's Coat (the common name for this plant), the leaves of the croton are unequalled by any foliage plant when it comes to intensity and variation of colour. But, in common with most plants, it will be found that the more colourful the leaves the more difficult the plant is likely to prove in cultivation. This is certainly so of the many crotons that are available, especially those in many shades of yellow, orange, and red.

The principal difficulty lies in the fact that it is not easy to provide the warm, humid, and light conditions that they enjoy, when you are trying to grow them indoors. Excessive fluctuation in temperature, amount of light, or watering will almost surely prove to be detrimental, if not fatal. For them to do well indoors, or in the greenhouse, a temperature of not less than 60°F. is needed, though higher temperatures in conditions that are not too dry would be even better. Adequate light is also essential if plants are to retain their colourful appearance; in poor light they are likely to turn green and not regain their attractive colouring. They are well content in a sunny window if compost is kept moist, for compost that is allowed to dry out excessively will, almost inevitably, result in loss of leaves. However, one should guard against the possibility of having compost permanently saturated, as totally wet conditions may prove equally harmful in time. Moist compost and moist conditions surrounding the pot is what one should aim for.

In dry atmospheric conditions a watchful eye should be kept for red spider mites on the undersides of leaves. To discourage red spider both sides of leaves should be regularly sprayed with water.

Cyclamen persicum (Primulaceae): For clean, fresh appearance the Florist's Cyclamen when well grown is probably one of the most attractive of pot plants. In recent years their beauty has been considerably enhanced by the introduction of what is known as the silver leaf varieties. These have silver and green mottled foliage, take a little longer to mature, but are well worth the little extra cost that is involved.

When purchasing it is advisable to seek plants that are not only crisp and fresh in appearance, but also have an ample supply of buds that will follow the few flowers that ought to be open when the purchase is made. It is completely futile and a waste of good money for anyone who lives in a very hot dry atmosphere to consider buying cyclamen plants. In such conditions their life is considerably reduced; leaves will turn brown, often quite dramatically, and the plant will be reduced to a miserable lot of dead flowers and leaves within a week.

Whatever else, cyclamen must have a cool, light room in which to grow, and a regular supply of fresh air will also be beneficial. In fact, 'cool, light, airy conditions' sums up the sort of environment that plants enjoy while they are growing in the greenhouses of the nurseryman. When these conditions are completely contrasted indoors it is impossible for plants to do well. Cyclamen plants should be well watered and allowed to dry out a little before being watered again. Plants may be watered from the top. It is a complete fallacy to think that the corm will rot if allowed to get wet, but it is possible to cause considerable damage if water is poured over the top of the plant, so allowing the flower and leaf stalks to become wet at their base. Fungus diseases result, and when detected must be treated with Benlate powder, or something similar.

After their natural flowering period, plants should be gradually allowed to die down and rest until such time as new growth is visible in the centre of the corm. Corms may then have the old compost removed before planting up in new compost with the corm partly exposed. Water sparingly until new growth is well under way. In the greenhouse it is better to grow new plants from seed sown in August/September of each year.

Dieffenbachia exotica (Araceae): Many Dieffenbachia (common name Dumb Cane) may be seen in the greenhouses of the better local parks departments, and they are among the most exotic of foliage plants, but few are suitable for indoor culture on account of their tenderness. It is possibly a bold statement, but I would put *D. exotica* among the easiest of indoor plants to care for if given reasonable conditions in which to grow. It is, nevertheless, the exception and one should not expect other dieffenbachias to grow anywhere nearly so well in room conditions. Moist, warm, shaded conditions are important; and moist peat or, better still, moss around the plant pot will be an advantage.

It is important to ensure that dieffenbachia plants do not have their main stems damaged, as the exuding sap, if allowed to get into the mouth can cause considerable discomfort, for the tongue is likely to swell up, causing loss of speech, hence the strange, but appropriate, common name. Fortunately, this is a most unlikely event and should not discourage you from purchasing this attractive and durable foliage plant.

Dracaena (Lilaceae): Many of these make excellent house plants and are reasonably easy to care for, while others fall into the almost impossible range. For the majority a temperature of not less than 60°F. is required, and a light position that affords some protection from strong, direct sunlight. The majority do better if they are watered with rainwater but this is not essential. The popular red-leaved *D. terminalis* is one that will respond better if treated in this way. The majority of dracaenas have a marked tendency to shed lower leaves as they increase in height, and this is particularly so in *D. marginata.* However, there is some compensation in that the silver-grey stems of this plant and many other dracaenas are attractive in themselves. It is also a durable house plant that improves considerably in appearance when the growing top is removed; two or three leading growths are the result, with the possible added attraction of an odd growth or two lower down the stem.

Ficus (Moraceae): Apart from the popular Rubber Plant there are many ficus plants available that make excellent indoor plants, some easy to care for, some difficult. The *benjamina* and *lyrata* varieties will, in time, develop into trees of considerable size, while the tiny *F. pumila* with its attractive small green leaves will be quite content to creep along the ground, or up a damp wall if there is one convenient—in the greenhouse, for example. A minimum temperature of 60°F. and a maximum of 70°F. is required, and protection from strong sunlight is essential—particularly for the *pumila* variety. Of the three mentioned *F. lyrata*, the fiddle-leaf fig, is the more difficult to care for, but the large, heavily-veined green leaves can make it well worth trying. The majority of these ficus plants take a little time to settle to a new environment, so one must expect the loss of a few leaves in the early stages. Cleaning of larger-leaved ficus with a damp cloth will improve their appearance; a weekly clean of this kind will do no harm. However, should anything other than water (chemical agents of any kind, for example) be used it is important that they be applied only as directed by the manufacturer.

Ficus robusta (Moraceae): This is the most recent and quite the best version of the plant that is generally known as the Rubber Plant, its predecessors being *F. elastica*, and *F. elastica decora*, which grows much more strongly, as the name suggests. A further characteristic is that it tends to produce strong side growths when it is 4–5 ft. in height; earlier plants did this at a height of 7–8 ft. Loss of lower leaves is the principal complaint with this and similar rubber plants, leaves often turning yellow and falling off for no apparent reason. Although it is quite natural for older plants to loose leaves as the stems become brown and woody, when less mature plants react in this way, a cultural fault of some kind should be suspected. The principal one, surprisingly enough, is not lack of attention; it is more often too much attention, particularly in watering. Rubber plants should be watered and allowed to dry out a little before any more water is given. Otherwise roots become waterlogged and soggy and begin to die off, making it impossible for them to maintain all the leaves on the plant.

Ficus plants will need potting on every second or third year into slightly larger pots, using J.I. No. 2 compost with a little extra peat. Potting of this particular ficus should not be undertaken just for the sake of it, as plants that are properly fed and cared for will continue to grow perfectly well in pots that may at times seem to be too small for them. If the plant is doing well in its present pot, it is usually best left alone. However, plants with leaves that are taking on a hard, yellow appearance and have their pots well filled with strong white roots will obviously benefit if they are repotted. This information applies to almost all the other house plants and is not confined to ficus.

Plants that are outgrowing their headroom will also present perplexing problems for the indoor gardener who is apprehensive about applying surgery to any of his plants. Actually, all the ficus can be very simply reduced in height at almost any time of the year (but preferably in winter when growth is dormant) by pruning the growth back to more manageable height with a pair of secateurs. To stop the wound bleeding, treat it with a proprietary sealing-compound—see your sundriesman about this.

Hedera/Ivy (Araliaceae): The many varieties of ivy are excellent in cool situations but, like the cyclamen, hopeless in rooms that are hot and dry. There are many green and variegated sorts to choose from, and all will do well in light, cool conditions, where the compost is not continually saturated with water. In poor light the variegated ones will quite quickly revert to green and lose their attractive appearance. Besides being good indoor plants, they will also do perfectly well out of doors as ground cover under shrubs, or as wall-plants. Plant them out in early summer so that they have a chance to become established before the worst of the winter comes along.

Hibiscus (Malvaceae): Becoming increasingly popular as indoor plants, the hibiscus is available in many shades of yellow, rose, and red. In a light, moderately sunny window in a warm room they are not too difficult to manage. It is essential that they be kept moist at all times, unless you wish to keep them in a dormant state during the winter, when you allow them to dry out and stay so until they are watered and brought back into growth in early spring. Individual flowers last for but a day or two at the most, but plants amply make up for this by producing a continual succession of them throughout the spring and summer months.

Monstera deliciosa (Araceae): Having large, glossy, green leaves that are deeply cut along either side, and perforated as they age, the Monstera is guaranteed to have considerable appeal, as all glossy-leaved plants seem to enjoy much attention. As with all the philodendron family, this one should be kept moist, warm, and shaded in order to get the best from it. If overwatered, plants will have a tendency to exude moisture from the edges of their leaves; furniture should be protected from the sticky substance that is produced in this way. Aerial roots of the monstera sometimes present a problem for the inexperienced indoor gardener. Rather than cut these off, it is better to tie them in tightly to the main stem of the plant and to direct such roots into the compost in the pot. Leaves of the monstera, like the ficus, may be cleaned, but the soft topmost leaves should not be handled as they are easily damaged and permanent marks will remain when the leaf matures.

Peperomias (Piperaceae): These stiff, compact little plants are ideal for the plant-collector who does not have a great deal of space at his disposal. *P. glabella* is a trailing variety that is excellent as a hanging basket subject. There are possibly half a dozen more that one can purchase with reasonable ease, and those with brighter variegated colouring, such as *P. magnolaefolia*, will require a very light position in order to do well. *P. hederifolia, caperata,* and *sanderiana* will need a light position but, at the same time, they will need protection from the sun. Keep at a temperature in the 55–65°F. region and avoid getting the compost too wet. As small plants, most of them will do very well in soilless mixtures.

Philodendron scandens (Araceae:) There are any number of philodendrons and this is one of the easiest to care for, needing conditions very similar to that described for the monstera plant. A peaty compost is needed when potting on, and it is advisable to provide some form of trellis framework for new growth to cling, or be tied to. (All the climbing plants will benefit from a similar simple structure.) Being an accommodating sort of plant, this one can equally well be used as a trailing plant for wall-containers.

Pilea (Urticaceae): Needing similar conditions to those required by the peperomias, except that they should be kept a little moister, the pileas are also grand little plants that take up very little space indoors. All of them will be improved for having their leading shoots pinched out regularly, which will encourage a much more bushy and pleasant appearance. Pilea Moon Valley is one of my favourites, having small bronze-coloured leaves that combine with most plants when done in a group. Another popular one is the silver-leaved aluminium plant which grows well in almost any light, warm, and airy position.

Poinsettia (Euphorbiaceae): Breeding of tougher varieties has made this the flowering pot-plant sensation of the present decade. In the past they were notoriously difficult, but we now find that, with no very special conditions, they will remain colourful, albeit a little dusty, for many months on end. Purchase from a good source and avoid getting them chilled on the way home from the supplier. A temperature of 60°F. is quite adequate, and the growing position should be the lightest one in the house. Let the compost dry out a little between waterings, and feed occasionally with a weak, balanced liquid fertilizer.

When leaves yellow and bracts begin to fall, the amount of water should be gradually reduced until the compost is almost dry. Cut the main stems down to about 5 in. from the pot and keep in a warm place until new growth is evident. At this time, watering should begin again, only a little to start with. When in active growth, the plant can be potted up into a slightly larger container using J.I. No. 3 compost. Water in and then keep on the dry side until they are growing freely, then water more heavily. Indoor plants will grow very much taller than those grown in the greenhouse that are chemically treated in order to keep them short. (The chemical is not available outside the trade.) To get coloured bracts to appear for a second time indoors, it is essential that plants be kept in a natural daylight only from about the end of September until bracts appear. Additional artificial light in the evening will stimulate leaf-production at the expense of flowering bracts.

Vines: Of these the most important are *Rhoicissus rhomboidea* and *Cissus antarctica*. The first-mentioned is one of the toughest of all the indoor plants, and it will often be seen growing, or at least trying to grow, in the most appalling conditions where other plants have long since given up the ghost. *C. antarctica* is a little more temperamental, and is particularly difficult in hot, dry situations; it is also easily damaged if fertilizer is given at excessive strength. Both are green and make fine climbing plants.

Saintpaulia (Gesneriaceae): This is surely at one and the same time one of the most popular and most perplexing of all indoor flowering plants. Some gardeners find them frustratingly impossible time after time, while others seem to manage them with no great bother. If you have no special facilities, a good arrangement is to grow them on a light, but not too sunny, kitchen windowsill during the day and to place them under a wall-or table-lamp in the evening. The extra light can make all the difference between success and failure. Use water with the chill off, and at all costs keep it off the leaves and flowers, which are very easily marked. Regular feeding with a weak liquid fertilizer is also needed, and a compost consisting of equal parts of J.I. No. 2 and fresh peat will provide a good potting-mixture.

Cuttings root with little difficulty in a peaty mixture. Firm, healthy leaves should be taken from the plant, with the entire stalk attached, and pushed gently into the peat just far enough to remain erect. In six to eight weeks the cuttings should have rooted sufficiently to be potted into the compost mentioned above. Make sure that plants are kept clean, and that all dead and dying leaves and flowers are removed before they begin to rot and affect the rest of the plant. Newer varieties have a considerable advantage in that flowers shrivel and die and stay on the stalk, whereas in the past they fell from the stalk and caused all sorts of problems with rotting and other fungus diseases.

Schefflera actinophylla: Finally an excellent plant for the house plant-grower who has few problems concerning space. In time the schefflera develops into a plant of considerable size, but never loses its graceful appearance and is a very popular subject for large office entrance-halls. It requires similar conditions to that of the monstera, though the atmosphere need not be quite so moist. Essentially a specimen plant, it will always look better when growing in stately fashion on its own rather than in a group with other plants around it.

Gardening Glossary

This glossary is not intended to contain (and could never hope to contain) all the terms which the week-end gardener will come across in his gardening life. It does, however, contain a large number of them and, in addition, defines many of the scientific terms which you may find throughout the book.

Accelerator: Either bacteria, or a chemical mixture usually containing nitrogen, added to a compost heap to speed up the humification process.

Acid: A soil is acid if there is *no* (or very little) lime in it. The degree of acidity is measured on a scale known as pH, in which pH 6·8 is a completely neutral soil. Acid soils have a pH lower than 6·8. while alkaline soils have higher values. Most plants prefer a slightly acid soil at a pH of about 6.6 (but see *calcicoles*).

Activator: Substance with properties similar to an accelerator (*q.v.*).

Air Layering: A method of wounding a branch and enclosing the area in moist sphagnum moss to encourage roots to develop above the wound. Once these have grown the branch bearing roots can be separated and planted out.

Alginates: Substances found in seaweed which help to improve the crumb structure of soil.

Alkaline: See *Acid*.

Ameliorant: Any material added to improve a situation, e.g. peat can be used as an ameliorant of sandy soils.

Annual: A plant which germinates, grows, flowers, sets seed, and dies in one year.

Aphicide: Chemical substance which will kill aphids (greenfly), e.g. Derris, Menazon.

Aphids: Commonly called greenfly. Very widely-distributed plant pests. As well as sucking food from the green parts of the plant, they cause leaf distortion and premature drop and are principal agents for the transmission of virus diseases. Root aphids attack the roots of lettuce and many brassicas. Aphid are not susceptible to all insecticides, but can be controlled by preparations containing Derris, Menazon and Carbaryl.

Available: A substance in the soil is 'available' when it is in a form capable of being absorbed by plant roots.

Axil: Usually 'leaf axil', meaning the angle made by the leaf where it joins the branch or stem.

Axillary Shoot: Each leaf bears a bud in the angle it makes with the stem. In most cases this bud remains dormant until the leaf dies or is removed, but in some cases (e.g. tomato, chrysanthemum), the bud develops into an axillary shoot which if left would become an axillary branch. Usually this branch adversely affects flowering and fruiting, the shoots should therefore be removed.

Basic Slag: A fertilizer containing up to 25% phosphate as well as a small percentage of lime.

Bastard Trenching: A system of digging in which after the top spit has been removed, the next spit is dug over and then covered with the top spit of the next row, and so on. Also called double digging.

Bedding Out: The process of transplanting half-hardy or tender annuals or perennials into flower-beds in order that the flowers or foliage may produce a massed effect.

Biennial: A plant which grows vegetatively in its first year, then flowers, fruits, and dies in its second year. Many vegetables, e.g. carrots, celery, etc. are biennials but may be forced to flower in their first year by frost or drought or injury. When this happens the plant is called a bolter.

Big Bud: A descriptive term for the buds of blackcurrant which have been attacked by a mite and in consequence have become much enlarged. Such buds usually abort and should be picked off and burned. A more serious consequence is that the big-bud mite normally transmits a virus disease which materially reduces the crop.

Black Leg: A disease which produces black dead areas at the base of the stem which will eventually wither and die. There are many fungi which cause black leg in different plants but the most common are probably black leg of potatoes caused by *Rhizoctonia solani* and black leg of brassicas caused by *Phoma lingam*.

Blanching: A method of preventing the stems of such plants as celery or leeks from becoming green by covering them with earth or some form of collar. If well done the blanched area should be white.

Bleed: If a plant is wounded, either accidentally or intentionally as by pruning, it may exude quantities of sap from the cut surface. It is then said to bleed. Formerly it was thought that plants could bleed to death but this is now known to be very unlikely.

Blindness: A plant is said to be blind if a bud does not mature or open. This is usually the result of inadequate feeding, water-logging, or insect attack.

Blower: A Brussels sprout which instead of being tight and hard has opened out and is soft and leafy.

Bolting: When a biennial plant comes into flower in the first year of its life, it is said to 'bolt', e.g. leek, celery.

Bone Meal: A slow-acting organic phosphatic (20%) fertilizer, which also contains some lime.

Brassica: A general name for cabbage, cauliflower, swede, Brussels sprouts. They are all susceptible to club root.

Budding: An operation often done on roses in which a bud of a very good variety is inserted at the base of the stem of a free-rooting variety. The bud will unite with the root-stock and, once established, the above-ground part of the root-stock is cut off leaving the bud to grow as the top of the plant. Similar to grafting, using a bud instead of a branch.

Bulb: Commonly applied to any swollen underground plant part, but technically it should be restricted to those bulbs which consist of swollen leaf bases, e.g. onion.

Bull Shoot: An excessively strong branch or stem which, if not removed, will dominate the plant and eventually, by using all the plant food, starve the rest of the branches.

Cabbage Lettuce: The type of lettuce which produces its leaves as a tight heart.

Cabbage Root Fly: The maggot of this fly may bore into the roots of all brassicas, causing wilting and eventually death. Can be controlled with calomel dust or BHC dusted around the base of the plants.

Calcareous: Containing lime or calcium.

Calcicole: A plant which grows well in a lime-rich alkaline soil, e.g. clematis, carnation.

Calcifuge: A plant which cannot grow in a soil rich in chalk or limestone, e.g. rhododendron, azalea, most Ericas.

Calomel Dust: Chemically this dust contains mercurous chloride which is a very effective killer of many soil pests and diseases such as cabbage root fly and club root.

Certified: Possessing a certificate of health, which usually means free of virus infection.

Chelate: A chelated compound is one in which the active ingredient will not be inactivated by the soil, e.g. iron chelates contain iron which can be used by the plant even in a lime-rich soil where normally all iron is unavailable.

Cheshunt Compound: A fungicide which is useful against soil-borne fungus diseases.

Chlorophyll: The green colouring material in leaves which is essential for the formation of sugars, etc. by plants in the presence of sunlight, carbon dioxide, and water.

Chlorosis: A yellowing of the leaves commonly found in chalk or limestone areas generally the result of a deficiency of iron. It is caused by a lack of chlorophyll formation.

Clamp: A method of storing such vegetables as potatoes or carrots involving protecting them from the frost by means of straw and soil.

Cloche: A number of glass panes or polythene sheets held together with wire in such a way that they form a continuous tunnel inside which plants can be grown, protected against extremes of weather.

Club Root: A disease of brassicas sometimes called 'finger-and-toe' which causes swelling of the roots and can lead to the death of the plant. The recommended control is calomel dust.

Colour Triad: Three colours which when used together in a flower-bed or border create a pleasing and harmonious effect.

Compatible: Two fruit-tree varieties which pollinate each other, and so produce fruit are said to be compatible. This is very important in fruit-growing; gardeners with room for only one tree must purchase a self-fertile variety to avoid the problems of incompatibility.

Compost: The product made by rotting down vegetable refuse of all types in a compost heap. It is a very rich source of humus which is essential to maintain the soil structure and population of micro-organisms. Alternatively the soil in which plants are potted, e.g. John Innes compost.

Compound Fertilizer: Contains many of the necessary plant foods, principally nitrogen, phosphorus, and potash.

Contact Insecticide: A type of insecticide such as DDT which kills insects when they come in contact with it. This is in contrast to a stomach insecticide which kills insects only after they have eaten the treated plants.

Cordon: Usually a fruit tree with a single stem and lateral branches in one plane only.

Corm: A thickened underground storage stem produced by certain species, e.g. crocus, gladiolus. It differs from a bulb in *not* consisting of leaf bases.

Cos Lettuce: Type of lettuce which bears many separate erect leaves but does not form a heart.

Cotyledons: Seed-leaves borne by plants before they produce their true leaves. Cotyledons are often fleshy and always have a very simple shape. Flowering plants are divided into two main classes based on the possession of one cotyledon (Monocotyledons) or two cotyledons (Dicotyledons).

Crocks: Pieces of broken pot or large pebbles put over the hole in a flower pot to stop soil being washed out, but still allowing slow drainage. The crocks should never block the hole completely.

Crop Rotation: A system of growing vegetables in such a manner that the same crop (or type of crop, e.g. brassica) does not occupy the same land for two years in succession. There are three-course rotations such as brassicas followed by potatoes, followed by root crops or peas and beans. There are also four-, five-, and six-course rotations.

Crown Bud: A term used in chrysanthemum production for the flower buds at the end of the lateral branches. Removal of the crown bud allows the development of second crown buds lower down the stem so that instead of a few large flowers you get many slightly smaller ones.

Crown: The branches of a tree. The central growing region of a plant such as strawberry, rhubarb, etc.

Crumb (soil): A number of small soil particles held together by humus and soil micro-organisms. The presence of a good crumb structure enables soils to drain easily and increases the fertility.

Cultivar: Natural plant species produce slight variants called varieties which may differ from the original in many ways, e.g. colour, shape, size. Such varieties of horticultural plants are called cultivars because they are maintained only in cultivation.

Curd: The white, edible part of a cauliflower.

Dalapon: A chemical used for killing weeds such as couch grass.

Damping-off: A disease of seedlings which causes them to rot at the base and die. Usually encouraged by over-watering and/or sowing too thickly. Controlled by using fresh soil and avoiding humid conditions, and watering with Cheshunt Compound.

Deciduous (Tree): Shedding leaves in the autumn.

Deficiency Disease: A disease whose prime cause is a shortage of a specific element in the soil, e.g. iron, boron, sulphur. The term is not normally used in connection with the major elements, nitrogen, phosphorus, or potash.

Derris: An insecticide based on an extract from the root of the tropical climber *Derris elliptica*. This is a good natural insecticide, effective against a wide range of insects. Unfortunately it is not very long lasting.

Dibber: A short round blunt-ended piece of wood which is pushed into the soil to make a hole when planting brassicas. The plant is then dropped into the hole and the dibber pushed in at the side of the hole and levered in such a way as to force the soil around the roots of the plant.

Dibble: The method of planting by using a dibber.

Disbudded: Has had the lateral or the leaf-axil buds removed.

Dormant: Resting, inactive, literally 'asleep'.

Double Digging: Involves removing the top soil and digging over the spit below it before replacing the top soil.

Double Flower: Flowers with more than the ordinary number of petals, e.g. many flowering cherries. They are often designated in catalogues as 'fl. pl.' meaning *'flore pleno'*.

Drainage Holes: Holes left in a lawn after the use of a hollow-tine fork; or a hole dug in a garden to watch the rise and fall of the water level after rain to see how effective the drainage is and at what level drains must be laid.

Drawn: Plants are said to be drawn if they become elongated and/or yellowish in colour as a result of being grown in shade or insufficient light.

Dressed: Seed treated with a fungicide to prevent rotting in the soil. Also applied to potatoes or bulbs or fruit which have been separated into different classes either by size or quality.

Dried Blood: A rich quick-acting source of nitrogen (14%), used mainly for house plants as it is too expensive for general garden use.

Drift: A large irregular-shaped group of plants of the same kind, e.g. a drift of bluebells at the edge of a wood.

Drift (2.4.D): The spread of fine dusts or sprays when applied in a wind. In a high wind, drift can travel miles and may cause serious damage.

Drill: A row of plants, usually vegetables, though sometimes applied to flowers.

Dutch Hoe: A hoe with two working edges generally used for weed-killing.

Dwarfing Stock: A root system on which any variety of apple, pear, plum, or cherry may be grafted to reduce very substantially the final height of the resultant tree.

Earthing-Up: The process of heaping soil around the base of plants usually to encourage the growth of roots from the stem, or to protect the root system from draught, light, or insect pests, or to blanch the stems.

Espalier: A system of training fruit trees so that the branches grow along horizontal wires about 18 in. or 2 ft. apart.

Etiolated: Long, spindly and yellow plants with poorly developed leaves. Plants grown in the dark or in poor light become etiolated.

Evergreen: Has green leaves all the year round, e.g. holly, pine.

F_1: Indicates a hybrid between two pure strains or species. Such hybrids often show increased size and strength and may ripen earlier.

Family Tree: A type of apple tree in which different varieties are grafted on the same root-stock. Thus it is possible on one tree to have an early and a late eater and an early and late cooker. Very good for small garden.

Flea Beetle: An insect which eats the edges of the leaves of brassicas. It will often destroy the cotyledons and so kill the plant. Control by BHC powder and derris. Typical flea-beetle damage is an indented edge.

Flocculate: The sticking together of small particles to form a larger crumb, e.g. lime will flocculate the small particles of a clay soil and give it a better crumb structure.

Four-Course Rotation: A system of crop rotation in which the same crop is grown in the same soil only once every four years.

Friable: A term applied to soil which has a good crumb structure and in which the particles do not stick together.

Fungus: A kind of plant composed of fine threads which cannot photosynthesize and is therefore obliged to obtain its food from dead or living organisms. In the latter category they can cause root rots, wilts, rusts, leaf spots, mildews, cankers, etc.

Fungicide: A chemical used to kill the fungi which cause mildews, rust, etc.

Furrow: The groove made in the soil in which the crop is planted. After planting, the furrow is usually filled in with soil to cover the seed.

F.Y.M.: Abbreviation for farmyard manure.

Garden Line: A very simple tool consisting two pieces of wood to which a length of string is attached. By pushing one stick into the ground and stretching the string taut to where the other stick is pushed in the soil, you have a straight line along which you can plant or sow.

Genus (pl. genera): A term in plant classification. Plants are divided into families, e.g. *Rosaceae;* each family into genera, e.g. *Rosa:* each genus into species e.g. *Rosa moyesii:* and each species into varieties or cultivars e.g. *R. moyesii var. pubescens.*

Good Heart: Applied to soil, it signifies fertile, well-drained, and in good condition for growing crops.

Grafting: The process whereby different plants can be induced to unite as one. The union can be successfully achieved only between closely related plants, e.g. different varieties of apple, lilac, or rhododendron.

Grape Stage: The stage in the development of a group of black-currant flowers when they look like a bunch of tiny green grapes.

Grass Box: The part of a lawn-mower where the grass is collected.

Green Manure: When green material such as weeds, rape, clover are dug into the ground to improve soil texture, they are termed green manures.

Ground Cover Plant: A prostrate or low-growing spreading plant which by shade and competition for food and water will help to exclude weeds.

Guano: Bird droppings that used to be widely used as manure.

Half-Ripe Wood: When a twig starts growing in the spring the wood is new, but as time passes it ripens and by July it is said to be half-ripe.

Half-Standard: Describes a fruit tree grown on a short stem 3–4 ft. in height before the first branches appear.

Hardening Off: The process of gradually exposing a plant which has been grown in shelter to the full rigours of outdoor conditions. The term is usually applied to half-hardy annuals.

Hardwood Cutting: A cutting taken when the wood is fully ripe in October or November.

Hardy Annual: An annual plant capable of surviving through winter if planted outside.

Haulm: The above-ground parts of a potato plant.

Heel: When a side shoot is pulled off a main branch for use as a cutting, a small piece of bark and a little wood often remain attached to the cutting. This is known as a heel and in some cases helps the cutting to root more easily.

Heeling-In: The process of temporarily planting trees or shrubs which arrive in bad weather. It usually involves covering the roots with soil in a shallow trench. Plants in this state will live for weeks or even two or three months.

Hollow-Tine: A fork whose prongs or tines are hollow, used to extract small cores from a lawn to improve drainage and aeration.

Hoof and Horn Meal: A slow-acting fertilizer which contains 14% nitrogen.

Hormone Rooting-Substance: A chemical which when applied to the base of a cutting hastens the production of roots.

Humification: The gradual conversion of plant and animal refuse to humus. The process usually occurs in compost heaps or in the soil itself.

Humus: The dark brown material produced by the biological decomposition of organic material such as compost, or farm-yard manure. In a garden, humus is of extreme importance in ensuring that the soil is fertile.

Hybrid: A plant resulting from the cross-fertilization of two different species (or varieties) of plant. They are symbolized by the sign ×, e.g. *Clematis* × *Jackmanii*. Plants grown from the seed of hybrid plants are very rarely identical with the parent.

Hybrid Tea: A modern type of rose-bush which bears its flowers singly as opposed to a 'floribunda' rose which has flowers in small bunches.

Hybrid Vigour: The additional strength and size often shown by hybrids between different species or varieties which are normally inbred.

Hydrochloric Acid: An acid used to detect the presence of lime in soil. It is cheap and easy to use.

Inert: Any material which is chemically inactive.

Inorganic: A chemical substance which does not contain the element carbon and was never part of a living organism.

Insecticide: Any chemical used to kill insects.

Intercropping: A system of growing one crop between the rows of another. For example, lettuce may be intercropped between tomatoes in a greenhouse.

Internode: The length of stem between two successive leaves, easily seen in chrysanthemums.

Iron Deficency: A shortage of available iron in the soil which causes yellowing of leaves and reduction of crop.

John Innes: A research institute which has given its name to a series of composts used for pot plants, sowing seed, and rooting cuttings. Usually called J.I. composts.

John Innes Base Fertilizer: A mixture of 2 parts of hoof and horn meal, 2 parts of superphosphate, and 1 part of sulphate of potash.

Lateral: A side branch. The term is used in fruit production as the fruit is usually borne on the laterals.

Layering: The process of inducing a wounded branch to produce roots by burying the wounded area in a light open compost.

Leaching: As water drains through the soil it dissolves and carries away the salts which act as plant foods. This process is called leaching.

Leader: Either the tip of the trunk of a tree which will continue upwards growth or a main branch which bears the fruiting laterals.

Leaf Mould: The humus-rich material formed from decaying leaves.

Leg: A short main stem: e.g. a gooseberry bush is grown on a leg, as distinct from a blackcurrant bush which has many main stems.

Lights: The glass or plastic covers of a cold frame.

Lime: A general term for calcium carbonate which when applied to the soil will remove acidity and improve drainage.

Loam: A soil which is neither too sandy nor has too much clay. This is the ideal garden soil and ranges from a sandy loam to a clay or stiff loam.

Major Element: Nitrogen, phosphorus, or potash when used in plant nutrition. So called because they are used in large quantities compared with trace or minor elements.

Malling IX: An apple root-stock which produces a dwarfed tree.

Metaldehyde: The active ingredient in many slug poisons.

Mist Propagation: A method of rooting cuttings in an atmosphere which is saturated with moisture.

Monoculture: The continuous cultivation of a single crop in the same soil over a long series of years.

Mosaic: A virus disease whose symptoms are the production of light yellow areas on the normally green leaf. Although such virus diseases rarely prove fatal, they always cause a marked reduction in the yield of the crop or the size of flowers, e.g. raspberry, potato, tomato, or dahlia mosaics.

Mulch: The application of organic material such as compost or peat to the surface of the soil around plants.

Naturalize: The establishment of bulbs in grass so that they grow and multiply.

Nitrate of Soda: A fertilizer containing 16% of nitrogen. Very quick acting.

Nitrification: Bacterial action which makes atmospheric or other nitrogen available to plants in the soil.

Nitro-chalk: A fertilizer containing 15% of nitrogen and some lime which makes it useful for acid soils.

Nitrogenous: Containing nitrogen.

Node: The point of a stem where a leaf or a bud is produced.

Onion Fly: An insect whose eggs hatch to form small white maggots which eat the onion bulb and roots. Can be controlled by calomel dust or lindane in May.

Onion Set: A small immature onion bulb wich can be planted and will grow to a mature onion plant with a large bulb. Often used in preference to seed. Applies also to shallots.

Organic Manure: Any material supplying plant food which has once been part of another living organism.

Overplant: Too many plants in an area. This leads to crowding and excessive competition effects, so that no plant can grow to best advantage.

Panning: The term used when a hard, maybe impervious, layer is formed in soil below the depth to which it is usually cultivated.

Paraquat: A substance which when applied to green leaves will kill the plant. It is therefore a total weedkiller. It is completely inactivated in soil and so planting can take place within a day of treating an area.

Pea Moth: A moth which lays its eggs in the pea-flower. When the pea-pod develops the larvae or maggot will hatch from the eggs and eat the peas in the pod.

Peat: Semi-fossilized plant remains, which, when added to soils

8

are slowly broken down to form humus. A good mulch or soil additive. It has an acid reaction.

Pelleted Seed: Seed covered with a coating of chemicals which ensures that the young seedling will have a good start in life.

Perennial: A plant which will grow from the same roots every year. Thus a tree is a perennial, and so is rhubarb.

pH: A symbol used to express the degree of acidity or alkalinity. It is usually followed by a number on a scale between 0 and 14. Thus *p*H 6.8 is neutral, a pH lower than this is acid and a higher value denotes alkalinity.

Phosphatic: Containing phosphorus.

Photosynthesis: A process occurring in leaves whereby chlorophyll using the sun's energy can act on carbon dioxide and water in such a way as to produce sugars and other plant foods.

Pinching Out: Taking a bud or side shoot between the forefinger and thumb and literally pinching it off.

Planting Out: When seedlings which have been pricked out and hardened off are old enough and the soil conditions are right, they are planted out in their final positions.

Plunge: Burying a flower-pot containing a house plant such as azalea up to its rim either in soil in the garden or in a cold frame.

Pollen: The yellow powder which contains the male reproductive cells. The pollen is usually produced in the part of a flower known as the anther.

Pollination: The transfer of the pollen to the female reproductive part, the stigma. This is usually followed by fertilization but this need not be so, as in incompatible varieties of apple.

Pollinator: Some varieties of fruit will not produce seeds or fruits unless they are pollinated by another variety of the same fruit. This latter is the pollinator.

Potassic: Containing potassium.

Potassium Sulphate: Fertilizer containing 48% of potash.

Pot-Bound: When the roots of the plant completely fill the flower-pot and there is therefore a restriction on further growth.

Potting On: Transfering a plant from a smaller to a larger pot.

Pre-emergence Weedkiller: A chemical which kills weeds before the main crop emerges from the soil.

Pricking Out: Transference of very young seedlings from the pot in which they germinated to orderly rows in a seed box to give them more room for growth.

Puddle: (a) To destroy the soil structure by trying to dig or work with it when it is it too wet;
(b) to plant after dipping the roots in a thick mixture of soil and water to improve early growth.

Radiation Frost: A frost arising on a clear night with no cloud so that the earth radiates and so loses its heat into the air. If this loss is great enough, a frost is produced.

Ramming Stick: A piece of wood with a handle and a broad flat end used for firming the soil in a plant-pot.

Re-Potting: Transferring a plant from one pot to another, not necessarily larger.

Residual Effect: The effect on a plant or crop of small quantities of a chemical which remain after the job for which the chemical has been originally used is finished, e.g. a substance used to control weeds among shrubs might have an adverse effect on later plantings of small annuals.

Rhizome: An underground stem which normally grows horizontally. It is often the means of spread of many weeds such as couch grass and pieces of rhizome form an easy means whereby a perennial may be divided, e.g. iris.

Ripewood Cuttings: Cuttings taken after the leaves have fallen, usually in October/November.

Root Aphis (Lettuce): A blue-grey aphis which causes the death of lettuce plants by attacking the roots. Control by applying BHC dust.

Root-Stock: The plant which supplies the root system to another plant, e.g. an apple grafted on a dwarfing stock of Malling IX. The latter is the root-stock.

Rotary Mower: A mower whose cutting blades rotate at a very high speed in a horizontal plane. Very good for all but the best lawns (such as golf-course greens, bowling-greens).

Runners: Stems which creep horizontally over the surface of the ground producing new plants at intervals, e.g. strawberry.

Scalping: Mowing a lawn so close that the blades remove the top layer of soil so producing bare patches.

Scion: The part of a grafted plant which contributes the stem and leaves.

Scorch: A general term which is applied to any condition which results in the production of dry, brown, dead areas on leaves or on a lawn.

Seed-Bed: An area of finely-divided, well-raked soil in which seed will be sown.

Seed-Leaves: The cotyledons.

Self-Blanching: Some varieties of vegetable, e.g. celery or leeks, are preferred when the edible parts are white or blanched. This used to be done by keeping this part of the plant in darkness by collars of cardboard or by heaping soil around the base of the plant. Now there are varieties which will be white under ordinary conditions and need no special treatment. These are self-blanching varieties.

Self-Clinging: Capable of adhering to a surface by means of suckers, tendrils, etc. although not supported by wires or trellis, e.g. ivy.

Self-Fertile: Able to produce fruit and seeds without pollen from another variety or species, e.g. James Grieve is a self-fertile apple, so problems of pollination do not arise.

Self-Seeding: A plant which by shedding its seed in the garden produces new plants. Generally refers to weeds or to such plants as nasturtium.

Set: See *Onion Set*.

Sick Soil: A soil in which one kind of plant has been grown for so many years producing such a build-up of pests and diseases, plus a depletion of necessary nutrients, that that plant can no longer be grown satisfactorily, e.g. potato-sick, rose-sick soil.

Side-Shoot: A shoot arising in the axil of a leaf *or* a lateral branch.

Simazin: A very persistent weedkiller which is often used on paths and drives.

Single-Digging: Digging to one spit depth.

Slaked: Has had water added to it, as in slaked lime, which is formed by the addition of water to quick lime. It is much safer to handle than quick lime, which is caustic and therefore very dangerous.

Soft Cutting: A cutting of soft green wood. Often called a tip cutting.

Soil-Conditioner: A substance, or mixture of substances, which will improve the crumb structure of soil, e.g. farmyard manure, compost, alginates.

Sole Plate: The metal plate on a cylinder lawn-mower against which the rotating blades cut the grass.

Species: A category of plant classification (see *Genus*). Most of the names known by gardeners are species names, e.g. *Begonia rex*.

Spit: The depth of the blade of a spade.

Spore: A very small frequently air-borne part of a fungus, fern, or other seedless plant which can grow to form a new plant. Spores therefore are one of the prime means of spread of plant diseases since they may travel many miles in a wind or even in moving water.

Sport: The sudden appearance of a plant or even part of a plant which is not typical, e.g. a pelargonium bearing red flowers may suddenly produce a white flower on a shoot. This is a sport, and new varieties are frequently derived from naturally-occurring sports.

Sprout: Short for Brussels sprout *or* for the young green shoots produced by a tuber such as potato. If a potato tuber is planted the sprouts will grow to become the new stems and leaves.

Spur: A fruit bud or a cluster of fruit buds, on, say, an apple tree. Continued pruning back of lateral branches encourages the production of spurs on the part of the lateral left unpruned.

Standard: The single main stem on which the crown of the tree is carried. A full standard is 5–6 ft. high. (See also *half-standard*).

Stomach Poison: An insecticide which must gain entry to the stomach of an insect before it can kill, e.g. arsenic.

Stool: A number of shoots coming out of ground to form a bush as in the case of blackcurrants. Sometimes when a tree is cut down a number of branches may arise from the cut stump, this too is called a stool.

Stopping: Removing a terminal bud (growing tip) in order to encourage the production of side shoots or breaks. Frequently done in chrysanthemums in order to increase the number of blooms per plant. Synonym of 'pinching'.

Stratified Seed: A technique for germinating thick-walled fleshy seeds, e.g. rose-seed. It involves putting a layer of sand in a box or pot and on top of that a layer of seed. This is covered with another layer of sand. The container is then put outside where it will be exposed to frost all winter or even for two winters. The seeds will either germinate in the boxes in the spring or they can be sieved out before they germinate and planted in the usual way.

Strike: When a cutting produces roots it is said to have struck.

Sub-Lateral: A main branch is a 'leader' which bears side branches termed 'laterals'. Side branches borne by laterals are sub-laterals.

Sub-Soiler: A tool for digging very deeply, even down to the sub-soil. It is normally a mechanical plough.

Sucker: An aerial shoot produced by the root stock of a grafted plant. If allowed to grow unchecked in, for example, roses, the suckers will eventually dominate the bush.

Sulphate of Ammonia: Probably the cheapest nitrogenous fertilizer (20% N_2).

Sulphur Shy: A variety of fruit which if treated with sulphur will drop its fruit, e.g. the gooseberry Leveller must not be sprayed with sulphur to control gooseberry mildew or the whole crop will drop off.

Superphosphate: A good quick-acting phosphatic fertilizer (18% P_2O_5).

Thin: When applied to seedlings, means to remove excess plants to allow ample room for those which are left to develop.

Thinnings: The seedlings removed from a row.

Three-Course Rotation: A system of cropping in which a given crop is grown in the same area of soil once every three years.

Tilth: The texture or the degree of fineness of division of soil, e.g. in a seed-bed you need a fine tilth.

Timing: The art of removing buds (stopping) of, say, chrysanthemum so that the flowers will be in perfect condition on a given date. Really only of consequence to those who compete at flower-shows.

Tine: One of the prongs of a fork (see *Hollow Tine*).

Tip-Bearer: Most fruit is borne on spurs or lateral branches, but in certain cases, e.g. Worcester Pearmain, the apples are borne at the tips of the branches. Thus normal pruning would remove the fruit buds, and such varieties require special treatment.

Toxin: Any poisonous substance.

Trace-Element: An element such as iron or boron which is necessary for plant health but only in very small (trace) quantities.

Transpiration: The process whereby water is lost from the leaves of plants.

Transplant: To remove a plant from one spot to another.

Trench: The furrow left when a spit of soil is removed. When applied to digging, trenching means double-digging.

Trickle-Bar: A perforated tube which is easily attached to a watering-can to give a wider and better-directed spray when using weedkillers such as paraquat.

Tuber: A swollen underground stem in which food is stored by plants. They can be used for propagation, e.g. potato tuber.

U.C. Compost: A compost developed by the University of California which consists of 25% clean sand plus 75% sphagnum peat, plus fertilizer.

Underplanting: Growing smaller plants in the shade of, or among, larger plants.

Variety: A variation from the typical form of a species. (See *Genus*).

Virus: An agent frequently spread by greenfly whose presence produces disease symptoms in plants.

Virus-Free Stock: Plants carefully selected and tested to be free of virus infection.

Wetting Agent: A chemical added to insecticides and fungicides to ensure that the liquid will not lie in distinct drops on the surface of leaves but will spread to form a continuous wetting film.

Wilting: The collapse of a leaf or plant due to lack of water.

Wind-Rock: Movement of a plant in the soil as a result of wind pressure on the top. Can cause root damage and death.

Index